Working Time in Comparative Perspective

Volume II

Life-Cycle Working Time and Nonstandard Work

Working Time
in Comparative Perspective

Volume II

Life-Cycle Working Time
and Nonstandard Work

Susan Houseman
and
Alice Nakamura
Editors

2001

W.E. Upjohn Institute for Employment Research
Kalamazoo, Michigan

The facts presented in this study and the observations and viewpoints expressed are the sole responsibility of the authors. They do not necessarily represent positions of the W.E. Upjohn Institute for Employment Research.

Cover design by J.R. Underhill.
Index prepared by Nancy Humphreys.
Printed in the United States of America.

Contents

Introduction and Overview

Susan Houseman
W.E. Upjohn Institute

Alice Nakamura
University of Alberta

This is the second of two volumes of selected papers presented at the conference "Changes in Working Time," which was jointly sponsored by the Canadian Employment Research Forum (CERF), the W.E. Upjohn Institute for Employment Research, and Statistics Canada in Ottawa, Ontario, June 13–15, 1996. The chapters in the first volume focus on the weekly hours that individuals work. These chapters examine recent changes in the distribution of weekly working time in Canada and the United States, the implications of the changing distribution of hours worked for earnings inequality, and efforts to reduce unemployment through mandated hours reductions.

The chapters in this volume study an expanded set of working-time issues, which may be loosely grouped under two topics: working time over the life cycle and nonstandard work arrangements. While the distribution of weekly work hours for the population has changed, so too has the amount that individuals work at various points in their life. Most notably, women with small children have increasingly joined the workforce, while labor force participation among older workers has declined. In addition, a growing number of adults are interrupting their careers to go back to school. Two of the chapters in this volume present an overview of life cycle working patterns and trends in Canada and the United States. Several other chapters study the decision to work at key points in the life cycle: one chapter looks at the payoffs to education among adults who have returned to school; two chapters examine the decision to work by mothers; and two chapters focus on retirement and work patterns among older adults.

Often individuals trying to balance school or family responsibilities with a job are part-time, temporary, self-employed, or home-based workers. These nonstandard employment arrangements may allow

1

them greater flexibility in scheduling to accommodate workers' other responsibilities. Similarly, older workers who have left a full-time, career job often work in a nonstandard employment arrangement as a transition to retirement. While many older workers seek part-time or temporary jobs as a bridge to retirement, many prime-age workers take on secondary part-time or temporary jobs, typically to meet special financial needs. Evidence that most types of nonstandard employment arrangements have been growing in Canada and the United States has led to concern about the implications for workers and firms.

Various nonstandard work arrangements are the focus of the last four chapters in this volume. Two chapters look at self-employment and home-based work as mechanisms for achieving greater scheduling flexibility among women. Another chapter compares moonlighting in Canada and the United States, describing the characteristics of workers who moonlight and offering explanations for the higher levels of moonlighting in the United States. The final chapter draws upon a survey of large companies to explain why employers are expanding their use of temporary help workers.

To help readers better understand the issues addressed in this volume and utilize the information contained in it, we provide a synopsis of each of the chapters below. For each chapter, we summarize the study's main objectives, the databases used, and the nature of some of the key findings. The chapters are organized into three groups by the aspects of working time that they consider.

The chapters in Part I examine general patterns and trends in working time over the life cycle for the United States and Canada, and they also introduce a number of the basic terms and concepts used in the rest of the volume.

In "The Life Cycle of Working Time in the United States and Canada: Long-Term Evidence," John D. Owen considers changes over the life cycle for working time in the United States and Canada since 1920. He notes that there have been important changes in weekly hours, in participation and employment rates, and in wages. The purpose of this chapter is to examine the relationship between changes in wage and life cycle labor supply patterns in the two countries.

Owen notes that a simple theory in which labor supply at each age is determined solely by contemporary conditions, without concerns about the future, does not explain life cycle variations in labor supply very well. Owen contrasts the implications of the simple model with the "life cycle theory" of Ghez and Becker. In their model, a young person's lifetime wealth is given by the initial stock of wealth that that person possesses plus the present value of all future income streams, including those from earnings. Owen also makes the important point that life cycle theory is not a theory about cross sections; rather, it is a theory about how the behavior of individuals changes as they age, and hence is a theory better examined with cohort data.

These insights provide the motivation for the empirical portions of this study, which study life cycle employment in the United States and Canada since 1920. The empirical work is based on a number of different data sources for both the United States and Canada that are detailed in a data appendix to the chapter. Owen concludes that the life cycle of working time has been remarkably similar in Canada and the United States, but that each country has experienced important changes in its life cycle patterns of employment. In particular, the level of male labor supply has declined over time, at first because of decline in the number of hours worked, but more recently because of decline in labor force participation. The decline in labor force participation has been especially large among young and older workers. Over the period studied, real wage growth slowed. Life cycle theory would predict that if workers anticipated the stagnation of wage growth, they would supply more labor in their early years. No support for this hypothesis was found, however.

In "Perspectives on Working Time over the Life Cycle," Michael Wolfson and Geoff Rowe utilize a new longitudinal microsimulation model developed by Statistics Canada—the LifePaths model—to examine statistical patterns of working time over the life cycle. Life-Paths provides a means for blending data on both cross-sectional time-use patterns and longitudinal labor force dynamics. It can be used to produce multistate life tables that relax some of the restrictive assumptions that underlie conventional working life tables, and it can be used to conduct a wide range of policy-related analyses as well.

The LifePaths model constructs estimates of birth cohort life cycles by synthesizing samples of hypothetical but realistic individual life histories. It therefore generalizes a variety of more traditional life table analyses, including working life tables, and affords a much wider variety of "views" of working time over the life cycle. More recent work has extended LifePaths from a single "period" cohort to a sequence of overlapping historical birth cohorts. This makes it possible to use the model to address questions of the intergenerational equity of public pensions, as well as issues of income adequacy, health, and the use of nonwork time.

One of the most striking results to emerge from the LifePaths representation of time use is a greater recognition of how our impressions of the importance of paid work over the life cycle are affected by the "granularity" of the time accounting that is used. Conventional approaches tend to go year by year, in which case a typical working lifetime can be expected to extend over 20–40 years of the life cycle. However, when finer units of time (e.g., hours and days) are used, the proportion of unit time intervals over the typical life cycle that are dominated by market work becomes a much smaller fraction.

Part II contains five chapters that examine individuals' work decisions at key points in the life cycle. In "Adults Returning to School— Payoffs from Studying at a Community College," Duane E. Leigh and Andrew M. Gill examine the choices of and the returns to different fields of study for returning adult students versus those who proceed on to college directly from high school. They use National Longitudinal Survey of Youth data through 1993 for respondents who were between 28 and 35 years of age. Leigh and Gill find substantial evidence that returning adults comprise a substantial share of those in postsecondary education. For instance, students in their thirties comprise 10 percent of those in two-year colleges and 37 percent of those in vocational or technical institutions. Sixteen percent of all BA degrees were earned by respondents classified as returning adults.

Leigh and Gill find that the size of the college earnings premium varies substantially by field of study, with the highest paying fields being engineering/computer science and social science/public service for men and nursing for women. Moreover, they find evidence, particularly for men, that returning adults are more sensitive to market wage differentials in choosing fields of study than are ones who continue on directly from high school.

In "Children's Effects on Women's Labor Market Attachment and Earnings," William E. Even and David A. Macpherson attempt to explain significant changes since the 1970s in the labor force attachment and earnings among women of childbearing age. Using data from the March Current Population Surveys over the 1976–1995 period, the authors document the dramatic rise in employment rates and the dramatic decline in the exit rates among civilian women aged 21 to 40. Not surprisingly, the exit rate among women with infants is the highest and among women with no children the lowest throughout the period. However, the differential in the exit rates across these groups narrowed dramatically over time: among women with some work history during the previous year, the exit rate among women with infants declined by 25.7 percentage points, whereas the exit rate among women with no children declined just 5.4 percentage points from 1976 to 1995. Even and Macpherson also find a convergence of exit rates by marital status. Interestingly, compared to previously married and never married women, married women were the most likely to exit employment in 1976, but by 1995 they were the least likely to exit employment.

Even and Macpherson try to explain this sharp decline in the exit rates among married women. By estimating probit models of exit behavior among married women over the 1976–1979 period and over the 1992–1995 period, however, they find that changes in observed characteristics explain only a small share of the large decline in exit rates between the two periods. The most striking finding in these probit models is that the presence of infants had a much smaller effect on the probability that a married woman would exit the labor force in the 1990s than in the 1970s. This finding indicates that the behavior of women, not their characteristics, has fundamentally changed over the period.

In wage models, the presence of children has a negative effect on women's earnings, a finding that is consistent with both theories of human capital and statistical discrimination. According to human capital theory, women who expect to exit the workforce when they have children would invest in less human capital. According to theories of statistical discrimination, employers would discriminate against hiring or promoting women of childbearing age into jobs that require large investments of human capital on the grounds that they are more likely than men to quit. Even and Macpherson, however, find that the adverse effect of children on women's wages has declined over time, especially among married women, which is consistent with the decline in their exit rates.

In the chapter "U.S. Health Policy and Mothers of Children with Disabilities," Janet Hunt-McCool examines the effects on the labor supply of mothers whose children suffer from disabilities or physical limitations. The health insurance options facing these mothers include no insurance; Medicaid (a free state/federal program for very low-income households); employment-based insurance, often conditional on full-time work and relatively high wages; and, if married, possible coverage by the spouse's employer-provided insurance policy. She notes that just under 60 percent of the U.S. population receives coverage from private carriers, while 18 percent have no insurance coverage, either private or public. Only 40 to 60 percent of the low-income population in each of the U.S. states is covered by Medicaid.

The data used in this study are from the 1987 National Medical Expenditure Survey (NMES), which collected information on medical care use and expenditures, health insurance coverage, and employment and hours worked in the United States. This analysis employs a subset of families with children between 1 and 17 years of age. These data are for 3,069 two-parent and 1,590 single-parent families in which the mothers were present. The sample of married mothers was further restricted to households in which husbands were employed full time as wage and salary workers. Multinomial logit estimates of the choice of usual hours of work per week are used to estimate the effects of child health status and the availability of private and public insurance on maternal labor supply. They are estimated separately for married and single mothers. The choices considered are no work, part-time hours (less than 35 hours per week), or work at full-time hours.

One of the main findings is that potentially chronic illnesses in children deter both single and married mothers from full- or part-time employment. This result differs from many previous studies that find a response only among married women. Women who do work are found to be more likely to choose limited hours or part-time work. Another main result is that health insurance on the job matters. These empirical results indicate that the odds of a woman opting for full-time work versus not working rise as the chance of being offered insurance increases. When the husband holds insurance, the mother is more likely to choose part-time work over full-time work, or, more often, to choose no work at all.

Hunt-McCool concludes that there are many reasons why the U.S. system of health insurance provision, in which coverage is tied to jobs, is inefficient or inequitable. She notes that the zero-sum alternative of Medicaid has its own set of disadvantages, including that lifetime income and wealth must remain very low to maintain this coverage, and market skills may depreciate with the limitations this imposes on work. She concludes that women will particularly suffer from the problems created by the employment/health insurance nexus since they routinely provide a large part of the nonmarket time their families require.

In "Early Retirees of a Telecommunications Firm—Patterns of Employment and Working Time," Gangaram Singh and Anil Verma investigate bridge employment among older workers, using data from the Survey of Work and Lifestyle Activities, a survey of former Bell Canada employees. In July 1995, a survey questionnaire was sent by mail to a sample of 3,614 individuals who had left the company between 1985 and 1995. This survey group consisted of all eligible individuals ages 45–50, and a randomly selected 50 percent of the over–50 age group. All of those aged 45–50 were included to try to ensure enough respondents from the "younger retirees" group. The response rate was 60 percent. This is a survey of persons who voluntarily retired from a long-term career job with what was Canada's largest telecommunications company. The majority of those included left Bell with a special financial settlement, and all of them were entitled to a private pension from Bell Canada at the time that the survey was conducted.

Singh and Verma find that 39 percent of the respondents had returned to work after their initial retirement from Bell and were still working, 2 percent were unemployed, and the remaining 59 percent were out of the workforce and hence still retired. For those who had returned to work, 82 percent reported having gone back to work in some form of nonstandard employment, while 18 percent had gone back to standard employment. In addition to providing descriptive statistics, the authors use a multinomial logit model to help explain the choices that these early retirees made between remaining retired, working in standard employment arrangements, and working in nonstandard employment arrangements. Most interestingly, they find that pension schemes that "clawback" benefits when retirees earn income reduce employment, particularly in full-time jobs.

Michael Baker and Dwayne Benjamin examine the effects of public pension schemes on retirement behavior in "Working Time Over the Life Cycle: Do Public Pensions Matter?" They point out that in 1980, over 60 percent of Canadian men between age 60 and 64 were working, whereas by 1994, this figure had fallen to 50 percent. Also, in the intervening years, early retirement provisions had been introduced into the Canadian Pension Plan (CPP), which governs pensions in all provinces besides Quebec, and into the Quebec Pension Plan (QPP). They examine whether there was any causal relationship between the change in pension policy and the increase in retirement rates. The approach they take is to make use of the difference in the time of introduction for the early retirement provisions in the CPP and the QPP. They rely primarily on time series evidence from the Canadian Labour Force Survey data. For portions of the study, they also utilize individual-level panel data from the Labour Market Activity Survey. Their analysis uncovers no strong evidence to suggest that major changes to the public pension schemes in Canada can explain the sharp decline in retirement age.

The chapters in Part III focus on various forms of nonstandard employment. The first three of these have to do with worker behavior and employment patterns. The fourth examines employer hiring practices.

In introducing her chapter, "Self-Employment and Schedule Flexibility for Married Females: Evidence for the United States from SIPP," Theresa J. Devine notes that as the employment rate for prime-age married women in the United States rose through the 1980s, their self-employment rate rose by more. She also points out that the findings to date on self-employment for married women suggest that many may be using this as a way to exercise more control over work schedules than is typically possible in the wage-and-salary sector. Her chapter presents new evidence on this work schedule hypothesis from the Survey of Income and Program Participation (SIPP).

Devine calls attention to a number of reasons why the SIPP data are particularly useful for investigating this work schedule hypothesis for the self-employment of married women. She points out that each SIPP interview collects relatively detailed information on job characteristics and work schedules (weeks worked, usual hours, and deviations from usual schedules of work). As well, SIPP is longitudinal, so changes in usual schedules and self-employment status can be measured, and SIPP interviews are just four months apart, which means that short-term changes can be measured quite accurately. SIPP also collects detailed information on business characteristics including husband/wife business ownership, legal status, and number of employees, all of which make this a rich data source for the study of self-employment in the United States.

Consistent with her hypothesis, Devine finds that the self-employed and wage-and-salary women report very different usual hours of work. Self-employed women rarely report 40 hours as their usual per week, while 40 is the number reported most often by wage-and-salary women. Usual hours of the self-employed are much more varied, both from one woman to another and over time for all individuals. Self-employed women also deviate from or change their own usual schedules more frequently than wage-and-salary women. Women who are only self-employed are less likely than wage-and-salary women to report that their part-time hours or the variability in their work schedules is due to insufficient work.

The data also suggest that the self-employment decisions of married women often depend on the employment circumstances of their husbands. Usual hours of self-employed women are more correlated with the usual hours of their husbands, particularly when their husbands are also self-employed. Additionally, more than half of the women who report self-employment during the period of a year had self-employed husbands.

In the chapter "Work Site and Work Hours: The Labor Force Flexibility of Home-Based Female Workers," Linda N. Edwards and Elizabeth Field-Hendrey examine the hypothesis that fixed costs of work play an important role in determining the probabilities of whether women work at home (home-based work), or out of the home (on-site work), or not at all. The data for their study are from the 5 percent Public Use Microdata Sample of housing units from the 1990 Census of Population of the United States. Identification of home-based workers is derived from answers to the journey to work question, which asks, "How did this person usually get to work last week?" The persons who responded that they "worked at home" are regarded as home-based workers. The sample was limited to those 25–55 years of age to avoid the years when large numbers of women either are still attending school or are retired.

Home-based women are found, on average, to differ greatly from on-site workers in both their personal characteristics and in the nature of their work. For example, 62.9 percent of the former are self-employed compared with 3.3 percent of the latter. Home-based workers are also found to have much more variety in their work schedules, both with respect to weekly hours and weeks worked per year. The authors conclude that their findings support the hypothesis that home-based work gives women greater flexibility in scheduling work and increases the labor force participation among women with high fixed costs of working, such as those with young children, with elderly relatives living in their home, with disabilities, and with long commutes to on-site work locations.

In "A Comparative Analysis of Moonlighting in Canada and the United States," Jean Kimmel and Lisa M. Powell provide a wealth of information for the United States and Canada about multiple job-holders and the jobs they hold. Their descriptive analysis provides information about differences across gender, age, education, marital status, region, and other characteristics. Separate information is provided about the primary jobs (PJ) versus the secondary jobs (SJ) that are held by multiple job-holders. They estimate PJ and SJ wage equations for each country and then use these to compute predicted wages that are included in probit models for the probability of moonlighting.

For the United States, the data are drawn from the May Current Population Survey (CPS), which contains a special supplement with information on multiple jobs. The CPS is a randomly drawn U.S. sample of households. The Canadian data are drawn from the Survey of Work Arrangements (SWA), which is a supplement to the November 1991 Canadian Labour Force Survey. While the Labour Force Survey does flag multiple job-holders, the SWA supplement provides additional information on work patterns, primary job union membership, occupational and industrial distributions of secondary jobs, secondary job wages, and the reason for moonlighting.

Kimmel and Powell find that moonlighting rates rise with the level of education, that unmarried females and married males are the most likely to moonlight, and that the total hours of work per week are much higher for moonlighters than nonmoonlighters. Although about two-thirds of moonlighters give financial reasons for taking a second job, moonlighters are not predominantly lower-income workers. Moonlighting rates are higher in the United States than in Canada, which Kimmel and Powell ascribe to the higher divorce rates and the lower unemployment rates in the United States.

In "Large Companies and the Changing Use of Temporary Workers: Trends and Impacts on Financial Measures of Performance," Shulamit Kahn, Fred Foulkes, and Jeffrey Heisler report findings from in-depth interviews with human resource executives at 35 large U.S. companies. They correlate changes in the way these companies use temporary workers with various financial measures of profitability. They also examine detailed case study results for selected firms in a narrowly defined manufacturing industry.

The authors find that many large companies are hiring more temporaries and are using them differently than in the past. For instance, temporary hiring is being used increasingly as a recruiting and screening mechanism for permanent employees. In addition, temps are increasingly being used as a way of dealing with variability in demand for labor that is both foreseen and unforeseen. The authors also look for correlations between use of temporary help agencies and financial performance, but find conflicting evidence in their cross-sectional and time-series analyses. However, as they note, it is difficult to tease out any causal relationship given their small sample size and the fact that human resources policies tend to be overshadowed by other factors in determining a company's financial performance.

Part I

1

The Life Cycle of Working Time in the United States and Canada
Long-Term Evidence

John D. Owen
Wayne State University

This chapter will discuss long-term changes in the life cycle of working time in the United States and Canada since 1920. The past 75 years have seen important changes in both weekly hours of work and in participation rates. These changes have been associated with equally remarkable movements in wages. This chapter will examine the relationship between these wage changes and the life cycle of labor supply in the two countries.

An international comparison can help us understand the extent to which labor supply developments in one's own country are unique or common to other nations. Nations differ in the structure of their economies, in labor market institutions, and, more generally, in their human relations climates; these factors can produce different labor market outcomes.

The next section offers an introduction to the economic analysis of life cycle variations in working time. The following section presents data on a number of age cross sections of labor supply as well as some cohort data, and discusses the implications for life cycle theory. The next sections present an empirical model of labor supply and provide the statistical results of testing this model, and the final section offers some conclusions. An appendix describes the data sources used for this study.

LIFE CYCLE THEORY AND LABOR SUPPLY

Economists have long been interested in why labor supply varies with age. The standard analysis is in terms of a choice between income and leisure, since diverting time from leisure to paid employment increases income. A higher price or opportunity cost of time is expected to discourage taking leisure; on the other hand, higher levels of income may yield a greater demand for leisure. Since the wage rate is both an approximate measure of the price of time and a principal determinant of the average person's income, changes in the wage rate, including those that occur over the life cycle, are expected to play an important role in determining the age distribution of labor supply.

In the simplest theory, labor supply at each age is determined by contemporary conditions, without regard to past or future concerns. For example, the labor supply of a 30-year-old in 1980 is determined by the wage rate available to him in that year, the wealth or nonlabor income that he might have, and other contemporary influences, but not by concerns about the future.

The effects of a high wage on labor supply at a given age are ambiguous in this simple theory since, as noted above, a higher opportunity cost of time discourages leisure while higher income is likely to increase it. We do know that over the past 150 years real hourly wages rose and the average level of male labor supply fell, yielding the famous backward sloping supply curve of labor. But these historical data on national aggregates may not give us a good prediction of how the number of hours worked will vary as an individual ages.

And indeed this simple theory does not explain life cycle variations very well. There are numerous empirical examples that are not consistent with a negative relation between age-specific wages and labor supply: new entrants into the labor force and those nearing retirement age typically earn less per hour yet supply fewer hours than those in the prime-age category, for example. More generally, we know that individuals do consider their likely futures when making decisions; for example, they save for their old age, when they expect to reduce their labor supply.

The life cycle theory of labor supply provides an alternative to this model.[1] Ghez and Becker (1975) pioneered in the development of this theory. In their model,[2] a young person's lifetime wealth is given by the initial stock of wealth he possesses plus the present value of all future income streams, including those from earnings. It is a perfect foresight model in which the individual can accurately predict these future events. On these assumptions, an individual's wealth does not vary over his lifetime; year-to-year changes in hourly wages only represent differences in the price of time.

Individuals maximize their lifetime utility, the present value of the utility gained in each year of adult life; the annual utility is a function of leisure and consumption in a given year. They can borrow as much as they like at a constant rate of interest and in any year work as many or as few hours as they like at the same hourly wage. The individual can then follow a utility-maximizing life plan for supplying labor, borrowing, and savings.

With wealth constant and higher wages in a given year simply representing a higher price of time, the individual will reduce the amount of leisure and increase labor supply when his wage is high, yielding a positive correlation of wages and labor supply.

The theory does not predict a perfect positive match between wages and hours over the life cycle, though. On the one hand, the market rate of interest encourages individuals to work hard and save when they are young; on the other hand, a common preference by individuals for present over future satisfactions provides an inducement to borrow and take leisure when young. If the rate of interest is high relative to the way the individual discounts the future, he is expected to have a peak in hours of work somewhat earlier than the peak in his hourly earnings.

The Ghez-Becker model makes some strong assumptions. Most people can not in fact readily predict how long-term trends in wages will affect their lives; even if they could, they face constraints in both credit and labor markets that would prevent them from taking full advantage of their predictions. Most of us cannot borrow as much as we might like at any interest rate, let alone a constant rate. In the labor market, part-time employment is often less well paid than full-time, while very long hours fatigue us, reducing our productivity and, often, the hourly return for our efforts. A temporary withdrawal from the labor force also imposes costs—lower earnings when the employee returns to seek new employment are common. Finally, the majority of full-time workers are employed at standard hours that constrain the ability of younger and older workers to have very different schedules.

Ghez and Becker did submit their theory to an empirical test, comparing the age distribution of hours per employed males with the age distribution of hourly wages, both for the year 1965. They found a very good fit: both hours and wages followed an inverted U path. Hours peaked before hourly wages, as their theory would predict if individuals faced a rate of interest that exceeded their personal rate of time preference.

This was not a satisfactory test of the theory, though; life cycle theory is a theory of the behavior of individuals, *not* age cross sections. The latter compares the labor supply of a number of cohorts at a moment of time; this need not trace out the experience of a single cohort.

EMPIRICAL DATA[3]

Age Cross Sections

Canadian and U.S. data on hours, labor force participation, employment, and earnings over the past 75 years provide us with a rich source of information. Long-term data on the age cross sections of male labor input (defined here as the proportion of the group employed times hours worked by those employed), reveal broadly similar patterns in Canada and the United States (Table 1). Data on child labor are not even collected, presumably because it has become so unusual. The labor of teenagers is reported and is relatively low.[4] Labor supply rises for those in their early twenties and is typically at a maximum for those in their late thirties. Those in the 45–64 age group work less, and those over 65 supply much less labor than those aged 45–64. We thus obtain an inverted U in each age cross section.

These inverted Us do change their shape over time. Earlier withdrawals from the labor force and later entry by young people, together with continued heavy participation by prime-age males, have yielded a more peaked distribution of labor supply in both countries.

Table 1 Hours of Labor Input, by Males

	Canada					United States				
	Age group					Age group				
	15–19	20–24	25–44	45–64	65+		16–19	20–24	25–44	45–64	65+
1995	8.6	23.1	33.6	28.1	3.2	1995	11.7	28.8	38.9	33.6	4.9
1990	11.9	26.9	35.4	29.5	3.5	1990	12.7	29.7	39.7	33.4	5.0
1985	10.5	25.9	34.6	29.5	3.8	1986	12.2	29.8	39.1	32.6	4.7
1980	13.9	29.3	36.4	32.0	4.7	1983	11.3	27.1	37.2	32.1	4.8
1975	14.1	29.1	37.0	33.3	6.1	1980	14.2	29.4	39.0	33.7	5.7
1970	12.2	29.9	38.3	35.5	8.2	1977	14.7	30.2	39.9	34.7	5.8
1965	13.5	34.7	41.2	38.0	10.0	1970	13.1	30.7	41.1	37.4	8.7
1960	14.1	34.2	40.3	37.6	11.3	1965	13.3	34.2	42.8	39.0	9.6
1955	17.4	36.9	41.8	38.8	12.5	1960	14.0	34.0	41.1	38.1	11.5
1950	21.7	39.7	44.4	41.4	16.7	1955	17.4	35.2	42.2	39.0	14.9
1946	24.2	38.4	44.7	42.7	20.0	1950	19.1	33.7	40.9	38.2	17.8
1941	25.1	44.2	50.5	49.0	21.7	1940	14.7	33.0	40.4	37.1	17.7
1931	23.1	39.3	44.3	43.4	22.7	1930	20.0	37.6	44.8	42.0	25.4
1921	31.3	45.2	50.3	49.6	27.3	1920	28.7	43.5	50.2	47.0	29.2

The age cross sections of wages for males in the two countries are also peaked. Hourly wages typically are very low for teenagers, rise with age, then peak in the late forties (somewhat later than the peak in labor supply).

There is one important difference between labor supply trends in Canada and the United States: the increase in Canadian unemployment over the past 15 years has now introduced a persistent, significant wedge between labor force and employment rates. However, this has not greatly influenced the relative distribution of labor input in the cross section, since there has been a substantial increase in the rate of unemployment among prime-age Canadian males, as well as higher rates among other age groups. When labor supply data obtained by multiplying hours per employed person by the labor force participation rate are compared with data using hours and the employment rate, little difference is observed in the relative age distribution of labor inputs.[5]

Time Series

Over the past 75 years, labor input per capita fell in each age group. In the earlier years of this period, reduced hours per employed male were the principal factor reducing labor input; in more recent years, declining rates of labor force participation and, most recently in Canada, higher rates of unemployment have been much more important.

Hours reduction in Canada also took a somewhat different course than in the United States. There was a sharp reduction from 1850 to 1950 in the United States, but very little reduction since for prime-age males.[6,7] Hours reduction continued for a few years longer in Canada; for example, the standard workweek in Canadian manufacturing fell from 50.3 hours in 1921 to 43.2 hours in 1950, but then dropped to 40.2 hours in 1965. But household data show little if any reduction in the past 20 years.[8]

Male labor force participation rates fell significantly in both countries; there was a long-term downward trend in every age group. The largest declines are seen among teenagers and those over 55. These trends have accelerated in recent decades, in the very years in which hours decline was moderated or ceased.

Because of higher unemployment, in Canada the decline in male employment rates was significantly sharper than that in labor force participation. Among males 15 and older, only 65 percent were employed in 1995. Even in the prime-age group—35–44 years—only 85 percent were employed.

Cohort Analysis

As noted above, life cycle theory is *not* a theory of age cross sections, but of individuals as they age, better measured by cohort data.[9] In both countries, cohort data show that the labor supply of male workers declines more with age than is indicated in the cross sections (compare Table 2 with Table 1). The basic reason for this difference is the downward time trend in male labor supply. Consider how inaccurate it is to use a cross section of U.S. males in, say, 1965 to evaluate the life cycle of labor supply of a man who is 67 years old in that year. Census data indicate that a 22-year-old in 1920 actually was likely to put in as much as 10 more hours per week, on average, than a 22-year-old was in 1965. Hence, an age cross section that compares 22-year-olds in 1965 with 67-year-olds in that year significantly underestimates the decline in labor supply with age that cohort actually experienced.

This cohort cross section discrepancy is now modulated somewhat differently than in earlier years. In both countries there has been a sharp decline in the proportion of males employed over 55 years of age, while hours of work have recently been flat. One result is that the discrepancy between cohort and cross-sectional data has become much smaller for the middle-age groups than for older groups. A cross-sectional age distribution of labor input in 1920 not only greatly exaggerated the input that a contemporary 17-year-old would supply in the last years of his working life, it also yielded substantial overestimates of his labor input in his twenties, thirties, and forties (see Table 1). More recently, though, while a 17-year-old in the 1960s did experience much more decline in his old age than would be predicted from a 1960s cross section, the cross-sectional data did not yield a bad prediction of his labor input as a middle-age worker. With weekly hours remaining fairly stable, the labor inputs of workers in their thirties or early forties were not falling very much in, say, the 1960–1980 period. (The forecasting error would be somewhat larger for Canadian workers because of the much larger increase in Canadian unemployment among the prime-age group.)

The Relation between Labor Input and Earnings

The real hourly earnings of males quadrupled in both countries over the past 75 years. The steep upward time trend in real wages in the first part of this period, from 1920 to about 1970, introduced major differences between age cross section and cohort earnings data. When wages rise at almost 2.5 percent per year,[10] the average wage at the end of a 50-year working life will be about triple the average wage at the beginning. Absent any changes in the age distribution of wages, the real hourly wage of a man in a given age group will then be more than three times as high in 1970 as in 1920. This rising trend yields a much more rapid increase in wages with age for a cohort than we see in the cross section. While the cohort gains both from this trend and from the benefits of the group's lifetime of job training and other useful work experience, we see only these latter effects in the cross section.

This has important implications for the life cycle theory of labor supply set forth above. Labor supply has tended to decline with age, while real hourly wage in the 1920–1970 period increased with age. As a result, data for the cohort entering in 1920 demonstrate a weak relationship between labor supply and wage. (See Figures 1 and 3.)

A representative worker in this cohort might achieve a four- or fivefold increase in his real wage over the next 50 years (due in part to improvements in his own skills and experience, and in part to the upward national trend in real wages), yet his labor input would decline by about 80 percent. Even if we compare the earnings of a man in his early twenties in this period with those he might earn in late middle age (say, 30 years later), we see a similar, if more moderate, result: a decline in labor input despite a more than threefold increase in his wage. Such facts challenge a life cycle theory that predicts that a future of rapidly rising wages will induce a cohort to take leisure when young and defer working until late in life.

The dramatic change in real wage growth in the past 25 years, from rapid increase to stagnation, affords another opportunity to consider the empirical usefulness of this theory. The relationship between labor input and wage in the cohort data now differs less from that found in the recent cross sections (compare Figures 2 and 4 with Figures 1 and 3, respectively); the cohort relation is now more uniformly positive, and so more like that in the cross section. An observer who relied only on these recent data might conclude that the simple life cycle theory is approximately correct.

The life cycle theory predicts that this major change in real wage growth (and hence in the way in which wage varies with age for the average person) would have produced large-scale changes in the life cycle of labor supply; the elimination of the trend reduces the incentive to supply more labor later in life, and so forecasts a shift toward supplying labor at earlier ages. It is difficult to see this effect in the cohort data in Table 2.

Figure 1 Labor Input versus Wage, Canada, 1921–1971

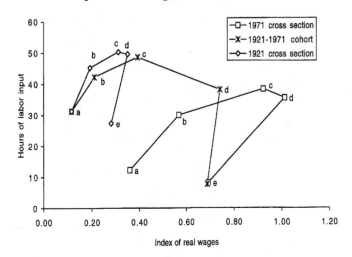

Figure 2 Labor Input versus Wage, Canada, 1941–1991

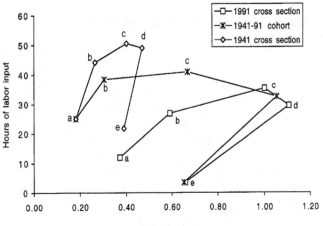

Key to Figure Legends

Legend	Age group (years)
a	Under 20
b	20–24
c	25–44
d	45–64
e	65 and older

Figure 3 Labor Input versus Wage, United States, 1920–1970

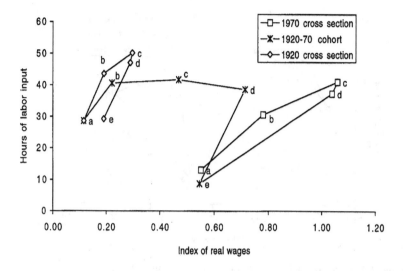

Figure 4 Labor Input versus Wage, United States, 1940–1990

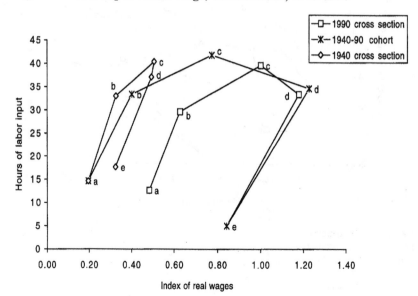

Table 2 Cohort Analysis of Hours of Labor Input

	Canada						United States				
	Year cohort born						Year cohort born				
Age	1904	1914	1924	1934	1944	Age	1903	1913	1923	1933	1943
16–19	31.3	23.1	25.1	20.9	14.0	16–19	28.7	20.0	14.7	19.1	14.0
20–24	42.2	41.8	38.4	36.3	30.2	20–24	40.6	35.3	33.3	35.2	34.2
24–44	48.6	44.6	40.9	39.5	36.7	24–44	41.7	40.8	41.8	40.6	39.9
45–64	38.1	36.5	32.5	29.5	28.1	45–64	38.6	38.3	34.7	32.8	33.6
65+	7.7	4.5	3.4			65+	8.7	5.7	5.0		

AN EMPIRICAL MODEL

The Basic Cohort Model

Such questions can be explored more systematically in a statistical treatment that uses multivariate analysis. Following Ghez and Becker, the behavior of a single cohort can be modeled with the log of labor input (I) being a function of a constant term, age (A), and the log of wage (W) at each age, i:

(1) $I_i = b_0^* + b_1 W_i + b_2 A_i$

In the Ghez-Becker model, b_2 is the product of the difference between the rate of interest and an index of individual time preference, and a measure of the substitutability of present and future consumption experiences; b_1 is a weighted average of this substitution possibility and the extent to which goods and time are substitutes within a single period;[11] and b_0^* reflects the influence of the cohort's wage (the present value of its earnings over its lifetime) as well as a constant.

The present study uses data from a number of birth cohorts (see Table 2). A Ghez-Becker type model can be rewritten for more than one cohort as

(2) $I_{ij} = b_0 + b_1 \left(W_{ij} - W_j \right) + b_2 A_{ij} + b_3 W_j,$

where i denotes age group, j denotes the jth birth cohort, and W_j is the log of cohort wage.[12] In this model, b_1 is expected to be positive, since the relative variation of wage over the lifetime of a given cohort is expected to increase labor supply. The constant b_2 will be negative if (as in the Ghez-Becker study) the market rate of interest exceeds the individual rate of time preference. The constant b_3 may be negative if there is a "backward sloping supply curve of labor," in the sense that those cohorts facing higher wages supply less labor over their lifetimes.

Eq. 2 can also be written as

$$(3) \quad I_i = b_0 + b_1 W_{ij} + b_2 A_{ij} + \left(b_3 - b_2\right)W_j$$

The age (A_{ij}) and the log of current wage (W_{ij}) of a cohort can readily be measured. Measuring the cohort wage is not so easy. A perfect foresight model would assume that each individual knows his future wages and hence could calculate their present value—a measure that would be consistent with the Ghez-Becker model. However, we lack full working life information for many of the cohorts in our data. One might, moreover, wish to consider other hypotheses about wage expectations. Several alternative models of cohort wage were developed to deal with these concerns. The first, W_j^1, simply assumed that the cohort wage of each cohort surpassed that of a cohort born a year earlier by the same percentage, g, so that $W_j^1 = W_0 + jg$, where W_0 is the logarithm of the cohort wage in a base year 0, and j is the number of years from the birth year of the base cohort to that of the jth cohort. For convenience, the base birth year chosen here was 1903. The age of an age group was taken at its midpoint. For example, those 14–19 years old in 1920 (the youngest cohort in the earliest year for which we had data) were assumed to be 17 years old then, or born in 1903. Or, to take another example, those 25–44 years old in 1950 were assumed to be born in 1916. In the first example, j was equal to 0; in the second, to 13.

W_0 is invariant. Hence, substituting in Eq. 3, we can write

$$(4) \quad I_{ij} = b_0 + b_1 W_{ij} + b_2 A_{ij} + \left(b_3 - b_1\right)\left(W_0 + jg\right)$$
$$= b_0' + b_1 W_{ij} + b_2 A_{ij} + \left(b_3 - b_1\right)jg.$$

Here the constant term is $b_0' = b_0 + (b_3 - b_1)W_0$.

A stochastic equation was used to estimate labor input in this first model:

(5) $I_{ij} = \beta_0' + \beta_1 W_{ij} + \beta_2 A_{ij} + (\beta_3 - \beta_1)gj + u_{ij}$,

where u_{ij} is a random disturbance term.

Cohort and Unexpected Period Effects

The break in wage regimes noted above (rapid wage growth followed by wage stagnation) offers an opportunity to carry out simple, informal tests of the importance of cohort and unexpected period effects on the life cycle of labor supply. The data were first divided into two periods, "early," 1920–1970, and "late," 1975–1995. The model was estimated for each of these periods separately.[13]

To explore this period hypothesis further, a dummy variable L, equal to 1 if after 1970, zero otherwise, was introduced as an independent variable and as multiplying each of the regressors, in an estimation of the 1920–1995 period:

(6) $I_{ij} = \beta_0' + \beta_1 W_{ij} + \beta_2 A_{ij} + (\beta_3 - \beta_1)gj + \beta_0^* L + \beta_1^* W_{ij} L + \beta_2^* A_{ij} L$

   $+ (\beta_3^* - \beta_1)gjL + u_{ij}$,

where u_{ij} is a random disturbance term.

If the life cycle or cohort theory is correct, and the cohort wage is defined accurately, we should expect little change in the coefficients between the early and late periods. By the same reasoning, Eq. 6 should not afford a better fit to the data than Eq. 5.

A change in wage regimes may also affect expected cohort wage. To explore this possibility, four other measures of expected cohort wage were constructed and used in alternative estimations. These measures assumed that those cohorts that had left the labor force by 1970—while wages were still rising—did use the average rate of growth of wages before 1970 to predict the long-term trend in their earnings; the log of the cohort wage for this group ($j < 0$) was measured as $W_0 + jg$, where g is the growth rate in average wages in the early period.

The alternative measures assumed that the change in wage regimes altered expectations for younger cohorts. All four assumed that those who entered the labor force after 1970 expected no upward trend in their wages (i.e., that $g = 0$ if $j \geq 50$).

This leaves a third group containing those who entered before 1970 but reached retirement age after that date (i.e., $0 \leq j \leq 50$). The first alternative $\left(W_j^2 \right)$ assumed constant cohort wage growth for those in this group up to 1970, but no growth after that date. The log of the cohort wage in this model, W_j^2, is then

if $j \leq 50$,

$$W_j^2 = W_0 + jg$$

(if $j \geq 50$,

$$W_j^2 = W_0 + 50g).^{14}$$

Variant 3 rejects the notion that the middle group didn't take future wage stagnation into account. The expected rate of growth of cohort wage for cohorts in this middle group is assumed instead to have declined linearly in the 1920–1970 period, from the growth rate expected by those entering in 1920 or earlier to the zero growth expected by those entering in 1970 or later. In this variant, the log of cohort wage for the middle group is

$$W_j^3 = W^0 + jg(1 - 0.01j).$$

This function is at a maximum at $j = 50$, and so predicts no further growth after 1970.[15]

The last variants $\left(W_j^4 \text{ and } W_j^5 \right)$ explicitly recognize that if wage stagnation occurred later in life, it might have less impact on life cycle decision making for two reasons: fewer years would be affected by the change in growth rates, and later years may be weighed less heavily than earlier years. The present value of the future wage trend was used to measure expected cohort wage in these variants. (The wage trends used continued to be the observed trend in the 1920–1970 period, and zero growth from 1970 onward.) W_j^4 used a real rate of discount of 4 percent; W_j^5 used a zero rate of discount. In these models, the log of cohort wage for the middle group is

$$W_j = W_0 + \int_0^{50-j} e^{g(j+t)-rt}\,dt + \left(e^{g50}\right)\left(\int_{50-j}^{50} e^{-rt}\,dt\right),$$

using r to denote the rate of discount.[16]

Multicollinearity

Current wages and cohort wages display similar upward trends, as do their logs, W_{ij} and W_j. In an alternative regression, it was assumed that the trend in the dependent variable was due to changes in the cohort wage. $\Delta I/\Delta yr$ was calculated for each period studied, and used to calculate an adjusted dependent variable $I'_{ij} = I_{ij} - j(\Delta I / \Delta yr)$. I'_{ij} was then regressed against age (A_{ij}) and the log of current wage (W_{ij}).

Canadian Unemployment

As noted above, the persistently high level of unemployment in Canada calls into question the use of labor input—hours per worker times proportion employed—as a measure of labor supply. To deal with this problem, alternative regressions were run with Canadian labor supply measured using labor force participation rate instead of proportion of population employed.

EMPIRICAL RESULTS

Table 3 presents the results of statistical estimations of the log of labor input, I, using the basic model set forth in Eq. 5 and data for Canada and the United States for the past 75 years. Part A presents results using the first measure of cohort wage $\left(W_j^1\right)$; the third measure $\left(W_j^3\right)$ is employed in part B.[17] (Space limitations prevent presentation of results for W_j^2, W_j^4, and W_j^5.) In each country, estimates are given for the entire 1920–1995 period, for the "early" period (1920–1970), and the "late" (1975–1995) period. Table 3, part C presents the results of an alternative method for standardizing for the cohort wage effect, using the adjusted dependent variable, I'_{ij} (defined above as $I - j(\Delta I / \Delta yr)$). (Note that the cohort wage effects in parentheses are based on the calculation used to obtain the adjusted dependent variable, not on a multi-

Table 3 Empirical Results[a]

A. Dependent variable: labor input
Cohort wage used: first (W_j^1)

	Canada			United States		
	1920–1995	1920–1970	1975–1995	1920–1995	1920–1970	1975–1995
Constant	7.3448	7.1733	5.3189	6.2422	6.5215	2.8810
	(31.750)	(29.024)	(9.251)	(18.933)	(30.496)	(4.782)
Wage	1.6480	1.4792	2.1984	1.2514	1.3803	2.7630
	(14.846)	(13.65)	(14.217)	(7.784)	(14.183)	(14.861)
Age	-0.0726	-0.0704	-0.0528	-0.0509	-0.0548	-0.0259
	(-18.064)	(-15.422)	(-7.101)	(-9.434)	(-14.481)	(-3.476)
Cohort wage	-2.4136	-1.8441	-3.9858	-1.8443	-1.6914	-3.1520
	(-17.231)	(-14.66)	(-1.928)	(-8.760)	(-14.694)	(2.730)
Cohort wage, adjusted coefficient	-0.7655	-0.3649	-1.7874	-0.5929	-0.3111	-0.3890
$\bar{R}^2$	0.829	0.844	0.915	0.544	0.856	0.888
N	70	45	25	75	40	35

B. Dependent variable: labor input
Cohort wage used: third (W_j^3)

	Canada			United States		
	1920–1995	1920–1970	1975–1995	1920–1995	1920–1970	1975–1995
Constant	7.3709	6.7760	5.5300	6.1160	6.2617	4.0160
	(25.726)	(22.982)	(9.206)	(19.914)	(22.572)	(5.796)

	1.7747	1.3779	2.4380	1.4960	1.3716	2.5470
Wage	(14.531)	(11.035)	(13.222)	(8.381)	(11.377)	(10.483)
Age	-0.0760	-0.0658	-0.0515	-0.0498	-0.0530	-0.0402
	(-18.522)	(-12.369)	(-8.421)	(-9.685)	(-11.386)	(-5.793)
Cohort wage	-3.0593	-2.2990	-1.6450	-2.0950	-2.1865	0.5358
	(-7.491)	(-7.503)	(-2.199)	(-9.050)	(-7.192)	(0.702)
Cohort wage, adjusted coefficient	-1.2846	-0.9211	0.7930	-0.5990	-0.8149	3.0828
$\bar{R}^2$	0.697	0.670	0.919	0.559	0.647	0.863
N	70	45	25	75	40	35

C. Dependent variable: I' = labor input net of calculated cohort wage effect

	Canada			United States		
	1920–1995	1920–1970	1975–1995	1920–1995	1920–1970	1975–1995
Constant	17.4540	17.7910	17.0970	13.7850	15.2160	4.8710
	(90.909)	(84.245)	(142.258)	(80.700)	(83.764)	(37.594)
Wage	0.4166	0.4490	2.2020	0.3168	0.3624	2.6430
	(2.908)	(3.027)	(14.256)	(2.421)	(2.768)	(13.313)
Age	-0.0222	-0.0190	-0.0462	-0.0169	-0.0107	-0.0447
	(-5.543)	(-4.809)	(-15.663)	(-4.550)	(-2.917)	(-13.562)
Cohort wage (calculated effect)	[-0.39]	[-0.30]	[-1.96]	[0.29]	[-0.22]	[0.30]
N	70	45	25	75	40	35

(continued)

Table 3 (continued)

D. Dependent variable: labor supply = hours × labor force participation rate

	Canada		
	1920–1995	1920–1970	1975–1995
Constant	7.3360	7.1623	5.3820
	(31.267)	(31.209)	(9.002)
Wage	1.5932	1.4260	2.1332
t-ratio	(14.152)	(14.176)	(13.265)
Age	−0.0718	−0.0695	−0.0535
t-ratio	(−17.606)	(−16.387)	(−6.916)
Cohort wage	−0.0406	−0.0437	−0.0117
t-ratio	(−16.310)	(−15.437)	(−1.634)
Cohort wage,			
Adjusted coefficient	1.5526	1.3823	2.1215
$\bar{R}^2$	0.826	0.868	0.910
N	70	45	25

[a] t-ratios are in parentheses.

variate analysis.) Part D of Table 3 presents estimations of labor supply in Canada, with the dependent variable defined as hours × labor force participation rate.

In every regression, the current wage variable has a positive, statistically significant effect on labor input, and age has a negative, significant effect. These two effects are consistent with the empirical findings in the Ghez-Becker study.

In the regressions for the entire period and for the early period in Table 3, the age coefficients range from –5.5 to –7.6 percent over the five models (W_j^1 through W_j^5). These are larger than expected (inasmuch as they are designed to reflect the difference between the available rate of return and individual time preference) and are much larger than those found by Ghez and Becker. When a correction is made for multicollinearity in Table 3, part C, the age coefficients for these periods are considerably smaller—between –1.1 percent and –2.2 percent—though still larger than the very small coefficients found by Ghez and Becker. The results in the present study indicate that when young people are faced with rapidly rising real wages, they are restrained from taking full advantage of the upward trend and postponing effort to their later years by a discrepancy between the market rate of interest and their own rate of time preference, and by uncertainty and other factors constraining the young. It was argued earlier that uncertainty about the future is a major constraint on life cycle variations in labor supply. In an interesting paper on the life cycle of savings, Nagatani (1972) argues that, under reasonable assumptions, such uncertainty can be "translated into a risk premium which adds to the market rate of interest in discounting future income." On this reasoning, the relatively large coefficients on age found here can be interpreted as reflecting not only the market rate of interest, but also an uncertainty premium.[18]

The elasticities of labor input with respect to current wage obtained for the entire period and for the early period are also rather large, ranging from 1.2 to 1.7, suggesting a high degree of substitutability of labor input between ages. However, when the adjusted dependent variables are used (Table 3, part C), the estimated current wage elasticities for these periods are more plausible, ranging from just 0.3 to 0.5.

The estimations for the "late" period are more difficult to interpret. Since there has been very little change in average real hourly wages in recent years, we should be able to focus more clearly here on life cycle variations in wages. While we do find good fits to the data in this period, the age and current wage coefficients are implausibly large, and they remain so even when an attempt is made to correct for multicollinearity (Table 3, part C). This may be the result of unobserved variables. In the Ghez-Becker model, these age and wage coefficients generate an inverted U in the life cycle of labor supply. Conversely, an increase in the steepness of this U in data will likely yield higher levels of these coefficients in a regression. However, this increased kurtosis may also reflect the influence of other, unobserved variables rather than a true change in the substitution elasticities that the age and wage coefficients represent in this model.

The relationship between labor supply and cohort wage in this late period is ambiguous, especially in the United States, where we see a decline in labor input per capita accompanied by a decline in the real average wage, yielding a calculated *positive* elasticity of about 0.3 (see Table 3, part C). This may be a result of the very small changes in real wages and labor supply in this period, i.e., −0.6 percent and −0.2 percent per annum, respectively. When change is this small, measurement errors can dominate real movement. Some economists have argued that the consumer price index has been upward biased over the past 20 years, by as much as 1 or 2 percent a year. If the measurement error was, say, 1.2 percent per year, then real wages actually increased at an annual rate of 0.6 percent, and the elasticity of labor supply with respect to wages was −0.3! One cannot, then, rely on the estimates of cohort wage effects in this period.

These estimations also provide evidence of a shift in labor supply relationship over time. The goodness of fit improves when separate regressions are run for the two subperiods. The adjusted R^2 values (see part A of Table 3) show a gain from 0.829 for the entire period to 0.844 and 0.915 for the two subperiods in the Canadian data, while this measure rises from 0.544 to 0.856 and 0.888 when U.S. data are employed. Moreover, when the entire period is used, with a dummy variable, "late period," introduced for interaction with all variables (as in Eq. 6), the adjusted R^2 rises from 0.829 to 0.902 for the Canadian data and from 0.544 to 0.886 for the U.S. data (not shown).

The alternative models of cohort wage W_j^2, W_j^3, W_j^4, and W_j^5 are designed to help us see how individuals reacted to the major change in the wage regime that occurred around 1970—to determine whether what appear to be unexpected period effects might actually be explained in terms of rational life cycle planning in a perfect foresight model. In this context, the results are somewhat disappointing. While the regression coefficients are broadly similar to those in the first model, the alternative models of cohort wage typically yield poorer fits, especially in the early subperiod (see parts A and B of Table 3). Unlike the basic model, the alternative models assume that younger workers in the early period forecasted wage stagnation and adjusted their labor supply accordingly. The results do not support that hypothesis. (Using alternative models has little impact in the late period, presumably because wages were flat in that period.)

Finally, when the alternative measure of labor supply, hours × labor force participation rate, is used for Canadian data (in Table 3, part C), the results are very similar to those obtained in parts A and B, when hours × employment rate is used. The one exception is in the late period, when the coefficient of cohort wage is insignificant.

CONCLUSIONS

1) The life cycle of working time has been remarkably similar in Canada and the United States. There are, of course, some differences. Canadian unemployment has been higher in recent years, reducing labor input. There are also smaller differences, especially in the timing of change; for example, the earlier achievement in the United States of a 40-hour standard workweek.

2) The age distribution of male labor supply is an inverted U. Over time, the peak has become more pronounced, as participation for young and old workers declined relative to those in their prime.

3) The level of male labor supply has declined over time: in earlier years, it was largely a result of reductions in working hours; more recently, it has been due to declining labor force participation.

4) Cohort data are a more appropriate measure of the life cycle of individual behavior than are cross-sectional data, but the cohort data show less regularity—especially for the U.S. cohort whose working lives spanned the entire 1920–1970 period, when wages were growing rapidly.

5) A multivariate estimation of the life cycle model performs well in the 1920–1970 period. When a number of cohorts are combined in a multiperiod analysis, and estimates of cohort wage, current wage, and age are used as independent variables, about 85 percent of the variation in labor input is accounted for in both countries. The signs of the independent variables are consistent with the model and, when they are corrected for multicollinearity, are of a plausible magnitude. The age coefficients do suggest that in a period of rapid growth in real hourly wages, a high level of uncertainty about the future, and possibly other factors, constrain young people from taking full advantage of this trend.

6) The model fits the data even better in the later period. This is seen both in a simple figure charting the experience of one cohort and in a multivariate, multicohort analysis. However, the magnitudes of the coefficients are implausibly large.

7) When the two periods are combined, significantly better results are obtained when a dummy variable representing the change in period is interacted with the independent variables. There are important changes in the regression coefficients.

8) An attempt was made to determine whether workers whose lives overlapped the early period, characterized by wage growth, and the later period of wage stagnation foresaw the change and adjusted their labor supply accordingly. No support was found for this hypothesis.

Notes

1. I follow Ghez and Becker in using this term to refer to decision making over an entire life cycle, rather than to decisions over a shorter period of time, such as a business cycle. For interesting examples of the use of different life cycle analyses using Canadian data, see Altonji and Ham (1990); Reilly (1994); and Roble, Magee, and Burbridge (1992).

2. For a positive assessment of this approach, see Browning, Deaton, and Irish (1985) and Rios-Rull (1993).

3. Sources discussed in the Data Appendix to this chapter.

4. This group provides the most difficult measurement problems. Different age categories are used by censuses and surveys in different years; there is an important, though difficult to measure, long-term trend from full- to part-time employment as student enrollment increases, and the way in which government agencies have measured (or have not measured) the role of student employment has changed.

5. Published sources of data and interpretations include Benimadhu (1987); Denton and Ostry (1967); Gartley (1993); Gower (1992); Morisette and Sunter (1994); Podoluk (1968); Rashid (1993); Simard (1986); Conference Board of Canada (1974); as well as the Canadian Censuses of 1921, 1931, 1941, 1951, 1961, and 1971; Historical Statistics of Canada (1965 and 1983 editions); Historical Labor Force Statistics; historical supplements of the Canadian Economic Observer; and Hourly Data from the Survey of 1981 Work History.

6. As measured by household data, at least. The establishment data collected by the United States Bureau of Labor Statistics indicate a sharper decline than do their household data, partly because of increased moonlighting (measured in the latter but not the former series) but also because of likely greater inaccuracy in the household data. Similar gaps between household and establishment data are seen in the Canadian statistics. Unfortunately, data collected from establishments are not obtained in conjunction with questions on the age distribution of the establishment's employment.

7. Since persistent, long-term variations in unemployment are usually small (much less important than variations in hours or labor force participation rates), very long-term analyses of labor inputs typically do not emphasize them. The long-lived increase in Canadian unemployment does require discussion.

8. Again, for prime-age males. Moreover, while the average changed little, there was an increase in the dispersion of hours. See Morisette and Sunter (1994) for an interesting discussion.

9. The census and labor force survey data used here are only imperfect measures of cohort behavior. As they age, cohorts are reduced by death and emigration, increased in numbers by immigrants. If those who die, emigrate, or immigrate supply, on balance, more or less labor than those who remain of the original cohort, the results observed in these sources will only approximate actual cohort behavior.

10. A typical rate of change in that period.

11. See Ghez and Becker (1975, p. 16). In real terms, the coefficient of the current wage is given by $-[\sigma_f(1 - s) + \sigma_c s]$ and the coefficient of age is $\sigma_c(r - \rho)$, where σ_c is the intertemporal elasticity of substitution, σ_f is the contemporary elasticity of substitution between goods and time, r is the real rate of interest, and ρ is the individual's rate of time preference. $s = WL/(WL + X)$ where W is the real wage rate, L is consumption time, and X is consumption of goods and services.

12. A comparison of Eqs. 1 and 2 indicate that $b^*_0 = b_0 + (b_3 - b_1)W_j$.

13. The data used were those for the years shown in Table 1, plus for the United States, 1993.
14. In estimating equations using the alternate measures of cohort wage, the constant term was interpreted in the same fashion as when the first measure of cohort wage was employed: in the third measure, for example, $\beta' = \beta_0 + (\beta_3 - \beta_1)W_0$ and the independent variable, cohort wage, in the regression was $W^3_j - W_0 = jg$ if $j \le 0$; = $jg(1 - 0.01j)$ if $0 \le j \le 50$; and $= 25g$ if $j > 50$.
15. Note that $W^3_j = jg$ at $j = 0$ (as in the earlier variants), and $25g$ at $j = 50$.
16. Regressions were also run that allowed for changed expectations within the late period. A sixth measure of cohort wage was employed here, $W^6_j = W_j(1 - \alpha y)$, where y = current year − 1970 and α is an estimable parameter. These regressions were not successful.
17. The estimations using W^3_j for the early period in Canada and the United States and for the entire period in Canada displayed significant autocorrelation. The results shown in Table 3 for these estimations were corrected for AR1 autocorrelation using the Cochran-Orcutt method.
18. The uncertainty premium here would be reflected in the lender's unwillingness to lend at a conventional rate of interest and the youth's unwillingness to borrow. The labor market constraints mentioned above would also contribute to large age constraints on individual behavior.

References

Altonji, Joseph G., and John C. Ham. 1990. "Intertemporal Substitution, Exogeneity and Surprises: Estimating Life Cycle Models for Canada." *Canadian Journal of Economics* 23(1):1–43.

Benimadhu, Prem. 1987. *Hours of Work: Trends and Attitudes in Canada.* Ottawa: Conference Board of Canada.

Browning, M., A. Deaton, and M. Irish. 1985. "A Profitable Approach to Labor Supply and Commodity Demands over the Life Cycle." *Econometrica* 53(3): 503–543.

Canada. 1927. "Dwellings, Families, Conjugal Conditions of Family Head, Children, Orphanhood, Wage-Earners." *1921 Census of Canada* vol. III, Ottawa.

_____. 1931. "Earnings of Wage Earners, Dwellings, Households, Families, Blind and Deaf-Mutes." *1931 Census of Canada* vol. V, Ottawa.

_____. 1946. "Earnings, Employment and Unemployment of Wage-Earners." *1941 Census of Canada* vol. VI, Ottawa.

_____. 1953. "Labour Force: Earnings and Employment of Wage-Earners." *1951 Census of Canada* vol. V, Ottawa.

_____. 1953. "Labour Force: Occupations and Industries." *1951 Census of Canada* vol. IV, Ottawa.

_____. 1965. "Wage Earners, Earnings and Employment." *1961 Census of Canada* vol. III, pt. 3, Ottawa.

_____. 1975. "Wage and Salary Income for Canada, Provinces and Census Divisions." *1971 Census of Canada* vol. III, Part 1, Ottawa.

_____. 1984. "Population: Employment Income Distributions." *1981 Census of Canada Nation series* vol. I, Ottawa.

_____. 1965. *Historical Statistics of Canada.* Cambridgeshire: Cambridge University Press.

Canadian Economic Observer Historical Statistical Supplement. Various issues. Toronto.

Conference Board of Canada. 1974. "The Altered Work Week, A Symposium." Ottawa.

Denton, Frank T., and Sylvia Ostry. 1967. *Historical Estimates of the Canadian Labour Force.* Ottawa: Dominion Bureau of Statistics.

Employment and Earnings. Various issues. Washington, D.C.: United States Department of Labor.

Gartley, John. 1993. *Focus on Canada: Earnings of Canadians.* Statistics Canada: Ottawa.

Ghez, Gilbert, and Gary S. Becker. 1975. *The Allocation of Time and Goods over the Life Cycle.* New York: National Bureau of Economic Research.

Gower, David. 1992. "A Note on Canadian Unemployment since 1921." Perspectives on Labour and Income, Autumn.

Monthly Labor Review. Various issues. Washington, D.C.: United States Department of Labor.

Morisette, Rene, and Deborah Sunter. 1994. "What Is Happening to Weekly Hours Worked in Canada." Analytic Studies Bureau research paper no. 65, Statistics Canada, Ottawa.

Nagatani, Keizo. 1972. "Life Savings: Theory and Fact." *American Economic Review* 62(3): 344–353.

Ostry, Sylvia, and Mahmoud Zaidi. 1979. *Labor Economics in Canada.* Toronto: Macmillan of Canada.

Owen, John D. 1986. *Working Lives: The American Work Force since 1920.* Lexington, Massachusetts: Lexington Books.

Podoluk, Jenny R. 1968. *Incomes of Canadians.* Ottawa: Dominion Bureau of Statistics.

Rashid, Abdul. 1993. "Seven Decades of Wage Change." *Perspectives on Labour and Income* (Summer): 9–21.

Reilly, Kevin T. 1994. "Annual Hours and Weeks in a Life Cycle Labor Supply Model: Canadian Evidence on Male Behavior." *Journal of Labor Economics* 12(3): 460–477.

Rios-Rull, Jose-Victor. 1993. "Working in the Market, Working at Home, and the Acquisition of Skills: A General-Equilibrium Approach." *American Economic Review* 53(3): 893–907.

Roble, A.L., L. Magee, and J.B. Burbridge. 1992. "Kernel Smoothed Consumption-Age Quantiles." *Canadian Journal of Economics* 25(3): 669–680.

Simard, Monique. 1986. "The Reduction and Rearrangement of Worktimes: A Priority and a Challenge." In *A New Work Agenda for Canada*. Toronto: Canadian Mental Health Association.

Statistics Canada. 1983. *Hourly Data from the Survey of 1981 Work History*. Ottawa.

_____. 1983. *Historical Statistics of Canada, Second edition*. Ottawa.

_____. 1994. *Earnings of Men and Women*. Ottawa.

_____. Various issues. *Historical Labour Force Statistics*. Ottawa.

_____. Various issues. *Labour Force Annual Averages*. Ottawa.

Data Appendix

United States: U.S. data for the 1977–1995 period from the *Monthly Labor Review*, various issues; *Employment and Earnings*, various issues, and unpublished data from the United States Department of Labor. Data for 1920–1977 from Owen (1986). Data for the recent period were relatively easy to obtain. When there was a change in data series in recent years, the Bureau of Labor Statistics personnel were very helpful in providing unpublished data. I am especially grateful to Steve Hipple for his assistance in this work.

Canada: Canadian data were obtained from a number of published and unpublished sources. I am especially grateful to David Gower, Regine Lafnier, Rene Morisette, and Abdul Rashid, all of Statistics Canada for their help in supplying and interpreting data.

Labor input per capita: This series required data on the employment rate and hours of work, by age and sex, over a 75-year period.

Employment rate: 1975–1995. *Labour Force Surveys*. Various issues, Table 1.

1946–1975. An employment rate was constructed for these years, then linked at 1975 to the Labour Force Survey data. Employment rate was measured as (labor force participation rate) × (1 – unemployment rate).

Labor force participation rate: *Historical Statistics of Canada*. 1983. Series 205–222.

Unemployment rate: *Historical Statistics of Canada*. 1983. Series 223–235.

1921–1946. An employment rate was constructed for these years, then linked to the later series.

Employment rate was again measured as (labor force participation rate) × (1 – unemployment rate).

Labor force participation rates were constructed from data in *Historical Statistics of Canada*. 1967. Series D107–123, and Denton and Ostry (1967).

Unemployment rate: Gower (1992). These national unemployment rate data were linked at 1946 with age divided data.

Hours: 1975–1995. Unpublished data from the *Labour Force Survey*, obtained from Statistics Canada.

1921–1975. A series of average hours was constructed. The ratio of female to male hours in 1975 was assumed to persist in this period. This ratio was used in conjunction with data on the changing proportions of males and females in the work force and with the series on average hours to estimate the average male workweek. Within the male work force, the age distribution of hours was assumed to correspond to 1975 ratios.

Average hours, 1966–1975. Unpublished data from Statistics Canada; linked to 1975 data.

Average hours, 1926–1966. Ostry and Zaidi (1979), pp. 80–81. Nonagricultural workers hours series; linked to 1966 data.

Average hours, 1921–1926. Ostry and Zaidi (1979), Standard hours in manufacturing. Linked to later series.

Wages: A time series of male real wages was constructed. Ratios of the wages of the different age groups to the male average were then multiplied by this average series to obtain wages for each age group.

Average male wages: 1995. *Employment, Earnings, and Hours*, February, 1996, p. 38.

1969–1994. Real earnings of male full-time, full year workers were obtained from *Earnings of Men and Women*, 1994, Text Table 1. (Hours reductions were minimal in that period, so that this series is a fair approximation of changes in hourly earnings.) Linked to 1995.

1920–1969. General index of wages (Deflated by Canadian CPI). *Historical Statistics of Canada* (1983), Series E209–219 for 1961–1969; E198–208 for 1920–1961. (This series endeavors to measure hourly earnings.) Linked at 1969 to later index.

Wage ratios: 1994. *Earnings of Men and Women*. 1994. Table 4. Average earnings of earners, full-year, full-time workers.

1980, 1990. Average earnings of earners, full-year, full-time workers. Unpublished data for *Earnings of Men and Women* from Statistics Canada.

1941. "Earnings, Employment and Unemployment of Wage-Earners, 1941." *1941 Census of Canada*, Volume VI. 1946 had both annual earnings and weeks worked by age and sex. The latter were divided by the former to obtain weekly earnings by age and sex.

1931. *Earnings of Wage Earners, Dwellings, Households, Families, Blind and Deaf-Mutes 1931 Census of Canada.* Vol. V. 1931 had weekly earnings by age and sex.

These five years were used to obtain through interpolation the wage ratios for the remaining years used in the statistical work.

2

Perspectives on Working Time over the Life Cycle

Michael Wolfson and Geoff Rowe
Statistics Canada

INTRODUCTION

A central topic in social statistics is patterns of work in a population. In addition to the longstanding interest in basic information like unemployment rates and employment/population ratios, there is increasing interest in the way individuals' working careers unfold over their lifetimes.

However, the requisite long-term longitudinal data on working careers are still largely unavailable in Canada and many other countries. As a result, statistical impressions have typically been generated either by examining trends in cross-sectional age-specific patterns, or by piecing together data using synthetic statistical methods. LifePaths, a microsimulation model recently developed by Statistics Canada (Wolfson 1995, 1997), provides an alternative means of combining information from different cross-sectional and longitudinal data sources to infer individual life paths. This model offers a means to estimate and display coherent pictures of work and other kinds of time use over various time scales ranging up to the full life cycle.

BACKGROUND—THE GENERAL SOCIAL SURVEY TIME-USE DATA AND LIFE TABLE APPROACHES

The most common perspectives on working time over the life cycle draw on cross-sectional labor force survey or population census data.

Figure 1 Population Age 15+, by Age, Sex, and Employment Status, 1991

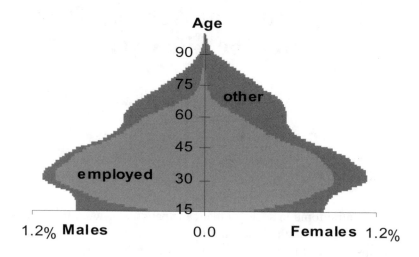

For example, Figure 1 shows a standard population pyramid from the 1991 Census. The proportion of individuals at single years of age is divided between those who were employed and those who were not, based on having positive labor market income in the previous calendar year.

Another less frequently presented perspective on working time over the life cycle draws on life table methods. The first such estimates for Canada were Denton and Ostry (1969), in turn updated by Gnanesekaran and Montigny (1975). More recently, Bélanger and Larrivée (1992) have made multistate life table estimates.

The original working life table efforts required only limited cross-sectional age-specific labor force participation and mortality rate data. These working life tables included two states: working and not working ("inactive"). Transitions between these states were based on age-specific labor force participation rates (for males only) and a series of simplifying assumptions. The key assumptions were that individuals could enter the labor market only once and could leave the labor market only once over their entire lifetime, and that overall, labor force participation rates first rise monotonically to an age where they are at a maximum, and then fall monotonically.

The more recent increment-decrement methods used by Bélanger and Larrivée relax these restrictive assumptions on transitions into and out of the labor force by using longitudinal microdata from the Labour Market Activity Survey (LMAS). These data allow gross flow transition probabilities to be estimated directly, so it is no longer necessary to infer these rates based on an assumed equality with net flows and by first-differencing age-specific participation rates. With increment/decrement methods, multiple exits and reentries to the labor force over a lifetime are not ruled out *a priori,* as in the earlier working life tables. However, strong simplifying assumptions are still embodied in the analysis. In particular, transition probabilities into and out of the labor force are assumed to be first order Markov, depending only on age, sex, and labor force status in the previous year, and nothing of subannual flows and seasonal patterns of employment is included.

Table 1 shows the two sets of estimates of working life expectancy in a comparable fashion. Notwithstanding the various simplifying assumptions, this series of male working life table summary results vividly displays the long-run trends of more time spent in schooling, ever earlier ages of retirement, a general reduction in working years, and hence a long-run decline in the ratio of working to inactive or retired years.

The last two rows give Bélanger and Larrivée results for 1986, first using the older gross equals net flow assumption (the 1986[a] row), and then using an increment/decrement life table based on gross transition probabilities (the 1986[b] row). The rather large 5.2-year difference in expected working life in these last two rows is indicative of the sensitivity of these kinds of results to the assumptions on transition rates.

However, both kinds of working life table assumptions, as well as the population pyramid in Figure 1, take the calendar year as the smallest time period and treat working within the year as a dichotomous variable. There is no allowance for part-time or part-year rather than full-time, full-year work, and nothing on unpaid work. Data from the 1992 General Social Survey (GSS) (Statistics Canada 1997), in contrast, suggest a high degree of heterogeneity in actual hours worked. For example, Figure 2 contrasts 1992 GSS data on hours of work in the reference day with 1991 Census data on hours of work (employed and

Table 1 Historical Stationary Male Life and Working Life Expectancies at Age 15

	Average age at			Number of years	
Year	Labor force entry	Retirement	Average age at death	Working	Retired
1921	17.5	62.7	67.6	45.2	4.9
1931	18.0	63.0	68.4	45.0	5.4
1941	18.2	63.1	69.1	44.9	6.0
1951	18.5	82.9	70.4	44.4	7.5
1961	19.2	63.0	71.2	43.8	8.2
1971	19.8	62.3	71.3	42.5	9.0
1986[a]	20.0	65.5	73.8	44.8	8.3
1986[b]	20.0	60.3	73.8	39.4	13.5

SOURCE: Adapted from Gnanasekaran and Montigny (1975) for decades 1921 to 1971 (Tables 2.1 and 12, 1975), and from Bélanger and Larrivée (1992) for the two 1986 rows (Tables 1 and 2, 1992).

NOTE: The Bélanger and Larrivée results were given only at age 16; age 15 results have been extrapolated. Working life expectancy is taken from Table 2 for both the active and inactive populations for the 1986[b] row. Also, they have only estimated the average age at death, and the expected number of working years, so the average age at retirement and number of years retired were derived based on the simple assumption that the average age at labor force entry was exactly 20. There also appears to be an inconsistency in the Gnanasekaran and Montigny results for 1971 average number of years working in comparison to all their other estimates, so this figure has been adjusted. The Bélanger and Larrivée definition of "working" is having worked at least one hour in a reference week in September of each year. The Gnanasekaran and Montigny definition for 1971 was essentially working or looking for work in the week prior to census enumeration, but then excluding summer students.

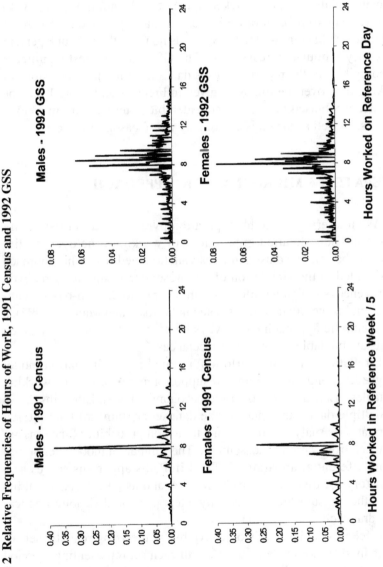

Figure 2 Relative Frequencies of Hours of Work, 1991 Census and 1992 GSS

Males - 1991 Census

Males - 1992 GSS

Females - 1991 Census

Females - 1992 GSS

Hours Worked in Reference Week / 5

Hours Worked on Reference Day

self-employed) in the reference week (the latter hours divided by 5 for comparability).

In common with similar survey data on hours worked in a week, the census data exhibit a marked spike corresponding to exactly 40 hours (nearly 40 percent of responses for males and about 25 percent for females). In contrast, the GSS reveals no more than about 8 percent of exactly 8-hour-day responses. The GSS data suggest significant rounding bias in the reported census data. In turn, the impressions of working time over the life cycle given in Figure 1 and Table 1 may be significantly biased due to this considerable heterogeneity in weekly patterns, as well as the omission of part-year (seasonal) work.

LIFEPATHS: A MICROANALYTIC APPROACH

As an alternative to the population pyramid and multistate life table approach, detailed impressions of working time over the life cycle can be generated using microsimulation methods. This approach is grounded in the simulation of a representative sample of realistic heterogeneous individual life paths, in contrast to the cell-based methods of multistate life tables. As noted in Wolfson and Manton (1992), a microanalytic approach can always be devised that nests any given multistate life table analysis as a special case.

LifePaths is a monte carlo longitudinal microsimulation model designed, among other things, to support generalizations of working life tables. Like any empirical socioeconomic model, LifePaths draws on multiple data sets, since no one data set contains all the required information. Analytical results like transition probability functions are estimated from various data sources. The simulation model then serves as an "inferential apparatus." The LifePaths apparatus serves as a repository for diverse empirical results, and as an inference engine where these results are synthetically integrated and their joint implications drawn out.

LifePaths achieves this objective by synthesizing realistic sets of full individual life cycle histories, with each set representing a period birth cohort. Generalized working life expectancies and associated life tables are then by-products. It is simply a matter of cross-tabulating the individual life histories comprising the cohort to construct working life table results analogous to those just presented. LifePaths' explicit microdata foundations further enable a wide range of "views" of cohort work patterns over the life cycle.

Unlike a life table, which follows groups of individuals, LifePaths generates one individual at a time, and follows him or her until death. LifePaths allows individuals to be highly heterogeneous, since each individual's life path is uniquely simulated. Also, LifePaths models individual dynamics in continuous time. LifePaths uses semi-Markov processes, usually represented by multivariate hazard functions or waiting time distributions. At any moment in time, an individual faces chances of making a number of transitions. For example, depending on his or her current state or set of attributes, this could be a transition into the labor force, or into a marital union.

In the current version of LifePaths, individuals are jointly characterized by the following basic attributes at each point in their lives:

- age—as a continuous variable;
- fertility—exact ages at the birth of children, and information on the presence of children in the familial home;
- nuptiality—unattached, in a common-law or marital union, separated, or divorced;
- work status—including labor force participation and employment status (hours per week, weeks in the year);
- school status—grade and type of institution if attending, educational attainment otherwise;
- work income—hourly rate, weekly and annual earnings;
- time use—17 categories, including various kinds of work, learning, leisure, and personal care; and
- spouse attributes—including age, educational attainment, and labor market experience.

In addition, a wide range of derived attributes can be constructed from these basic attributes.

The core of the LifePaths model is the set of processes by which the trajectories for each attribute are generated. A brief sketch is given in the following paragraphs.

Demography. Fertility is modeled as a sequel to conception, which in turn is modeled as a series of piecewise constant hazard rates, conditional on age, marital status, and number of previous live births. The main data source is birth registrations, supplemented by data from the 1983 Family History Survey to account for biases arising from conceptions while single or in a common-law union that are then followed by a marriage before the birth of the child. Mortality rates are conditional on age, sex, and marital status, and are based on death registrations. In both cases, the population census provides the denominators.

Union formation and dissolution are represented by a series of hazard functions (Rowe 1989). From the single state, there are competing risks of entering a common-law union or a legal marriage. Marriage breakdown involves risks of separation and subsequent divorce. These hazards have been separately estimated for men and women, and depend in a complex way on previous history. For example, a woman's "risk" of entry to a union is positively related to being pregnant, and is highest shortly following labor force entry. Risk of separation for a woman is higher if there are no young children at home, if the woman was a teenage bride, and if she has recent work experience.

Educational Progression. Transition rates for progression through elementary and secondary school were constructed to be as close to jointly consistent as possible with the 1986 and 1991 population census data on the school attendance rates of children of the relevant ages. Progression through postsecondary institutions (colleges, trade schools, universities) is based on hazard rates jointly estimated from the National Graduates Survey (NGS), administrative data on school enrollments, and the LMAS for cases where young people quit work to return to and continue their studies.

Labor Market. Labor market experience is simulated in two main parts: whether or not employed, and earnings from employment. The first of these, transitions into and out of employment, is estimated from the LMAS separately for males and females, and also separately for first entry, second and subsequent entry, and exit from employment. First entry is represented by waiting time distributions, while the other transitions are represented by multivariate hazard functions. Sex and educational attainment are important determinants of the waiting time to first employment. Reentry hazards depend on sex, educational attainment, and duration of the current spell of nonemployment, and for women the presence of infant children has an additional depressing effect.

Earnings are in turn based on employment status as just described, and separate models for weekly hours of work, and hourly wages. Upon first entry to employment, a weekly hours value is randomly assigned, drawn from an age-, sex- and educational attainment-specific distribution, in turn based on data from a combination of NGS, LMAS, and the Survey of Consumer Finances (SCF, the annual household income distribution survey). Subsequently, the weekly hours variable is updated as a function of age, sex, last year's weekly hours, and educational attainment. At the same time that weekly hours is assigned, each individual is assigned a percentile rank for hourly earnings. The hourly earnings rate is then "looked up" from age-, sex- and educational attainment–specific distributions. Percentile ranks are adjusted from year to year based on estimates of rank order "churning" from the LMAS.

Daily Time Use. The 1992 General Social Survey (GSS) collected 24-hour time-use diary data for about 9,000 individuals, evenly distributed by age, sex, day of the week, and month of the year. The GSS also collected basic data on educational attainment, employment status, and family status. After extensive analysis of these data, a LifePaths module was created that imputes to every simulated person-day one vector of time spent over a 24-hour period in each of a series of 17 activities. (Special assumptions have been made for children under age 15 and the elderly living in institutions, since they were not covered by the GSS.)

The statistical analysis indicated that age, sex, day of the week, marital status, presence of young children, educational attainment, and main activity (i.e., student, employed or self-employed, other) were all significantly associated with these vector patterns. Thus, all of these attributes, as generated by other LifePaths processes, were used in the imputation. The imputation process was also designed to reproduce the observed variability in time-use patterns among individuals with the same attributes, based on using the distribution of vector residuals from a multivariate regression analysis. Further details are given in the appendix.

The multivariate life cycle histories generated by a LifePaths simulation enable basic working life table results to be extended in several directions. Annual patterns of paid work can be examined in more detail, going beyond a two-way breakdown between working and nonworking years. For example, part-time work, hours worked per week, subannual spells of unemployment or withdrawal from the labor force, periods where work and school are simultaneously pursued, and self-employment are all taken into account. In addition, the time aspects of work are combined with earnings, formal schooling, and familial context (e.g., living alone or with other family members).

PRELIMINARY RESULTS

Before presenting results based on LifePaths simulations, Figure 3 shows the 1992 GSS time-use patterns in a manner analogous to "employment" in the population pyramid in Figure 1. This time, however, instead of distributing total person-years in the population by age, sex, and a dichotomous characterization of employment, Figure 3 shows the distribution of total person-hours in the population by age, sex, and main type of activity. The 1992 detailed time-use patterns have been combined with the same census population data for 1991 as

Figure 3 Total Population Age 15+ by Age, Sex, and Main Activity, 1991

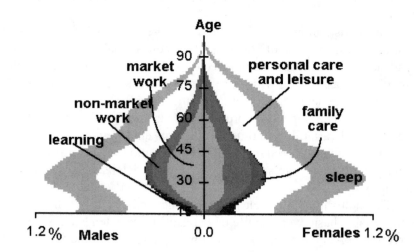

in Figure 1 by reweighing the GSS sample to correspond not only to census counts of individuals by age and sex, but also by labor force status, census family size, and the age of the head of the census family.

Perhaps the most dramatic change from Figure 1 to Figure 3 is in the apparent importance of paid or "market" work. Using a binary classification on person-years as in Figure 1 gives the impression that employment is a major use of time. On the other hand, using daily hours as in Figure 3 suggests that paid work is of much lesser relative importance in the daily (or even waking) lives of Canadians. This pair of figures also indicates the limitations of conventional demographic dependency ratios, which use raw counts of individuals of working age (e.g., age 20 to 64) as the denominator. In the context of Figure 3, such ratios clearly understate the degree of economic dependence of many individuals in society.

BASIC LIFEPATHS RESULTS

The baseline LifePaths simulation consists, fundamentally, of a sample of complete (synthetic) individual life cycle histories. This longitudinal micro database of sampled life histories is too complex to be examined directly, so we offer here only selected summary "views" of the underlying microcosm.

To start, Figure 4 shows the population pyramid for the base case simulation scenario. This is similar to Figures 1 and 3 except that the population envelope is the steady-state or period life table population, rather than an actual population distribution by age and sex. It is based on late 1980s and early 1990s transition probability functions, as sketched above. As expected, at higher ages, the survival curve for females falls more slowly than that for males, a counterpart to (or, more accurately, the underlying reason for) females' higher life expectancy. (The blip in the age 99 interval reflects the fact that this is actually the age ≥ 99 interval.)

Figure 4 also shows the population broken down into three socioeconomic categories—"employed," "in school," and "other." "School" starts at grade 1, so day care and kindergarten are part of "other." Since the LifePaths framework tracks individuals through time contin-

Figure 4 LifePaths Population (person-years) by Major Activity, Age, and Sex

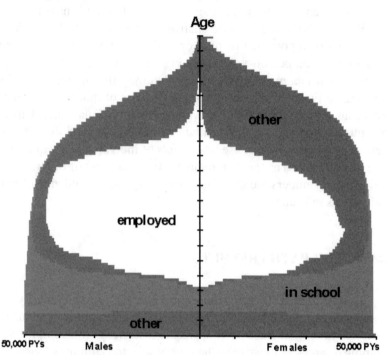

uously, some arbitrary classifications have been applied in years where individuals engage in more than one activity. Specifically, for a person-year to be considered "employed" in this diagram, the individual had to be working at least 15 hours per week, and the plurality of time during the year had to be spent working at this hours-per-week rate. Thus, someone who spent 5 months as a student, 4 months working at least 15 hours per week, and the remaining 3 months of the year working less than 15 hours per week (including not working at all) would be considered in "school" that year; while if the 5 and 4 were reversed, they would be considered "employed." (Definitions such as these are under the control of the LifePaths user.) The diagram shows that virtually everyone is in school by age 8, a few start leaving at age 16, most have left by age 20, but there is a tail of both males and females who are in school through their twenties.

No one appears to make a transition directly from school to employment, though we return to this point in a later figure. Instead, a perhaps surprising proportion of individuals are in the "other" category, which includes the unemployment as well as those not in the labor force (e.g., homemakers, the retired). As expected, males are more likely to be employed at various ages than are females. There is a bit of a dip in the employed profile for women in the prime child-bearing years. Men show a relatively sharper decline in participation in the age 60–65 age range than women, whose participation begins dropping at earlier ages.

Parenthetically, Figure 4 corresponds to Sir Richard Stone's "active sequence" (i.e., transitions among working and learning states) in his proposed System of Social and Demographic Statistics (United

Figure 5   LifePaths Population (person-years) by Family Status, Age, and Sex

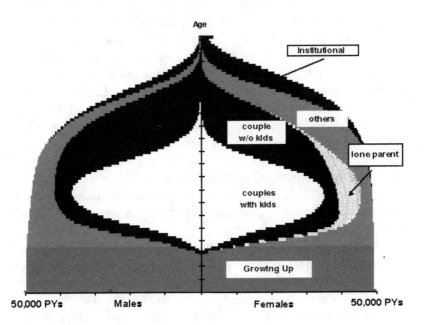

Nations 1975). Figure 5 gives the corresponding LifePaths view for Canada of his "passive sequence," the other main demographic focus in the SSDS. It uses the same population pyramid graphic form, and refers to exactly the same underlying LifePaths synthetic population, but classifies individuals along a different dimension: family status. By definition, all individuals under age 18 are classified as "growing up" unless they are married or have a child. Also, whenever a marriage breaks down, any children are assumed to remain with the mother. This assumption explains why there are female but no male lone parents. (Future versions will incorporate more realistic data on custody arrangements.)

Comparing the male and female curves for the married states (couples with and without children) shows the male curves displaced a few years toward higher ages. This is a reflection of the general pattern where husbands tend to be a few years older than their wives. Figure 5 also shows there are many more widows than widowers ("others" at higher ages). This is a consequence of both the positive average age difference between husbands and wives, and the greater life expectancy of women. Finally, the diagram indicates the much higher rates of institutionalization of women (principally in nursing or chronic care facilities), due in turn to their greater longevity and higher prevalence of health problems at older ages, and the fact that similarly incapacitated males more often have a wife who can care for them at home.

Figures 4 and 5 show only two rather straightforward "views" (in this case, cross-tabulations) of the full underlying LifePaths microcosm—a multivariate longitudinal micro data set for a synthetic "early 1990s" period birth cohort. Exactly this same underlying longitudinal micro data set can be tabulated to generate a view of the flows between states rather than stocks within each state. For example, Table 2 displays the flows corresponding to the stocks in Figure 4. Each cell of the table presents the average number of individuals making each kind of transition each year (within each age range) for a cohort of 100,000 births.

The first transition is from "other" (early childhood or preschool) to "school." Figure 4 indicates that all male and female children make this transition by ages 6 and 7. The next major transition is at the end of "school," where the peak flow rate to "work" occurs around age 20 for both males and females. A smaller number, also peaking at about

Table 2 LifePaths Gross Flows between Major Activities Average Persons per Year, by Age and Sex

Age	Other→school	School→work	School→other	Other→work	Work→other
Females					
15–19	91	3727	1215	912	1202
20–24	493	5397	1236	4695	5388
25–29	179	1339	229	6352	5185
30–34	59	394	86	5231	4849
35–39	67	190	56	3319	3749
40–44	74	191	45	2807	2957
45–49	73	159	47	2411	3291
50–54	27	91	19	2165	3352
55–59	3	56	18	1499	3436
60–64	0	15	6	586	2882
65+	0	0	0	721	1260
Males					
15–19	137	3505	1431	803	1302
20–24	719	5151	1574	3913	4175
25–29	222	1423	224	4157	2562
30–34	82	478	69	2899	2571
35–39	41	215	42	2455	2291
40–44	33	164	33	2153	2076
45–49	19	105	19	2000	2107
50–54	4	42	3	1997	2021
55–59	5	88	15	1955	3456
60–64	0	30	7	1373	4756
65+	0	0	0	971	2405

NOTE: From early adult ages to the 60s, the main flows are between the "work" and "other" categories. Note that all these flows are gross rather than net. It is notable that the net flow between work and other (based on comparing the gross flows) shifts direction toward "other" in the 40–45 age range for females, but remains quite small for males through age 50. This is followed by retirement peaks in the 55–65 age range, the one for males being more pronounced.

age 20, move from school to "other" activity. Recall that the "other" category is any person-year where the plurality of the year (i.e., at least a tiny bit more than one-third) was spent neither as a student nor working more than 15 hours per week.

In addition to stocks and flows of individuals in various categories of activity, LifePaths also supports data views showing sojourn times, which are the lengths of time individuals spend in various states. Such sojourn times have already been illustrated in Table 1 above, giving earlier life table estimates of working life expectancy. A major additional capability in LifePaths, given its explicit micro data foundations, is the option of viewing uni- or bivariate distributions of durations or sojourn times across the population. For example, Figure 6 shows the joint distribution for males and females of years spent mainly in school and mainly in employment, as a 3-d plot of simulated frequencies.

This graph indicates modes at around 12 years of school, for both men and women, and about 30 years of employment for women compared to 35 to 40 for men. The expected distribution of years of school

Figure 6 LifePaths Joint Distribution of School and Work Sojourn Times

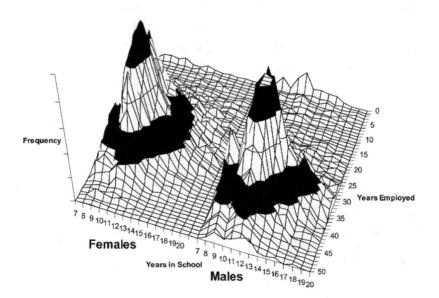

is a bit wider for men, while the distribution of years of employment is considerably wider for women.

Note that a year of employment in Figure 6 is based on the amount of time (essentially week by week) that LifePaths is simulating the individual as "employed" (yes or no, based on labor force dynamics estimated from the LMAS). This is similar to an annual average of monthly labor force surveys, which is essentially the proportion of weeks employed. Years of schooling are analogously defined.

However, impressions of working life expectancy are sensitive to the precise way work time is measured. For example, Figure 7 compares three definitions for a subsample of individual life histories generated by a LifePaths simulation. The straight line represents lifetime work in hours, based on the most detailed time use data imputed from the GSS. This ranges up to 10 years for women, and 12 years for men, where these are years of working 24 hours per day and 365 days per year.

The two clouds of points in Figure 7 represent annualized definitions like those used in Figures 1 and 6. The solid squares correspond in concept to Figure 6, the amount of time LifePaths is simulating the individual as "employed" (yes or no). The hollow squares then apply a calendar year window, and count a year as "employed" if at any time during the year, the individual was "employed" in the sense of the solid squares. This latter definition corresponds to Figure 1, where the census data counted an individual as employed if he or she had strictly positive labor market income in the calendar year.

The slopes of the point clouds suggest (reassuringly) that every "solid" year of work (24 hours per day, 365 days per year) is associated with about three years of work as more conventionally defined. However, each solid year of work is also associated with a considerable scatter in the point cloud, representing the fact that annual dichotomous representations of working time are a considerable homogenization of reality.

Finally, Figure 8 gives another set of views of the LifePaths cohort. This is also a small subsample of the cohort simulated. This time, individuals were "checked" every three months during their entire lifetimes. At each "check" time, their cumulative time spent in market work, nonmarket work, and leisure was recorded. The various curves in Figure 8 show individuals' trajectories through the life cycle of time

Figure 7 Lifetime Work Durations, Three Definitions

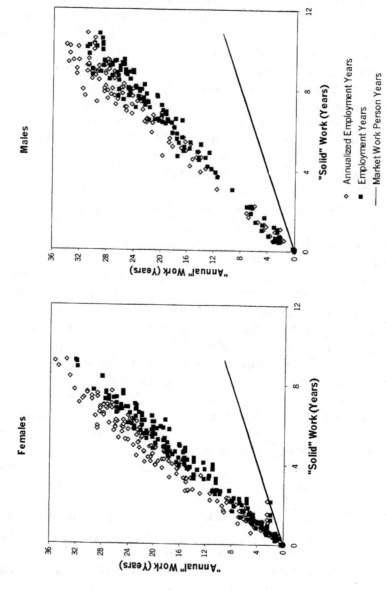

Females

Males

◇ Annualized Employment Years

■ Employment Years

— Market Work Person Years

Figure 8 Sample LifePaths

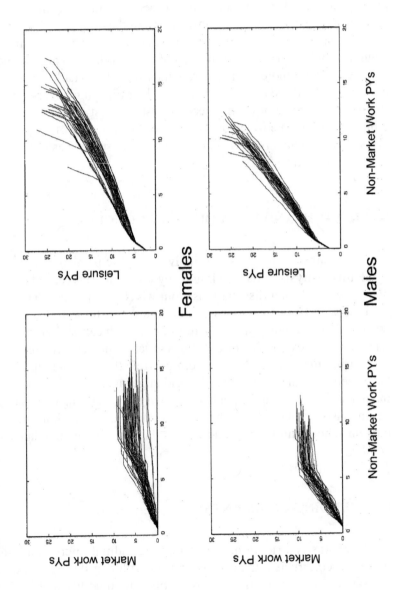

spent in pairs of these activities. For example, the graph in the upper left shows time spent in nonmarket work along the horizontal axis, and time spent in market work along the vertical. In all cases, individuals move from the origin in the southwest toward the northeast.

Comparing the left pair of graphs, men tend to spend less time in nonmarket work (the slope of their set of curves is higher) than women, while women far more often interrupt their periods of market work and have intervals where they spend most of their time in nonmarket work (indicated by trajectories that head almost due east). Judging by the typical slopes of the trajectories in the right-hand pair of graphs, for every hour of nonmarket work, men spend almost twice as much time in leisure as women.

VALIDATION AND DATA QUALITY CONCERNS

The synthetic microcosm of individuals' life paths on which this LifePaths analysis is based should, by construction, reproduce the major marginal joint distributions from which it was built. This was the case with labor force participation rates, fertility rates, mortality rates, union formation and dissolution rates, educational enrollment rates, and age/sex-specific distributions of labor market earnings.

During the course of constructing LifePaths, these comparisons have been continually checked. By and large, agreement is good. The main instances of disagreement arise when the underlying data sources are inconsistent with each other (for example, as with administrative data on school enrollments and census data on school attendance by children).

CONCLUDING COMMENTS

LifePaths is a richly multivariate longitudinal microsimulation model. It constructs estimates of birth cohort life cycles by synthesizing samples of hypothetical but realistic individual life histories. It therefore generalizes a variety of life table analyses, including working life tables, and affords a much wider variety of "views" of working time over the life cycle. More recent work has extended LifePaths from a single "period" cohort to a sequence of overlapping historical birth cohorts; for example, to consider questions of the intergenerational equity of public pensions (Wolfson et al. 1998), and the intersection of adequate income, health, and leisure time (Wolfson and Rowe 1998).

One of the most striking results in this LifePaths analysis is the difference in impressions of the importance of paid work over the life cycle depending on the "granularity" of the time accounting. Conventional approaches, when viewing the entire life cycle, tend to go year by year, so that a typical life cycle can be expected to involve 20 to 40 years of work. However, when the analysis uses much finer units of time (e.g., hours and days), it becomes clear that paid work is a much smaller part of life.

References

Bélanger, Alain, and Daniel Larrivée. 1992. "New Approach for Constructing Canadian Working Life Times, 1986–1987." *Statistical Journal of the United Nations ECE* 9(1): 27–49.

Denton, Frank T., and Sylvia Ostry. 1969. *Working Life Tables for Canadian Males.* Ottawa: The Queens Printer.

Gnanasekaran, K.S., and G. Montigny. 1975. *Working Life Tables for Males in Canada and Provinces 1971.* Occasional paper, Statistics Canada Catalogue 71-524E, Ottawa.

Rowe, G. 1989. "Union Dissolution in a Changing Social Context." In *The Family in Crisis: A Population Crisis?*, J. Legare, T.R. Balakrishnan, and R.P. Beaujot, eds. Ottawa: Royal Society of Canada, pp. 141–163.

Statistics Canada. 1997. "Overview of the 1992 General Social Survey on Time Use (GSS-7)." Working paper no. 9, Statistics Canada, Ottawa.

United Nations. 1975. *Towards a System of Social and Demographic Statistics.* New York: United Nations.

Wolfson, M.C., and K.G. Manton. 1992. *A Review of Models of Population Health Expectancy: A Microsimulation Perspective.* Analytical Studies Branch research paper series, No. 45, Statistics Canada, Ottawa.

Wolfson, M.C. 1995. "Socio-Economic Statistics and Public Policy: A New Role for Microsimulation Modeling." Invited paper to the 50th session of the International Statistical Institute, Beijing, August 21–29.

————. 1997. "Sketching LifePaths: A New Framework for Socio-Economic Statistics." In *Simulating Social Phenomena*, R. Conte, R. Hegselmann, and P. Tierna, eds. Lecture Notes in Economics and Mathematical Systems 456, Springer Verlag, Berlin.

Wolfson, M.C., and G. Rowe. 1998. "Public Pension Reforms – Analyses Based on the LifePaths Generational Accounting Framework." 26th General Conference of the International Association for Research in Income and Wealth, Cambridge, United Kingdom.

Wolfson, M.C., G. Rowe, X. Lin, and S.F. Gribble. 1998. "Historical Generational Accounting with Heterogeneous Populations." In *Government Finances and Generational Equity*, M. Corak, ed. Ottawa: Statistics Canada, pp. 107–125.

Appendix: Microsimulation of Patterns of Time Use

This appendix provides further detail on the methodology by which the time use data collected in the 1992 General Social Survey (GSS) (Statistics Canada 1997) were imputed to the individual histories simulated by LifePaths. These GSS data by nature provide a cross section of the time-use patterns of Canadians in 1992, and cannot directly provide a view of time use over the life course. LifePaths simulations therefore require an imputation of time use patterns over the lifetimes of synthetic individuals.

Structuring and Interpreting the Data

For these purposes, GSS time uses were partitioned into 17 mutually exclusive activity types:

1) employment	7) self-employment	13) commuting
2) family care	8) domestic work	14) volunteer work
3) adult education	9) formal education	15) sleep/nap
4) shopping	10) personal care	16) social leisure
5) active leisure	11) serviced leisure (movies, etc.)	17) passive leisure (tv, etc.)
6) reading	12) other	

Given this classification of activities, the GSS data set can be thought of as an array of 8,815 rows, each 17 columns wide (each row corresponding to one of the 8,815 respondents with a complete set of responses). About 60 percent of all the cells of this array indicate zero reported time use. However, for two reasons, these zeros should not necessarily be interpreted as representing a complete absence of time engaged in a given activity:

- reported time use activities are "main" activities that partition the day into mutually exclusive periods (for example, joint time use such as reading for leisure while travelling to work on the bus would be reported as commuting); and

- there is evidence of substantial rounding in the responses (for example, 32 percent of reported durations of sleep are even multiples of an hour, while 16 percent are even multiples of half an hour).

Moreover, it is important to distinguish between two types of zeros in this overall array:

- Response zeros—zeros that represent activities that are engaged in with small probability, for short intervals or that are unlikely to be a main activity. Ideally, the expected values of such zeros in the observed GSS data should be represented as small positive quantities.

- Structural zeros—zero time spent in an activity that is likely to be a main activity, where such a zero is reasonable in relation to the stage in the life cycle. For example, retirement usually implies no paid work. Such zeros should be modeled as zeros—they are essentially impossible events.

Zero time spent in an activity was operationally identified as a structural zero for:

- Employment or self-employment—if the main activity in the previous seven days was either retirement, long-term illness, maternity/paternity leave, or other nonwork if no work was reported in the previous year.
- Commuting—where both employment and self-employment are structural zeros.
- Formal education—if employment and/or self-employment are nonzero.
- Family care— if no spouse or child were present in the household.

About 12,000 structural zeros were identified by these definitions, representing about 13 percent of the zeros in the data array.

Regression Analysis

A sequence of three equations was then estimated as the basis for imputing daily time-use patterns to the individual trajectories simulated by LifePaths. In all cases, k indexes the 17 activities, and i the individual respondents to the GSS. These equations were estimated from the GSS 8815 by 17 array.

The first set of logistic equations describes the patterns of occurrence of structural zeros:

(A1) $E(ZERO_{ik}) \approx \left(1 + \exp\left[-X_{ij}^{*}\beta_{jk}\right]\right)^{-1}$

The second set of 17 log-linear equations provide estimates patterns of time use conditional on the structural zeros estimated in the first equation:

(A2) $E(GSS_{ik}ZERO_{ik} = 0) = \exp\left[X_{ij}\beta_{jk} + \beta_{i}\right]$

where GSS_{ik} = the proportion of daily time spent by individual i in activity k. A special feature of this second set of equations is the term i representing a constant term for every respondent in the sample. These individual level constants represent a constraint on each individual's predicted time-use pattern (i.e., it must sum to 100 percent of 24 hours). The individual level constants may also be interpreted as reflecting random factors at the individual level that can be further modeled.

The third set of equations then captures patterns in individual variability of time spent in each activity. Residual variances are defined in terms of differences in square-root proportions, rather than the more usual log differences, to avoid problems with response and structural zeros (since the log residual ($\ln(0) - \ln(u)$) is undefined). As well as being defined for zeros, the vector distance measure expressed in terms of differences in square roots is a true distance (i.e., satisfying $d(x,y) \geq 0$, $d(x,y) = d(y,x)$ and $d(x,y) + (d(y,z) \geq d(x,z))$ and is unique in that respect among common distance measures on the unit simplex.

(A3) $SD_i = \sqrt{\left(\Sigma \left(\sqrt{GSS_{ik}} - \sqrt{\exp\left[X_{ij}\beta_{jk} + \beta_i \right]} \right)^2 \right)}.$

$= \exp\left[X_{ij}\theta_{jk} + \delta\varepsilon_i \right],$

where $\varepsilon \approx \text{Normal}\left(0, \delta^2 \right)$. In other words, it is being assumed that the standard deviations (SD_1) of time-use proportions are log normal, though with means depending on X_{ij}.

Estimation for Eqs. A1 and A2 was carried out by iterative proportionate adjustment, while Eq. A3 was estimated by least squares.

The choice of predictor variables in each of the equations was constrained by what was available both on the GSS and in the LifePaths model. The following variables were used:

Predictor variables	Definitions
Reference day	Sunday, . . . , Saturday
Sex	male, female
Age group	15–17, 18–19, 20–24, 25–29, . . . , 65–69, 70+
Marital situation	married or CLU (spouse not working last week), married or CLU (spouse worked last week), never married, widowed, divorced or separated.

Children	no children at home, all children at home aged 5+, one or more children at home aged <5
Education attainment	less than secondary school, secondary school only, at least some postsecondary.
Respondent's work	mainly a full time student last week, working last week, not working and not mainly a full time student last week.
Response rounding	zero responses in multiples of one-half hour, 1 response in a multiple of one-half hour, two responses in multiples of one-half hour, more than three responses in multiples of one-half hour.

An evaluation of the fit of these equations is difficult both because of the zeros in the data, and because the statistical properties of entries in time use diaries are difficult to specify. The following evaluation measures were calculated by analogy to statistical models of count data and should be taken as merely suggestive of the explanatory power of each variable.

Reduction in deviance due to addition of independent variables	Structural zero model		Time-use model	
	(Equation 1)		(Equation 2)	
Variable	Deviance	# Fitted parameters	Deviance	# Fitted parameters
Reference day	17.1 ns	42	4645**	119
Sex	875.0**	12	923.1**	34
Age group	4611.8**	78	1241**	221
Marital situation	29.1 ns	24	198.5**	68
Children	230.5**	18	1325**	51
Education attainment	327.9**	18	389.7**	51
Work	—	—	4355**	51
Rounding	—	—	48.55 ns	68

NOTE: ** denotes significance at 5%; "ns" denotes not significant at 5%.

Imputation algorithm

Finally, given the estimated set of equations, imputation of the 17 element time-use activity vectors was based on an algorithm that started with annual features, and then successively expanded the imputation to weekly and ultimately daily features. For each individual life cycle history simulated by Life-Paths, and for each year, the following procedure was implemented.
Starting at the annual level,

- choose ZERO day - based on a uniform random number ranging from 1 to 365. Note that the interval between successive ZERO days will range from 1 to 729 days.

- on ZERO day, it is decided whether or not a structural zero will be imputed to market work, commuting, formal learning and/or care for family members for the next "year" (actually until the next ZERO day), based on probabilities determined from the logistic regression Eq. A1 estimated from GSS data.

Given these annual level imputations, the process next focuses on a week: Starting at the annual level,

- choose a random REF day, based on a uniform random number ranging from 1 to 7. Note that the interval between successive REF days will range from 1 to 13 days.

- on REF day each week, one of the actual 8,815 empirical residual vectors RESID is chosen at random. The residual vectors are in standardized form:

$$RESID = [(\sqrt{(GSS)} - \sqrt{\text{fitted from equation 2})}]/SD.$$

- also on REF day, a random heterogeneity term ($\delta\varepsilon$) is generated from the log-normal distribution represented by Eq. A3.

Finally, the imputation algorithm determines a set of daily activity patterns for all 365 days of the year (actually, all the days until the next ZERO day):

- each day, the appropriate average time use vector (AVG) is determined—corresponding to the day of week, sex, age, marital situation, presence of children, employment/schooling and education attainment—by applying Eq. A2 to the LifePaths variables pertaining to that day. A corresponding calculation, based on Eq. A3, provides the heterogeneity term (SD) appropriate to the day of the week, etc. and to $\delta\varepsilon$.

- subsequently, the average, residual, and heterogeneity terms are combined.

$$\sqrt{ } \; (AVG) + RESID \times SD$$

The added variability due to the RESID and SD terms preserves correlations among time use activities and accounts for interindividual variation. By varying RESID and SD only on a weekly basis, some (possibly spurious) correlation is induced between days of a given week.

- impossible time uses are set to zero—for example,

    age < 6: preschool: domestic work, formal learning and reading;

    age < 12: family care;

    age < 15: market work, commuting and adult education;

    institutional: market work, commuting, family care, domestic work, and volunteer work.

Likewise, structural zeros as prescribed above are set if necessary conditions are still met:

- employment time use = 0, if no work simulated for the previous 12 months
- self-employment time use = 0, if no work simulated for the previous 12 months
- commuting time use = 0, if no work simulated for the previous 12 months
- formal learning time use = 0, if currently employed
- family care time use = 0, if no spouse & no children are present at home
- finally, negative [$\sqrt{ }$ (AVG) + RESID × SD] combinations are set to zero, with the remaining values transformed and scaled to sum to 1.0.

The algorithm thus provides simulated time use proportions that will approximately reproduce time use averages, variances and covariances as observed in the GSS data.

Note

The work reported here is very much a team effort, principally by members of the Socio-Economic Modeling Group of the Analytical Studies Branch, Statistics Canada.

Very helpful suggestions were provided by Alice Nakamura, though we remain responsible for any errors and infelicities in this chapter.

Part II

3

Adults Returning to School—Payoffs from Studying at a Community College

Duane E. Leigh
Washington State University

Andrew M. Gill
California State University at Fullerton

In his well-known survey article, Willis (1986, p. 526) pointed out that as an empirical tool, the Mincer human capital earnings function is one of the great success stories of modern labor economics. As he noted, the Mincer earnings function has been used in hundreds of studies using data from virtually every historical period and country for which suitable data exist. The great advantage of the Mincer earnings function is that, with a few simplifying assumptions, the internal rate of return to education can be estimated from cross-section data limited to information on current earnings of those in the labor force, their age, and their years of schooling. One of these simplifying assumptions is that individuals complete their schooling early in their lifetimes and only then enter the labor force, the state in which they remain until retirement.[1]

Accumulating evidence indicates, contrary to this Mincerian assumption, that the work and schooling patterns of U.S. workers are such that schooling investments no longer necessarily occur early in life. An early article by Corman (1983) showed for the 1970s that a growing proportion of postsecondary students were older than the traditional college ages of 18 to 22. Moreover, an increasing number of these older students enrolled in nondegree programs at postsecondary vocational schools. More recently, several studies have appeared demonstrating the empirical significance of nontraditional schooling patterns (see Light 1995; Oettinger 1995; and Leigh and Gill 1997). Using the National Longitudinal Survey of Youth (NLSY), all three of these studies indicate that school enrollment histories are frequently characterized by lengthy interruptions in attendance. For example, Light reports that 35 percent of white males who left school for the first time between 1979 and 1988 returned to school before 1989.

Another strand of the education literature makes it clear that community colleges, rather than vocational schools, have become the major alternative to four-year colleges in meeting society's demand for postsecondary education and training.[2] Labor economists and policymakers' interest in community colleges has recently been stimulated by a widely cited working paper by Kane and Rouse (1993). (The published version of this paper is Kane and Rouse 1995a.) Using data from the National Longitudinal Survey of the Class of 1972 (NLS72), as well as the NLSY, their study provides evidence of a substantial return to college credits, whether provided by a two- or four-year college and whether the credits lead to a degree or not. The Kane-Rouse study does not, however, address the issue of nontraditional schooling patterns. Specifically, they do not distinguish between returning adults and continuing high school graduates in estimating the earnings effects of postsecondary education. Leigh and Gill (1997) made this distinction and find that returns to community college training are positive and of essentially the same size for returning adults as they are for continuing students. Among males, in fact, returning adults enjoy an earnings increment from nondegree community college programs above that received by comparable continuing students.

One explanation of differential returns to alternative groups of people possessing the same level of education is that individuals in the two groups made different choices regarding their major field of study. At the level of four-year educational institutions, there is considerable evidence that the returns to college vary widely by major field (Altonji 1993; Berger 1988; Grogger and Eide 1995; James et al. 1989; and Rumberger and Thomas 1993). Grogger and Eide, for example, showed that a substantial portion of the rising college wage premium observed during the 1980s can be attributed to the decisions of college students to select more financially remunerative majors.

Differential returns to alternative fields of study have attracted much less attention at the community college level. In one of the few available empirical studies, Jacobson, LaLonde, and Sullivan (1997) examined a large sample of displaced workers in their mid thirties who participated in a classroom program operated at a community college located in Allegheny County, Pennsylvania. This study suggested that there is a good deal of variation in the returns to what the authors term "hard" and "easy" classes.[3] The authors found that there is no gain for completing easy courses, while substantial labor market returns are enjoyed by those who make it through hard courses. In a second empirical study, Grubb (1992) showed using NLS72 data that substantial variation in annual earnings exists by field of study at two-year institutions and proprietary schools. Once work experience has been controlled for, however, most of the positive earnings impacts disappear, leading him to question why individuals choose to enroll in these postsecondary institutions.

It is interesting to note that Grubb's results in his 1992 paper and in a closely related 1993 paper are in direct conflict with evidence presented by Kane and Rouse (1993) in their analysis of NLS72 data. Recently, Kane and Rouse (1995b) reexamined Grubb's NLS72 sample finding, after correcting for the mislabeling and mismeasurement of several key variables, that both men and women who attended a two-year college earn more than comparable high school graduates, whether or not they completed the degree. Moreover, these positive labor market effects remain even after controlling for labor market experience.

Using NLSY data, we examine the payoffs to returning adults from studying at a community college. Our objectives are twofold. First, we seek to establish whether returning adults differ from continuing high school graduates in terms of the field-of-study choices they make. An important element of this aspect of our analysis is investigating gender differences in community college field of study. Second, we estimate the earnings effect of community college schooling for returning adults as opposed to continuing students, exploring how these effects vary by major field of study and demographic characteristics including gender.

THE DATA

Kane and Rouse (1993) developed a useful hierarchy for organizing the detailed information on postsecondary education programs available in the NLSY. Following their empirical strategy, we first establish whether a respondent has completed a postsecondary degree. Working backward from 1991, we record the highest degree reported. Thus an individual who had earned an Associate of Arts (AA) degree and later a Bachelor of Arts (BA) degree would be classified as a BA degree holder. Next, respondents without postsecondary degrees are classified by the type of college they attended; that is, a two- or four-year institution. Again, it is the most recent college attended that takes precedence. Finally, individuals for whom we could not assign a highest degree or a postsecondary educational institution attended were checked for participation in an occupational training program, excluding regular school programs. This question appears in the training (as opposed to the regular schooling) section of each questionnaire, and a number of possible sources of occupational training are listed. Following the classification scheme of Kane and Rouse, we classify respondents by whether or not they attended an occupational training program in a vocational or technical institute. A summary of these variable definitions appears in Table 1.

Table 1 Definitions of Postsecondary Education Variables

Variable[a]	Definition
Highest degree	
AA	Obtained an AA degree
BA	Obtained a BA or BS degree
Graduate degree	Obtained an MA, Ph.D., or professional degree
Other	Most recent college attended is a two-year institution and earned no degree
Most recent college attended	
Two-year	Most recent college attended is a two-year institution and earned no degree
Four-year	Most recent college attended is a four-year institution and earned no degree
Voc/tech	Attended a vocational or technical institute occupational training program but did not attend college. (Note: This excludes apprenticeships, correspondence courses, and other forms of training.)

[a] Categories are mutually exclusive.

To make our results comparable to those of Kane and Rouse, we impose the following restrictions on our NLSY sample:

1) Respondents must have been working but not self-employed in 1993.

2) Respondents must not have been enrolled in school in 1993.

3) Respondents must have participated in all waves of the survey.

4) Respondents must have reported a 1993 hourly wage rate of between $1.67 and $100.

The third restriction allows us to easily construct a measure of actual work experience. Restriction 4 has the effect of trimming from the sample a handful of respondents who reported extremely high or low wage rates. These restrictions result in a total sample of 5,015 respondents. Note that we do not restrict from our sample high school dropouts.

Since we are interested in distinguishing postsecondary educational enrollment of returning adults as opposed to continuing high school students, it is crucial for us to determine the timing of the variables specified in Table 1. NLSY data provide information on the year the highest degree was obtained, the year the most recent educational institution (two- and four-year) was attended, and the last year training in a voc/tech institution was received. Using this information, we can calculate the age at which a respondent obtained his or her highest degree, last attended college, or was last enrolled in a voc/tech. Table 2 presents frequency distributions for the age at which respondents earned an AA or BA degree, most recently attended a two-year college, or last attended a voc/tech.

To better understand how these frequency distributions were calculated, it may be useful to focus on the distributions shown in columns 1 and 4 for AA and BA degree holders, respectively. (Age of two-year college attendance and of voc/tech enrollment are constructed in the same manner.) Letting AGEDEG represent the age at which the highest postsecondary degree was awarded,

$$AGEDEG = YRDEG - 79 + AGE79,$$

Table 2 Percentage Distributions of Age at which Respondents Received an AA or BA Degree, Last Attended a Two-Year College, or Last Participated in a Voc/Tech Program

| | Postsecondary education variables | | | | | |
| | 1 | 2 | 3 | 4 | 5 | 6 |
Age	AA degree	Two-year college	Voc/tech	BA degree	Grad degree	BA returnees
<18	0.3	1.8	9.6	0.1	--	--
18	1.8	9.1	11.0	0.3	0.5	--
19	13.3	15.5	8.9	0.2	--	--
20	15.9	10.5	7.5	1.2	0.5	3.2
21	14.1	8.5	6.8	30.7	0.0	1.6
22	9.7	7.2	6.4	27.4	4.9	6.4
23	8.9	6.7	5.5	16.4	6.9	6.5
24	5.4	5.6	7.8	8.0	12.2	8.1
25	6.1	7.5	6.2	4.1	18.6	14.5
26	4.6	6.8	6.2	3.5	10.3	11.3
27	6.4	4.2	6.4	3.1	16.7	16.1
28	3.8	2.9	5.9	1.6	13.2	6.5
29	2.0	3.4	4.3	1.2	5.9	8.1
30+	7.7	10.3	7.5	2.2	10.3	17.7
N	391	789	438	835	204	62
% of total sample	(7.8)	(15.7)	(8.7)	(16.7)	(4.1)	(1.2)

NOTE: The sample includes respondents working but not self-employed in 1993, excludes those enrolled in school in 1993, includes those who participated in all waves of the survey, and includes those reporting a 1993 hourly wage rate of between $1.67 and $100 ($N = 5,000$).

where YRDEG is the year the respondent reported his or her highest degree was awarded, and AGE79 is the respondent's age in 1979. The distribution presented in column 1 is specific to respondents who reported that their highest degree is the AA, and column 4 is specific to BA degree holders. Overall, nearly 8 percent and 17 percent, respectively, of the sample possess AA and BA degrees, another nearly 16 percent attended a community college, and an additional almost 9 percent were enrolled in a voc/tech. Across all seven of the postsecondary education variables defined in Table 1, we were unable to calculate AGEDEG for just 15 individuals. Thus our analysis is based on a sample of 5,000 respondents.

Our main interest in presenting Table 2 is to gain insight into the number of respondents represented in the table who can reasonably be interpreted as returning adults as opposed to continuing high school students. Looking specifically at community college attendance in columns 1 and 2, the central tendency of the distributions is, as expected, at about age 20 for the AA degree and at about age 19 for two-year college students. Nevertheless, there are a considerable number of students in their mid twenties and older who returned to school at a community college and earned the AA. The particular age chosen to distinguish returning adults from continuing students is inevitably somewhat arbitrary.[4] However, it seems reasonable to follow Corman (1983) in choosing an age threshold of 25, since such a threshold would allow an individual who graduated from high school at 18 to accumulate four or five years of work experience before enrolling in a community college and graduating with an AA degree at 25. Using age 25 as our threshold, about 31 percent of AA degree holders and 35 percent of two-year college students are classified as returning adults. Indeed, fully 10 percent of two-year college students are in their thirties. In column 3, about 37 percent of voc/tech students are classified as returning adults, while just 16 percent of BA degrees in column 4 were earned by respondents we classify as returning adults.

The last two columns of Table 2 examine the quantitative importance of two often-heard statements, namely, that large numbers of "mid career" students obtain advanced and professional university degrees at older ages, and that many BA degree holders return to local community colleges to enroll in nondegree vocational programs. Column 5 indicates that about 4 percent of our sample earned graduate or professional degrees. Of these individuals, just 10 percent are 30 years of age or older when they received their degree. The central tendency of the distribution seems to be at about age 25 or 26, indicating, at least for our sample, that it is fairly uncommon for college graduates with substantial labor market experience to return to school to study for an advanced or professional degree. Column 6 suggests that it is even less common for BA degree holders to subsequently enroll in a two-year college program.

Stratifying the data by gender, Table 3 compares community college field-of-study choices made by returning adults and continuing high school students. Represented in the table are all AA recipients and enrollees in nondegree two-year college programs in our sample. Table 2 indicates that a total of 1,180 respondents are either AA degree holders or two-year college attendees. The sample size reported in Table 3 is slightly smaller at 1,110 respondents because we were unable to assign a field of study to 70 individuals.[5] It is also worth noting that although males outnumber females in the total sample of 5,000 respondents (2,555 males vs. 2,445 females), females are considerably more likely than males (25.8 percent versus 19.4 percent) to enroll in a community college.

Aggregating the NLSY codes for detailed fields of study at postsecondary educational institutions, the fields of study we distinguish in Table 3 are the following:

• business and management,

• nursing,

Table 3 Distributions of Field Study of AA Degree Recipients and Two-Year College Attendees, by Gender, Age of Threshold of 25 and Older

Field of study	Males			Females		
	All	Continuing students	Returning adults	All	Continuing students	Returning adults
Business	0.209	0.217	0.194	0.325	0.357	0.268
Nursing	0.012	0.012	0.012	0.119	0.116	0.125
Health professions/ physical sciences	0.070	0.058	0.094	0.124	0.111	0.147
Engineering/ computer science	0.320	0.299	0.363	0.117	0.111	0.130
Education	0.047	0.046	0.050	0.080	0.063	0.112
Social science/ public service	0.094	0.088	0.106	0.064	0.065	0.063
Letters, humanities, and other	0.248	0.281	0.181	0.170	0.178	0.156
N	488	328	160	622	398	224

- health professions (excluding nursing), physical sciences, and agricultural and natural resources,
- engineering, computer and information sciences, mathematics, and architecture and environmental design,
- education,
- social sciences, psychology, and public affairs and services, and
- letters, area studies, communications, fine and applied arts, foreign languages, home economics, law, theology, and interdisciplinary studies.

At the community college level, the fields of study health professions/physical sciences and engineering/computer science correspond, respectively, to science technology and engineering technology education. These two fields warrant special notice in view of a National Science Foundation program—the Advance Technological Education program—designed to promote curriculum development and program improvement for technician training in the application of advanced technologies. In a recent NSF report that is part of this program, Burton and Celebuski (1995) discussed the important role of community colleges in contributing to the nation's resources in science and engineering. As they suggested, two-year colleges ". . . take seriously their service to the community by offering courses designed to help the workforce upgrade and renew job skills and [to help] others to pursue lifelong learning."[6] The authors also pointed out an interesting contrast between the time trends in degrees earned and in course enrollment for the two technology programs. For the 1989–1992 period, while the number of engineering technology associate degrees awarded fell and science technology degrees flattened out, course enrollment in engineering technology and science technology programs increased by 11 percent and 30 percent, respectively. Their interpretation of this evidence is that community college students are enrolling in courses to obtain specific course work rather than an AA degree.

In Table 3, nearly one-third of males in our community college subsample indicate an engineering/computer science field of study. The next most popular field at about 21 percent is business, with about 7 percent of the sample emphasizing course work in the health professions/physical sciences (excluding nursing). Among women, the most popular field of study by far is business, at about one-third of the sub-sample. Approximately 12 percent of female respondents is found in each of three fields including nursing, health professions/physical sciences, and engineering/computer science. Differences by gender in choice of field of study also show up in data for four-year institutions. Rumberger and Thomas (1993) reported for the 1985–1986 period that the most popular college majors of employed male BA recipients are, in descending order, business, science/mathematics, and engineering. In contrast, the top three majors for employed female BA holders are health professions, education, and business.

Making the returning adult/continuing student distinction, the major difference shown for males in Table 3 is that returning adults are 10 percentage points less likely than continuing students to have enrolled in course work in the letters, humanities, and other category. The bulk of this difference is explained by a more than 6 percentage point greater representation of returning adults in engineering/computer science. One interpretation of this evidence is that male returning adults are more interested, relative to male continuing students, in fields of study that have immediate application in the labor market. For females, returning adults are seen to be about 9 percentage points less likely to be studying business courses than continuing students. On the other hand, female returning adults are about 5 percentage points and 4 percentage points, respectively, more likely to report as their field of study education and health professions/physical sciences.

ESTIMATED RETURNS

Using an age threshold like age 25, our empirical strategy for estimating the labor market payoffs to postsecondary education programs is to define a dummy variable ADULT representing returning adults. This variable is then interacted with the education variables in an earnings regression with which we can estimate the payoffs to postsecondary education programs for returning adults as distinct from continuing students. To simplify the discussion, suppose that we collapse the postsecondary education outcomes into a composite variable called POSTSEC. Our regression framework would thus look as follows:

(1) $\ln W = a_1 + a_2 \text{POSTSEC} + a_3(\text{POSTSEC} \times \text{ADULT}) + a_4 X + u,$

where W is a measure of earnings, X is a vector of control variables, and u is a disturbance term. Controlling for factors expected to affect earnings in X, a_1 is our estimate of the return to postsecondary education for continuing high school graduates, while a_2 measures how this payoff may differ for returning adults.

Columns 1 and 4 of Table 4, which is taken from our companion paper (Leigh and Gill 1997), report return estimates to alternative types of postsecondary education in terms of the hourly wage rate and annual earnings measured as of 1993. Following the specification of Kane and Rouse (1993), control variables in the regressions include age in 1979, race/ethnicity, actual weeks worked, weeks worked squared, Armed Forces Qualification Test score, region and urban residence in 1993, and part-time employment in 1993. Because we do not restrict our sample to high school graduates, we also include a dummy variable measuring less than 12 years of schooling.

As noted in the first section, a key finding presented by Kane and Rouse (1993) is that community college programs generate positive wage differentials, even for those not completing an AA degree. In Table 4 this result shows up strongly for men and somewhat less strongly for women. Relative to high school graduates, estimated differentials for males enrolled in two-year college programs are seen to be 10.2 percent and 18.9 percent, respectively, measured in terms of hourly wages and annual earnings. The two-year nondegree point estimates for women are lower at 5.7 percent and 4.4 percent, although return estimates to AA degrees are higher for women than for men. Also apparent in the table is confirmation of the Kane-Rouse finding that enrollees at two- and four-year colleges who did not earn degrees fared about equally well in the labor market.[7]

Following the empirical strategy laid out in Eq. 1, columns 2 and 3 and columns 5 and 6 of Table 4 present for hourly wages and annual earnings, respectively, estimates of the returns to education for continuing students and the increments in these returns, which may be either positive or negative, for returning adults. The age threshold distinguishing returning adults in these results is receipt of degree or most recent postsecondary school attendance at an age not younger than 25. Beginning with males, a glance down columns 3 and 6 indicates as

86

Table 4 Returns to Selected Categories of Postsecondary Education, by Gender, Age Threshold of 25 and Older[a,b]

Explanatory variables	Col. 1	2	3	4	5	6
	Log hourly wage			Log annual earnings		
	All	Continuing students	ADULT increment	All	Continuing students	ADULT increment
Males						
Highest degree						
AA	0.200**	0.209**	−0.028	0.218**	0.198**	0.071
	(0.036)	(0.042)	(0.070)	(0.055)	(0.063)	(0.105)
BA	0.311**	0.354**	−0.137**	0.440**	0.464**	−0.140*
	(0.029)	(0.031)	(0.055)	(0.044)	(0.046)	(0.083)
Most recent college						
Two-year	0.102**	0.075**	0.084*	0.189**	0.157**	0.101
	(0.027)	(0.031)	(0.046)	(0.041)	(0.047)	(0.070)
Four-year	0.103**	0.136**	−0.110**	0.075**	0.226**	−0.168**
	(0.031)	(0.035)	(0.056)	(0.047)	(0.053)	(0.084)
Voc/tech	0.035	0.011	0.072	0.108**	0.099*	0.028
	(0.029)	(0.034)	(0.054)	(0.045)	(0.053)	(0.084)
Adj. R^2	0.339	0.342		0.325	0.327	
N	2,555	2,555		2,446	2,446	

Females

Highest degree

AA	0.243**	0.235**	0.026	0.263**	0.228**	0.083
	(0.031)	(0.035)	(0.055)	(0.057)	(0.065)	(0.101)
BA	0.336**	0.320**	0.100*	0.407**	0.380**	0.170*
	(0.028)	(0.030)	(0.053)	(0.051)	(0.054)	(0.094)
Most recent college						
Two-year	0.057**	0.051*	0.015	0.044	0.054	-0.023
	(0.025)	(0.029)	(0.038)	(0.046)	(0.053)	(0.071)
Four-year	0.073**	0.063**	0.037	0.007	0.009	0.000
	(0.028)	(0.032)	(0.050)	(0.052)	(0.059)	(0.090)
Voc/tech	-0.013	-0.004	-0.025	-0.003	0.032	-0.090
	(0.032)	(0.041)	(0.059)	(0.060)	(0.075)	(0.110)
Adj. R^2	0.406	0.406		0.413	0.413	
N	2,445	2,445		2,311	2,311	

[a] Control variables included in the regressions are race/ethnicity, age in 1979, total weeks worked, weeks worked squared, AFQT score, and dummy variables for 1993 residence classified by region and urban/rural, high school dropout, and part-time employment in 1993. Graduate degree and other postsecondary degree are also included.

[b] ** indicates significance at the 5% level; * indicates significance at the 10% level Standard errors are in parentheses.

many negative adult increment estimates as positive estimates. The positive estimates appear for AA degrees and two-year college programs. In particular, incremental effects of two-year college programs of 8.4 percent and 10.1 percent, respectively, are reported in the hourly wage and annual earnings equations. That is, a nondegree community college program boosts earnings for returning adult males by 8 to 10 percent more than it does for male continuing students. In contrast, there is little evidence of a positive additional effect for returning adult males of an AA degree. Estimated adult increments are uniformly negative (and statistically significant) for BA degree holders and enrollees in four-year college programs.

A note of caution is worth mentioning in connection with our estimated returns to a BA degree and potentially also to attendance at a four-year college. While Table 2 shows that receipt of a BA is concentrated at the ages of 21 and 22, it is certainly possible that at least some older BA degree recipients we classify as returning adults are really continuing students who took longer than normal to complete their degree requirements. For example, a respondent receiving a BA at age 25, rather than being a returning adult, might be a continuing student who needed seven or eight years to complete the degree because he or she was only able to attend college on a part-time basis. The problem of misclassifying returning adults is less of an issue for community college students because of the shorter length of their programs.[8]

Turning to females, with one exception the ADULT increment estimates are small and/or statistically insignificant. The exception is receipt of a BA degree. In contrast to the results for men, completion of a BA is estimated to increase the wages of returning adult females by 10 percent and annual earnings by 17 percent relative to the wages and earnings of continuing students.[9]

The positive incremental effect we estimate for returning adult males enrolled in nondegree two-year programs might be due to 1) older males choosing in greater numbers to study more remunerative fields, or 2) older males enjoying a larger payoff to the same fields of study compared to younger males. We considered the first of these possibilities in Table 3. Turning to the second, Tables 5 and 6 report estimated returns to community college fields of study for males and females, respectively. In Table 5, for example, all the male observations in our sample are used in estimation except for a small number of

Table 5 Returns to Community College Fields of Study for Males, Age Threshold of 25 and Older[a,b]

Field of study	Log hourly wage			Log annual earnings		
	All	Continuing students	ADULT increment	All	Continuing students	ADULT increment
Business	0.123***	0.112**	0.039	0.193**	0.142*	0.162
	(0.044)	(0.051)	(0.088)	(0.067)	(0.079)	(0.132)
Health/science, incl. nursing	0.112*	0.273**	−0.379**	0.062	0.221*	−0.385*
	(0.067)	(0.087)	(0.131)	(0.100)	(0.129)	(0.197)
Engineering/computer science	0.171**	0.129**	0.115*	0.237**	0.208**	0.082
	(0.038)	(0.045)	(0.068)	(0.056)	(0.067)	(0.102)
Education	0.069	0.070	−0.001	0.116	0.084	0.090
	(0.087)	(0.107)	(0.179)	(0.132)	(0.164)	(0.269)
Social science/public service	0.150**	0.109	0.112	0.273**	0.212*	0.165
	(0.063)	(0.078)	(0.125)	(0.093)	(0.115)	(0.185)
Letters, humanities, and other	0.095**	0.070	0.105	0.156**	0.125*	0.137
	(0.041)	(0.046)	(0.087)	(0.061)	(0.068)	(0.131)
Mean dep. var.	2.401	2.401		10.040	10.040	
Adj. R^2	0.339	0.341		0.328	0.329	
N	2,521	2,521		2,413	2,413	

[a] Included in the regressions, in addition to the control variables specified in the note to Table 4, are BA degree, four-year college, graduate degree, other degree, and voc/tech.
[b] **indicates significance at the 5% level; *indicates ignificance at the 10% level. Standard errors are in parentheses.

Table 6 Returns to Community College Fields of Study for Females, Age Threshold of 25 and Older[a,b]

Field of study	Log hourly wage			Log annual earnings		
	All	Continuing students	ADULT increment	All	Continuing students	ADULT increments
Business	0.064**	0.068*	-0.013	0.103*	0.103	0.001
	(0.032)	(0.036)	(0.059)	(0.059)	(0.067)	(0.110)
Nursing	0.276**	0.263**	0.035	0.381**	0.348**	0.085
	(0.048)	(0.059)	(0.092)	(0.088)	(0.110)	(0.169)
Health/science	0.181**	0.222**	-0.094	-0.005	0.003	-0.017
	(0.047)	(0.061)	(0.089)	(0.086)	(0.111)	(0.162)
Engineering/computer science	0.085*	0.112*	-0.068	0.086	0.124	-0.097
	(0.048)	(0.060)	(0.092)	(0.090)	(0.113)	(0.173)
Education	0.126**	0.039	0.174	0.088	0.023	0.129
	(0.057)	(0.079)	(0.109)	(0.104)	(0.144)	(0.199)
Social science/public service	0.099	0.085	0.039	0.164	0.056	0.287
	(0.063)	(0.077)	(0.128)	(0.117)	(0.147)	(0.233)
Letters, humanities, and other	0.058	0.059	-0.004	-0.026	0.032	-0.178
	(0.041)	(0.049)	(0.080)	(0.075)	(0.089)	(0.146)
Mean dep. var.	2.220	2.220		9.646	9.646	
Adj. R^2	0.403	0.402		0.413	0.413	
N	2,409	2,409		2,277	2,277	

[a] Included in the regressions, in addition to the control variables specified in the note to Table 4, are BA degree, four-year college, graduate degree, other degree, and voc/tech.

[b] ** indicates significance at the 5% level; * indicates significance at the 10% level. Standard errors are in parentheses.

males who attended a community college but failed to report a field of study. The regressions estimated are the same as those in Table 4 except that separate field-of-study variables measured for all AA degree and two-year college respondents are used in place of the AA and two-year college variables. The reference category is, as before, high school graduates.

For males in Table 5, all of the return estimates are positive, as expected, in both the wage and annual earnings equations. However, there are sizable differences in returns across fields. (Note that for males, nursing is included in the health professions/physical sciences category.) Point estimates in the wage regression range from a low of 6.9 percent for education to highs of 15.0 percent for social science/public service and 17.1 percent for engineering/computer science. Even greater variation is exhibited for annual earnings, with point estimates ranging from 6.2 percent for health professions/physical sciences to 23.7 percent for engineering/computer science and 27.3 percent for social science/public service.

Compared with males, the female estimates in Table 6 tend to be lower at the low end and higher at the high end. In the wage equation, for example, estimates range from 5.8 percent for the letters, humanities, and other category up to 27.6 percent for nursing. Nursing has an even larger return estimate of 38.1 percent in the annual earnings equation.

Comparing these return estimates with the field-of-study decisions reflected in Table 3, the evidence, at least for males, is consistent with our earlier speculation that returning adults may be more sensitive to market wage differentials in making their career training decisions than are continuing students. The relatively low-wage field of letters, humanities, and other is the choice of a lower percentage of returning adult males than male continuing students, while the high-wage engineering/computer science field attracts a relatively high percentage of returning adult males.

We might also briefly compare the variation exhibited in these community college return estimates to variation in returns calculated for four-year institutions. Holding constant a variety of demographic, labor market, and other variables, Rumberger and Thomas (1993) report that starting annual salaries of males majoring in engineering or in a health-related field—the highest-paying of the seven fields they examine—are over one-third higher than starting salaries for male humanities graduates (their reference category). Consistent with our community college findings, the variation in returns to BA degrees appears to be greater for females than males. Rumberger and Thomas report that female engineering and health profession majors command starting salaries that are over 40 percent higher than the salaries of female humanities majors.

A final result to note in Tables 5 and 6 draws on the returning adult/ continuing student distinction. Large standard errors lead to estimated adult increments that for women are uniformly not significantly different from zero at customary significance levels. This evidence is consistent with our Table 4 finding for females that neither an AA degree nor a two-year nondegree program provides an additional return to returning adults above that received by continuing students. For males, we estimate statistically significant adult increments, of opposite signs, for engineering/computer science and health professions/physical sciences. The large negative estimates for health professions/physical sciences in both the wage and the earnings regressions appear to be an anomaly associated, at least in part, with the very low wages and annual earnings of just two returning adult males with nursing training whose earnings strongly influence the coefficient estimates because of a small cell size. The more reliable result is the positive 11.5 percent increment in wages we obtain for returning adult males with training in engineering/computer science. Recalling the estimated returns presented in Table 4, it appears that the incremental effect of 8 to 10 percent reported there for returning adult males in two-year programs is associated with a disproportionate representation of returning adults in engineering/ computer science coupled with a statistically significant incremental effect, at least for wages, of engineering/computer science.

For all male community college enrollees (both AA recipients and nondegree two-year program attendees), Table 7 presents the results of a decomposition analysis intended to measure the extent to which differences in wages between returning adults and continuing students are due to differences in choice of major field of study versus differences in the returns to any selected major. The column 1 differences in major field are based on Table 3, while the differences in returns to alternative majors shown in column 2 make use of the adult increments reported in Table 5. Table 7 makes it clear that the positive wage differential

**Table 7 Decomposition of the Effects of Community College Field
of Study on the Wages of Male Returning Adults
and Continuing Students**

Field of study	Differences in choice of field[a]	Differences in returns[b]	Total
Business	–0.003	0.008	0.005
Health/science, including nursing	0.010	–0.040	–0.030
Engineering/computer science	0.008	0.042	0.050
Education	0.000	0.000	0.000
Social science/public service	0.002	0.012	0.014
Letters, humanities, and other	–0.007	0.019	0.012
Total[c]	0.011	0.040	0.051

[a] Weighted by coefficients estimated for continuing students.
[b] Weighted by field-of-study choices made by returning adults.
[c] Totals may be off due to rounding.

enjoyed by returning adult males who attended a community college is largely driven by a favorable difference in returns estimated for training in engineering/computer science.

CONCLUSION

Using NLSY data through 1993 (when respondents were between 28 and 35 years of age), this study examined the payoffs to studying at a community college, looking specifically at choices among and the returns to different fields of study for returning adult students as opposed to continuing high school graduates. We report that it is not uncommon for respondents in their mid twenties or even thirties to return to school in a community college program. Among community college students, NLSY data allow us to distinguish between AA degree recipients and those who attended a community college program but did not receive an AA.

Our results indicate, not surprisingly, that both male and female community college attendees earn at least as much as comparable high school graduates regardless of their field of study. The size of the earnings premium varies substantially by field of study, however, with engineering/computer science and social science/public service the highest paying fields for men, and nursing the highest paying field for women. Looking at the distributions of respondents by field of study, there are substantial differences between men and women and between returning adults and continuing students. A question that is yet to be answered is explaining the greater propensity of women to enroll in community colleges.

Comparing the field-of-study distributions with our estimated earnings premiums, there is evidence, particularly for men, that returning adults are more sensitive to market wage differentials in making career training decisions than are continuing students. Especially noteworthy are the findings for engineering/computer science, the field of study distinguished in NLSY data that corresponds to community college engineering technology programs. We find that 1) engineering/computer science attracts a relatively high percentage of returning adults compared to continuing students, and 2) returning adults in engineering/computer science programs command an 11.5 percent wage premium relative to comparable continuing students. Thus our earlier result (Leigh and Gill 1997) indicating an incremental earnings effect of 8 to 10 percent from two-year nondegree programs seems to be associated with both more-than-proportionate enrollment of older adult males in the relatively high paying field of engineering/computer science and a higher return to returning adults from engineer/computer science programs. This finding is consistent with Burton and Celebuski's (1995) evidence that students in engineering technology programs are increasingly enrolling in courses to obtain some specific course work rather than an AA degree. Further research is needed to determine whether the incremental earnings effect for returning adult males enrolling in engineering technology programs can be accounted for by their greater participation in nondegree short courses and customized technical courses developed by community colleges to meet the particular skill requirements of local employers.

Notes

The comments of our discussant, Shelly Lundberg, are gratefully acknowledged. Susan Houseman also provided us with a number of helpful comments.

1. The other assumptions are that the only cost of schooling is foregone earnings, and that the length of each individual's working life is independent of his or her years of education.

2. Kane and Rouse (1995a) pointed out that community colleges currently enroll more than half of first-time, first-year postsecondary school students, and an even larger share of those whose decisions to attend college are affected by state and federal financial aid programs. Grubb (1991) and Osterman and Batt (1993) documented the long-term shift in emphasis from academic to vocational programs within community college systems, making them natural subcontractors for government-sponsored retraining programs.

3. Hard classes are defined as academic math and science courses and as vocational courses in nursing, other health-related fields, trades and repair, and computer information systems. All other vocational and academic courses are classified as easy courses.

4. In our companion paper (Leigh and Gill 1997), we experimented with different threshold ages and with an alternative approach to making the returning adult/continuing student distinction based on a gap in continuous school enrollment.

5. In the NLSY, field of study is asked in a sequence of questions providing detail about the respondent's two- and four-year college program rather than about his or her highest degree. Hence, there is not perfect matching between the available information on highest degree and college field of study.

6. Burton and Celebuski (1995) also mentioned that community colleges 1) support a diversity of learning objectives, including remedial courses that prepare students for further career-oriented training as well as courses for transfer to four-year institutions; and 2) provide access to higher education for many who might otherwise not have the opportunity, including large numbers of minority and female students.

7. An apparent anomaly in the female earnings regression in column 4 is the small and statistically insignificant return estimates for two-year and especially for four-year college programs. We find that our annual earnings estimates are quite sensitive to the inclusion of female respondents with very low annual earnings. Imposing a lower bound restriction of just $1,500 per year, for example, raises our estimates to 6.1 percent (from 4.4 percent) and 8.1 percent (from 0.7 percent), respectively, for two- and four-year colleges. These coefficient estimates are also statistically significant.

8. Distinguishing returning adults from continuing high school students by a gap in continuity of schooling rather than AGEDEG, we reported in Leigh and Gill (1997) that the negative incremental effects for the BA degree and for four-year college disappear for returning adult males. Positive incremental effects of a BA

degree for returning adult women, noted below in the text, also disappear. However, the estimated return to males for nondegree two-year college programs remains in the 8 to 10 percent interval.

9. In our companion paper (Leigh and Gill 1997), we also attempted to control for self-selection in the decisions to enroll in a postsecondary education program, and among those choosing to enroll, determining choice of educational institution. Our approach to the self-selection issue is simply to augment the regression model summarized in Table 4 with explanatory variables—measures of family background and motivation—expected to influence both enrollment and choice of educational institution. The results suggest the presence of a small upward bias in measured returns to education and a slight narrowing of returning adult/continuing student differentials. Nevertheless, the incremental impact of a nondegree community college program for returning adults remains at 8 to 10 percent in terms of wages and annual earnings.

References

Altonji, Joseph G. 1993. "The Demand for and Return to Education when Education Outcomes Are Uncertain." *Journal of Labor Economics* 11(January, Part 1): 48–83.

Berger, Mark C. 1988. "Predicted Future Earnings and Choice of College Major." *Industrial and Labor Relations Review* 41(April): 418–429.

Burton, Lawrence, and Carin A. Celebuski. 1995. *Technical Education in Two-Year Colleges.* HES Survey Number 17, National Science Foundation, Division of Science Resources Studies.

Corman, Hope. 1983. "Postsecondary Education Enrollment Responses by Recent High School Graduates and Older Adults." *Journal of Human Resources* 18(Spring): 246–267.

Grogger, Jeff, and Eric Eide. 1995. "Changes in College Skills and the Rise in the College Wage Premium." *Journal of Human Resources* 30(Spring): 280–310.

Grubb, W. Norton. 1991. "The Decline of Community College Transfer Rates: Evidence from National Longitudinal Surveys." *Journal of Higher Education* 62: 194–222.

_____. 1992. "Postsecondary Vocational Education and the Sub-baccalaureate Labor Market: New Evidence on Economic Returns." *Economics of Education Review* 11: 225–248.

_____. 1993. "The Varied Economic Returns to Postsecondary Education: New Evidence from the Class of 1972." *Journal of Human Resources* 30(Winter): 205–221.

Jacobson, Louis S., Robert J. LaLonde, and Daniel G. Sullivan. 1997. "The Returns from Classroom Training for Displaced Workers." Working paper, Westat, Inc., Rockville, Maryland.

James, Estelle, Nabeel Alsalam, Joseph C. Conaty, and Duc-Le To. 1989. "College Quality and Future Earnings: Where Should You Send Your Child to College?" *American Economic Review Papers and Proceedings* 79(May): 247–252.

Kane, Thomas J., and Cecilia E. Rouse. 1993. "Labor Market Returns to Two- and Four-Year Colleges: Is a Credit a Credit and Do Degrees Matter?" Working paper no. 4268. National Bureau of Economic Research, Cambridge, Massachusetts.

_____. 1995a. "Labor Market Returns to Two- and Four-Year College." *American Economic Review* 85(June): 600–614.

_____. 1995b. "Comment on W. Norton Grubb: 'The Varied Economic Returns to Postsecondary Education: New Evidence from the Class of 1972.'" *Journal of Human Resources* 30(Winter): 205–221.

Leigh, Duane E., and Andrew M. Gill. 1997. "Labor Market Returns to Community Colleges: Evidence for Returning Adults." *Journal of Human Resources* 32 (Spring): 334–353.

Light, Audrey. 1995. "The Effects of Interrupted Schooling on Wages." *Journal of Human Resources* 30(Summer): 472–502.

Oettinger, Gerald S. 1995. "Do Borrowing Constraints Cause School Interruption?" Working paper, Texas A&M University, College Station, Texas.

Osterman, Paul, and Rosemary Batt. 1993. "Employer-Centered Training for International Competitiveness: Lessons from State Programs." *Journal of Policy Analysis and Management* 122(Summer): 456–477.

Rumberger, Russell W., and Scott L. Thomas. 1993. "The Economic Returns to College Major, Quality and Performance: A Multilevel Analysis of Recent Graduates." *Economics of Education Review* 12: 1–19.

Willis, Robert J. 1986. "Wage Determinants: A Survey and Reinterpretation of Human Capital Earnings Functions." In *Handbook of Labor Economics,* Vol. I, Orley C. Ashenfelter and Richard Layard, eds. Amsterdam: North Holland, pp. 525–602.

4
Children's Effects on Women's Labor Market Attachment and Earnings

William E. Even
Miami University

David A. Macpherson
Florida State University

Economic explanations of sex differentials in the labor market often rest upon the fact that women are more likely to exit the labor market than men. As numerous studies have demonstrated, childbearing is an important reason why women exit the labor market. Over the past 20 years, the effect of children on women's labor market attachment has diminished considerably. For example, the percent of women exiting work after having a child dropped from 58 to 24 percent between 1976 and 1995.

This study's first objective is to document the changing pattern of women's labor force exits over the past 20 years, particularly as it relates to childbearing. The analysis reveals a dramatic decline in exit rates among women, particularly among married women with infants. The second objective is to determine why this dramatic decrease in exit rates occurred. Among the explanations explored are increased education, earnings, and a movement of women into occupations where labor force attachment has a larger return. The results reveal that, despite a wide range of available information on standard labor supply variables, very little of the decrease in exit rates can be accounted for. Alternative explanations for the decline in exit rates are discussed.

The final objective of the study is to test an important prediction of the economic theory of sex differences in the labor market; namely, if the impact of children on labor force attachment has diminished over time, their indirect effect on wages should be decreasing as well. There is strong evidence in support of this proposition.

BACKGROUND

The fact that women have more frequent career interruptions than men is the foundation for two well-established economic theories of male/female wage differentials. According to the human capital theory, the fact that women are more likely to withdraw from the labor force than men results in several gender-related differences that lead to lower wages among women. For example, women will accumulate less human capital through labor market experience and be less willing to invest in training (general or specific) since the return on such investments is reduced by a higher quit rate. Also, given their higher quit rates, women may select into occupations that impose a lower penalty for an interruption. For example, women may choose jobs in which skills depreciate slowly during a period out of the labor force and jobs with less firm-specific training.

A higher quit rate among women will also reduce their wages if employers practice statistical discrimination. According to this theory, sex-related differences in quit rates lead employers to discriminate against women if there are hiring or training costs that make quits costly to the employer.[1]

Since these two theories imply that continuity of employment is an important determinant of wages, the relative constancy of the male/female wage gap as labor force participation rates increased rapidly between 1950 and 1980 was initially viewed as evidence against the theories. However, several studies note that rising female labor force participation does not necessarily generate an increase in the continuity of women's employment. That is, for example, suppose that 30 percent of the women work 100 percent of the time. If there is an increase in labor force participation among women that work less than 100 percent of the time, the average degree of continuity among women will fall.

Several studies document that increased employment continuity did not always accompany rising labor force participation rates. For example, Goldin (1989) shows that the average work experience of employed married women did not change substantially since 1920 despite the fact that the labor force participation rate of women increased sevenfold. Also, O'Neill (1985) finds that average tenure of working women fell during the 1960s and early 1970s as labor force participation rates rose.

Since the mid 1970s, women's labor force continuity has improved. O'Neill and Polachek (1993) report that working women's labor market experience has been rising since the mid 1970s, thus contributing to a narrowing of the wage gap during the 1980s. Also, Shaw (1994) finds that the degree of persistence in young women's hours worked has increased over time.

Among employed women, the probability of a career interruption rises substantially around childbirth. Furthermore, Shapiro and Mott (1994) demonstrate that employment behavior surrounding a woman's first birth is an important predictor of labor market behavior 15 to 20 years into the future. Thus, examination of trends in women's employment behavior surrounding childbirth provides an important forecast of future labor market attachment and the direction of sex differences in earnings and occupations.

Among studies that focus on the impact of children on women's labor supply, an important issue is whether the model conditions on prior labor supply behavior. For example, while Klerman and Leibowitz (1994) examine the labor supply behavior of all women with a child less than a year of age, Even (1987) restricts his analysis to women that were working during pregnancy.[2] Nakamura and Nakamura (1994) discuss the desirability of conditioning on prior labor supply. They make the argument that, in cases where prediction accuracy is paramount, prior labor supply and child status variables should be included in the model since they control for unobserved differences in "tastes for work."

Whether labor supply models should be conditioned on prior labor market experience depends largely on the investigator's objective. For example, when an employer is deciding whether to invest in the training of a woman, the key statistic is not the percentage of all women that work, but rather the probability that a working woman will exit the labor force.

In this study, focus is placed on employment following childbirth among women that worked in the year prior to the birth. In this sense, the study is an analysis of conditional labor supply. There are two reasons for the emphasis on employment following childbirth. First, childbirth is one of the most important reasons that women withdraw from the labor force early in their careers. Second, as noted by Shapiro and Mott (1994), employment following childbirth is a very strong predictor of future labor market attachment.

The study adds to the literature in several ways. First, it is the only study to examine trends in conditional employment following childbirth over the past 20 years. Second, it is the first to attempt to account for the tremendous increase in labor market attachment that has occurred. Finally, it examines whether the predictions of human capital and statistical discrimination theories are borne out in terms of changing wage patterns predicted by the decline in women's exit rates.

THE DATA

The data for the analysis are drawn from the March Current Population Survey (CPS) for the years 1976 through 1995.[3] The sample is restricted to civilian women aged 21–40 in the week of the survey. We exclude women under age 21 because of the complications that arise from school attendance and employment. We exclude those over age 40 to focus on women in their childbearing years.

An advantage of the March CPS data is that it includes information on employment status in the week prior to the survey and also asks a variety of questions about employment and earnings in the prior year.[4] Thus, it is possible to examine employment transitions by comparing employment status last year with employment in the week prior to the survey. For the analysis, anyone who reports more than one week of employment in the prior year is defined as employed last year. Anyone who reports that they worked in the week prior to the survey or is on leave (paid or unpaid) is defined as employed this year.

Figure 1 Employment Rates of Women Aged 21–40

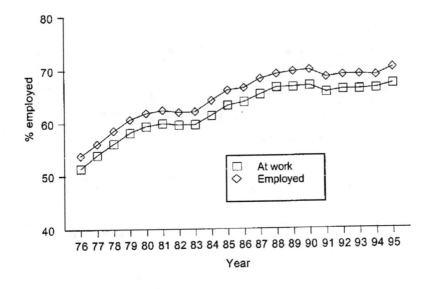

TRENDS IN WOMEN'S EMPLOYMENT

In Figure 1, the percentage of 21- to 40-year-old women employed is presented for the years 1976 through 1995. Over the period, the employment rate rose from 53.8 to 70.2. The growth in the employment rate has subsided over the past 10 years. Whereas it rose at an average of 1.2 percentage points per year between 1976 and 1985, average growth was only 0.4 percentage points per year since 1985.

Employment rates by child status are presented in Figure 2. There are several notable points. First, employment rates are highest among women without children and lowest among women with infants (defined here as a child less than one year of age). Second, the differences in employment rates according to child status fell dramatically over time. For example, the employment rate of women with an infant rose 30.7 percentage points (from 22.4 to 53.1) percent between 1976 and 1995. Among women with no children, the employment rate rose only 4.4 percentage points (from 77.4 to 81.8). For women whose

Figure 2 Percentage of 21- to 40-Year-Old Women Employed, by Age of Youngest Child

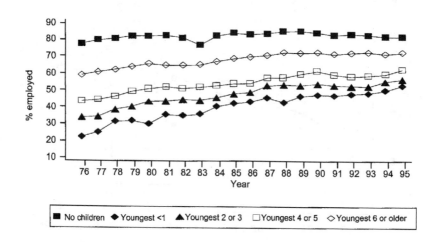

Figure 3 Percentage of Women Employed, by Marital Status

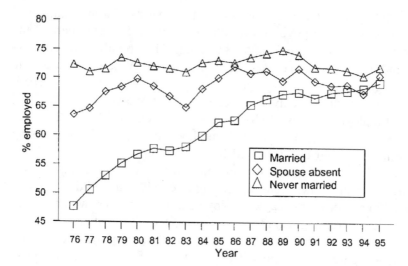

youngest child was more than one year old, the increase in the employment rates lies between these extremes.

Figure 3 presents employment rates by marital status. Consistent
with the fact that the greatest increase in employment has occurred
among women with children is that employment rates are rising more
rapidly among married than never-married women. The rate of growth
in previously married (i.e., divorced, widowed, or separated) women's
employment rates lies between these two extremes. Between 1976 and
1995, the employment rate rose 21.6 percentage points (from 47.7 to
69.3) among married women; rose 7.0 percentage points (from 63.5 to
70.5) among previously married women; and fell by 0.3 percentage
points (from 72.3 to 72.0) among never-married women. It is likely
that the greatest growth in employment rates among married women is
related to the fact that employment has risen most among women with
young children.

TRENDS IN EXIT BEHAVIOR

The evidence on employment rates makes it clear that the percentage of women employed has increased dramatically over time, particularly among women with young children. This does not, however,
necessarily imply that there has been an increase in women's labor
force attachment. In fact, within certain limits, it is possible to have a
simultaneous increase in the percentage of women employed and the
percentage of women who exit the labor force from one year to the
next.

Because the predictions of human capital and statistical discrimination models rest upon gender differences in exit rates, not employment rates, this section examines trends in exit behavior, with a focus
on what occurs following childbirth. The analysis is restricted to
women who were employed in the year prior to the March survey.
Among such women, two types of exits are defined on the basis of the
woman's reported activity in the week prior to the survey. A *work exit*
occurs if a woman reports she did not work in the week prior to the survey. An *employment exit* occurs if a woman reports that she did not
work and was not on leave (paid or unpaid) from her employer. Given

Figure 4 Work versus Employment Exits of Women

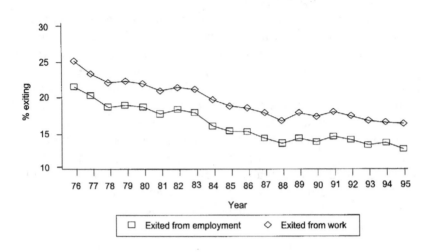

Year

☐ Exited from employment   ◇ Exited from work

A woman is defined as employed if she worked or was on leave in the week prior to survey.

its more comprehensive definition, the percentage of women who exit work will always exceed the percentage that exit employment.

Figure 4 presents work and employment exits for all women aged 21–40. Between 1976 and 1995, women's employment exit rates fell 8.9 percentage points (from 21.5 to 12.6), and the work exit rate fell 8.7 percentage points (from 25.0 to 16.3). The fact that the absolute decrease in exit rates is virtually the same for work and employment exits suggests that the percentage of employed women that go on leave has been stable over time.

The fact that exit rates have fallen so dramatically over time among women implies that gender differences in earnings and human capital accumulation should be falling, *ceteris paribus*. With greater labor force attachment, women should be more willing to seek jobs that require specific training, and employers should be more willing to hire women into such jobs. Also, with women's improved labor force attachment, differences in labor market experience between men and women should be on the decline.

Figure 5 Women's Work Exit Rates, by Age of Youngest Child

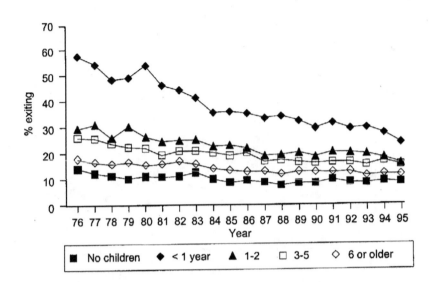

Employment exit rates, by child status, are presented in Figure 5. Across the entire time period, exit rates are highest for women with an infant and lowest among those with no children. The difference in exit rates among groups has dropped dramatically over time, however. Whereas the exit rates of women with an infant fell 25.7 percentage points (from 57.6 to 23.9), those for women with no children fell only 5.4 percentage points (from 14.3 to 8.9). For women with children more than a year old, the decline in the exit rate was somewhere between these two extremes. In general, exit rates have decreased for women with every child status examined, and there has been a narrowing of differences across child status groups.

The reduced effect of children on exit rates is consistent with the convergence of exit rates across marital status presented in Figure 6. In 1976, the exit rates were 24.3, 16.1, and 18.6 for married, previously married, and never-married women, respectively. By 1995, exit rates had fallen for the three groups to 12.2, 13.1, and 16.5, respectively. While exit rates fell for all three groups, they fell most for married and then previously married women. In fact, whereas married women had

Figure 6 Work Exit Rates, by Marital Status

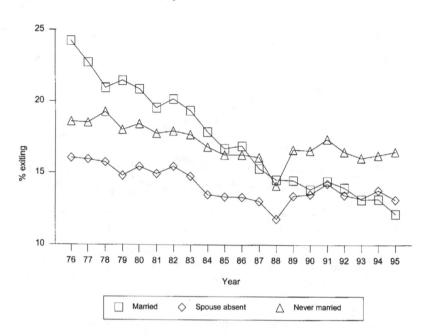

the highest exit rates in 1976, by 1995 they had the lowest exit rates.
Given that married women are more likely to be affected by childbearing, the greater decline in their exit rates is not entirely surprising. It is,
however, rather surprising that married women today have lower exit
rates than never-married women. Given that never-married women are
not likely to have a partner who can generate income when she is out of
work, it is surprising that such women are more likely to exit employment. One possible explanation is that never-married women are more
likely to be eligible for federal income support programs and face
greater disincentives for work.

In summary, exit rates fell dramatically over the past 20 years, particularly among women with young children and married women. The
economic impetus and consequences of this dramatic change are the
subject of the next two sections.

WHY HAVE MARRIED WOMEN'S EXIT
RATES DECLINED?

The standard theory of women's employment decisions rests on a comparison of market and reservation wages. A woman's reservation wage is the minimum wage at which she is willing to accept employment. A woman works if the wage rate offered in the market exceeds the reservation wage. For a woman to exit, either the reservation wage must increase or the market wage must decrease. In most circumstances, women's market wages are not likely to fall with time since on-the-job training and the accumulation of experience will naturally increase their wages. The exception occurs when there is a decrease in labor demand, causing employers to cut wages. It is probably the case, however, that most working women's exits result from sudden changes in their reservation wages. For example, the birth of a child will likely increase the reservation wage and increase the likelihood that a woman exits the labor force. Nakamura and Nakamura (1996) show that several nonwage variables (e.g., marital status, child birth, husband's income) have large effects on women's employment.

An important consideration in the wage/reservation theory is the impact of human capital accumulation and depreciation. Mincer and Polachek (1974) describe the relevant wage rate as the "full wage," which includes 1) the market wage, 2) the present value of the reduction in future earnings caused by the increased depreciation of human capital during time out of the labor force, and 3) the present value of the loss in future earnings associated with the foregone accumulation of human capital. Using this expanded definition of the relevant wage rate, *ceteris paribus*, the greater the depreciation of wages during time out of the labor force, the less likely a woman will exit. Similarly, the greater the foregone growth in wages during time out of the labor force, the less likely a woman will exit.

There are several pieces of empirical evidence consistent with the notion that labor force withdrawals reduce earnings and that women select into occupations that penalize exits the least. Mincer and Polachek (1974) find that wage deterioration during time out of the labor force is highest for those with the highest level of schooling and in high-skill occupations. Moreover, Polachek (1981) shows that women tend to select into the occupations that have the lowest atrophy rates. Light and Manuelita (1995) report that women's wages fall less than men's after a temporary departure from the labor market and that they rebound more quickly after reentry. Also, Hirsch and Macpherson (1995) show that occupations with a disproportionate share of women tend to have less training. In general, the greater frequency of labor force exits impacts the types of jobs that women enter and their earnings growth.

Given these considerations, a model of women's exit behavior must control for several factors: the market wage, factors influencing the reservation wage, and factors that influence the impact of an exit on future wages. Possible explanations for the decline in exit rates are higher market wages, lower reservation wages, or a movement of women into jobs that have greater wage growth and/or depreciation rates.

The CPS data include information on wage rates. Several variables that are likely to influence the reservation wage are also available, such as marital status, other family income (excluding transfer payments that would be endogenous to the woman's work decision), children in various age groups, and the woman's age and race. Finally, occupation and industry controls are included to account for differences in the level of training and skill atrophy across jobs.

Since the earlier examination of trends in exit rates by marital status reveals that most of the decline has occurred among married women, it appears that separate analysis by marital status is in order. For the sake of brevity, focus is placed only on married women in this section. In work not reported here, the relative stability of exit rates among never-married and previously married women is consistent with the observed changes in their characteristics.[5]

Among married women who worked in the year prior to the survey, there are several factors that may have contributed to the rapid decline in their exit rates between 1976 and 1995. Some possible explanations are provided by the sample means in Table 1. First, the average number of children fell slightly from 1.6 to 1.5. This may have contributed to a modest decline in exit rates because many exits are associated with childbearing. Second, women's education has increased over time. The average number of years of education among married women increased from 12.7 to 13.6, and the percentage of married women with college degrees increased from 18.08 to 26.9. Higher levels of education could reduce exit rates by improving women's wages. Finally, the percentage of women who are self-employed rose from 3.5 to 7.3. The flexibility of some types of self-employment could make it easier for women to stay at home with an infant and continue working. Also, for some self-employed workers there will be investments in capital or reputation that could drive up the opportunity cost of staying out of the labor force.

Table 1 Sample Means for Married Women Aged 21–40 Who Were Employed in the Prior Year

Year	Education (years)	Have a college degree (%)	Self-employed (%)	Number of children	Sample size
1976	12.66	17.97	3.49	1.61	7,952
1977	12.73	18.77	3.89	1.58	10,047
1978	12.74	18.93	4.59	1.54	9,790
1979	12.83	19.38	4.44	1.52	10,481
1980	12.88	19.80	4.85	1.49	12,683
1981	12.91	19.34	5.29	1.47	12,627
1982	12.97	20.56	5.50	1.47	11,367
1983	13.09	22.09	5.54	1.41	11,405
1984	13.19	23.62	6.40	1.43	11,407
1985	13.17	22.90	5.81	1.42	11,744
1986	13.17	22.69	5.83	1.43	11,763
1987	13.22	23.23	5.97	1.44	11,872
1988	13.23	23.41	6.41	1.44	11,755
1989	13.28	25.01	6.12	1.44	11,020
1990	13.29	25.07	6.21	1.45	11,736
1991	13.35	25.58	6.38	1.46	11,372
1992	13.33	24.46	6.35	1.46	11,192
1993	13.44	25.98	6.12	1.46	10,951
1994	13.51	26.06	6.72	1.47	10,282
1995	13.55	26.89	7.31	1.46	10,097

To determine the extent to which the above changes have contributed to married women's declining exit rates, a decomposition of the change in exit rates over time is performed. The comparison is made between 1976–1979 (1970s) and 1992–1995 (1990s) exit rates. A probit model of exit rates is estimated for 1976–1979. Using the 1976–1979 probit coefficients, a predicted exit rate is generated for women in 1992–1995. The difference in the 1976–1979 exit rate and that predicted for 1992–1995 is the change in the exit rate that can be accounted for by changes in observed characteristics of working women. Using the approach described in Even and Macpherson (1990), it is also possible to calculate how much of the change in exit rates can be attributed to changes in a particular explanatory variable.

Table 2 presents the estimated probit models of exit behavior for the 1976–1979 and 1993–1995 samples. Most of the results are consistent with expectations. Focusing on the probit model for the 1976–1979 sample momentarily, the effect of children on the probability of exit is quite substantial when the child is an infant but diminishes rapidly as the child ages. A child under the age of one increases the probability of an exit by 26.7 percent. The effect drops sharply to 8.9 percent for a child aged 1 to 2, and falls gradually to 0.8 percent for children aged 13–16. Children 17 and over have a statistically insignificant effect on exits.

A higher real wage has a statistically significant but diminishing negative effect on the probability of an exit.[6] While the effect of real wages is statistically significant at the 0.01 level, quantitatively the effect is quite small. At the mean value of the minimum wage in 1973–1976, a $1 increase in the real wage reduces the probability of an exit by only 0.03 percentage points. This effect is minuscule in comparison to the effect of young children on the probability of an exit.

The type of job held by women also has an important effect on the probability of exiting. Consistent with expectations, self-employed women are 10.2 percent less likely to exit than female wage and salary workers in the private sector. Also, there are significant differences in the probability of an exit across industry and occupation. The differences across industry and occupation could reflect variations in the cost of an exit from the labor force due to variations in training or skill depreciation rates.

Table 2 Probit Estimates of Exit Model for Married Women Aged 21–40

	1976–1979		1992–1995	
	dp/dx	t-statistics	dp/dx	t-statistics
Intercept	0.05	1.38	–0.07	–2.72
Number of children of age				
<1	0.27	39.43	0.10	23.04
1	0.09	11.52	0.04	7.67
2	0.05	6.62	0.03	7.21
3	0.04	6.14	0.02	5.07
4	0.04	5.36	0.02	4.94
5	0.03	3.76	0.02	3.78
6–7	0.02	4.68	0.02	4.63
8–9	0.02	3.35	0.01	1.41
10–13	0.01	2.29	0.00	0.39
14–17	–0.01	–1.43	0.00	0.45
Education				
HS graduate	–0.03	–4.95	–0.04	–6.26
Some college	–0.03	–3.78	–0.04	–6.15
College graduate	–0.04	–4.20	–0.04	–5.10
Race				
Black	–0.06	–6.73	0.01	1.37
Other nonwhite	–0.02	–1.57	0.01	1.24
Real wage	0.00	–9.24	0.00	–10.66
(Real wage)^2/100	0.00	10.93	0.00	12.03
Other income/100	0.08	3.13	0.00	–0.15
(Other income)^2/100	0.00	1.93	0.00	3.91
Part-time	0.08	16.78	0.08	22.37
Age				
24–26	–0.03	–3.86	–0.03	3.93
27–29	–0.04	–5.64	–0.04	–5.46
30–32	–0.07	–8.03	–0.05	–7.73
33–35	–0.08	–8.72	–0.06	–8.53

(continued)

Table 2 (continued)

	1976–1979		1992–1995	
	dp/dx	t-statistics	dp/dx	t-statistics
36–38	–0.09	–8.75	–0.06	–8.75
39–40	–0.10	–9.24	–0.07	–8.63
Public sector employee	–0.02	–2.68	–0.01	–2.20
Self-employed	–0.10	–9.02	–0.05	–7.56
Sample size	38,270		42,522	
Scale factor	0.28		0.18	
Log likelihood	–18,247.17		–14,767.78	

NOTES: The partial derivatives (dp/dx) are evaluated at the sample means of the independent variables. The partial derivative divided by the scale factor yields the associated probit coefficient. The model also includes controls for the amount of training required in the 3-digit occupation, as well as 8 region, 12 occupation, and 12 industry dummies.

Other results consistent with predictions are the fact that more educated women, who are generally believed to have more firm-specific training, are less likely to exit. Also, other sources of family income increase the probability of an exit by increasing the reservation wage through an income effect.

Comparing the 1976–1979 estimates with those for 1992–1995 reveals a high degree of similarity. The most notable difference is that infants have a much smaller effect on exit probabilities in the 1990s than in the 1970s. Whereas having an infant increased the probability of an exit by 26.7 percentage points in the 1970s, the effect fell to 10.4 percent in the 1990s.

The decomposition of the change in married women's exit rates is presented in Table 3. The exit rate fell by 9.6 percentage points between the 1976–1979 and 1992–1995 sample. Using the 1970s probit coefficients, only 2.3 percentage points of this decline can be accounted for by changes in married women's observed characteristics. With the 1990s coefficients, 2.1 percentage points are accounted for. In either case, about one-fourth of the decline in married women's exit rates can be accounted for by the long list of control variables included in the probit models.

Table 3   Factors Contributing to Change in Exit Rates among Married Women between 1976–1979 and 1992–1995

Base-year coefficients	1976–79	1992–95
Variable		
Children	0.43	0.22
Education	–0.28	–0.36
Race	0.02	0.01
Wage	–0.25	–0.23
Other income	–0.10	0.00
Occupation	0.00	–0.24
Industry	0.11	0.05
Part-time	–0.09	–0.10
Region	–0.09	–0.06
Age	–1.11	–0.89
Public	0.08	0.06
Self-employed	–0.21	–0.12
Occupation characteristics	–0.77	–0.46
Total explained	–2.27	–2.14
Total unexplained	–7.30	–7.43
Total change	–9.57	–9.57

Table 4   Factors Contributing to Change in Exit Rates among Married Women with a Child under One between 1976–1979 and 1992–1995

Base-year coefficients	1976–79	1992–95
Variable		
Children	–0.09	–0.09
Education	–0.07	0.06
Race	–0.02	–0.05
Wage	0.00	0.00
Other income	–0.21	0.16
Occupation	0.22	–0.66
Industry	0.18	0.26
Part-time	0.11	0.22
Region	0.20	–0.08
Age	–1.90	–2.56
Public	0.10	0.10
Self-employed	–0.52	–0.33
Occupational characteristics	–1.36	–0.83
Total explained	–3.83	–4.20
Total unexplained	–22.89	–22.52
Total change	–26.72	–26.72

Given the fact that childbirth is arguably the most important cause of women's exits in the labor force and that the impact has dramatically fallen over time, a focus on behavior surrounding childbirth is instructive. As in the prior section, focus here is placed upon the behavior of married women.

In Table 4, a decomposition of the change in exit rates between the 1970s and 1990s sample is presented.[7] Of the 26.7 percentage point decline in exit rates, only 3.8 (4.2) percentage points can be accounted for by the characteristics included when using the 1970s (1990s) probit coefficients. Thus, less than one-sixth of the decline in exit rates can be accounted for by changes in observed worker characteristics.

THE IMPLICATIONS OF GREATER LABOR FORCE ATTACHMENT FOR WOMEN'S EARNINGS

The greater likelihood of labor force exits among women is often pointed to as a cause of several gender-related differences in labor market outcomes. This section investigates whether the large decline in women's exit rates has resulted in the wage effects predicted by human capital and statistical discrimination theory. In particular, the changing pattern of exit rates has implications for women's wages through their effect on job choices and the level of training received.

One important change in exit rates is that, whereas married women had substantially higher exit rates than previously married or single women in the 1970s, they have slightly lower exit rates in the 1990s. To the extent that married women and their employers incorporate this behavior into their human capital decisions, married women's investments in training should have increased. Also, whereas married women should have been more inclined to be in traditionally "female" occupations in the 1970s, this tendency should have diminished over time. Finally, as married women's investments in human capital improve, and as employers practice less statistical discrimination against them, married women's wages should have improved relative to other women.

Another important change in exit rates is the remarkable decrease in the effect of childbirth on exit rates, particularly among married women. Since children have a smaller effect on the probability of an exit, their negative effect on wages should have diminished over time, especially among married women.

Table 5 presents log-wage regressions for the 1970s and 1990s. In the first two columns, estimates are presented for all women aged 21–40. Consistent with the hypothesized effect, the impact of children on wages has diminished over time. Whereas each child reduced wages by 3.4 percentage points in the 1970s, the effect had fallen to 2.5 percent by the 1990s.[8] Consistent with the dramatic reduction in married women's exit rates relative to single and previously married women is the fact that married women's wages have increased relatively. In the 1970s, married women had slightly higher wages (0.009) than other women, though the difference was statistically insignificant. By the

Table 5 Log-Wage Regressions by Marital Status[a]

Variable	All women		Married women		Previously married women		Never-married women	
	1976–79	1992–95	1976–79	1992–95	1976–79	1992–95	1976–79	1992–95
Intercept	1.491	1.452	1.492	1.586	1.543	1.31	1.507	1.367
	38.78[b]	41.24	30.99	33.66	13.48	12.74	18.80	21.12
Number of children	−0.034	−0.025	−0.031	−0.016	−0.035	−0.038	−0.031	−0.048
	−16.92	−11.71	−12.28	−6.11	−7.30	−7.40	−5.67	−8.53
Years of education (reference group < 12 years)								
12	0.10	0.119	0.072	0.101	0.133	0.149	0.187	0.125
	14.92	14.61	8.65	9.06	9.25	8.69	10.32	7.40
13–15	0.133	0.211	0.109	0.198	0.173	0.237	0.194	0.199
	17.40	24.82	11.11	16.86	10.25	12.96	10.45	11.64
16 or more	0.225	0.39	0.202	0.39	0.301	0.417	0.272	0.353
	24.78	41.30	17.16	30.22	12.96	17.93	13.41	19.26
Race (reference group white)								
Black	0.03	−0.04	0.051	−0.03	0.025	−0.045	−0.018	−0.049
	4.21	−5.75	4.97	−2.59	1.79	−2.98	−1.35	−4.54
Other race	0.023	−0.018	0.034	−0.033	−0.027	0.007	0.018	−0.001
	1.72	−2.11	1.99	−2.77	0.78	0.31	0.70	−0.05

Part-time worker	0.042	−0.016	0.054	−0.002	0.07	−0.036	0.008	−0.038
	8.38	−3.34	8.60	−0.37	4.91	−2.67	0.65	−4.18
Age (reference group aged 21–23)								
24–26	0.108	0.101	0.102	0.109	0.055	0.071	0.126	0.101
	16.23	13.11	10.85	8.22	2.74	2.38	11.47	9.75
27–29	0.168	0.197	0.152	0.191	0.123	0.147	0.204	0.212
	23.82	25.25	15.96	15.06	6.29	5.19	14.60	18.06
30–32	0.195	0.261	0.171	0.253	0.151	0.192	0.272	0.286
	25.84	33.45	17.15	20.29	7.67	6.97	15.31	22.52
33–35	0.222	0.298	0.199	0.288	0.166	0.254	0.314	0.307
	27.72	37.62	19.02	23.07	8.09	9.33	14.77	21.76
36–38	0.237	0.32	0.204	0.306	0.232	0.27	0.311	0.349
	28.64	39.87	19.05	24.48	11.17	9.97	12.83	22.17
39–40	0.222	0.329	0.197	0.31	0.186	0.277	0.314	0.393
	23.48	37.33	16.40	23.46	8.16	9.85	9.97	20.17
Public sector employee	−0.005	−0.041	0.002	−0.041	0.006	0.001	−0.019	−0.054
	−0.70	−5.96	0.22	−4.57	0.36	0.05	−1.46	−4.16
Self-employed	−0.276	−0.18	−0.298	−0.201	−0.15	−0.126	−0.141	−0.105
	−22.90	−18.97	−21.62	−18.21	−4.43	−4.54	−3.34	−3.97

(continued)

Table 5 (continued)

Variable	All women		Married women		Previously married women		Never-married women	
	1976–79	1992–95	1976–79	1992–95	1976–79	1992–95	1976–79	1992–95
Marital status (reference group never married)								
Married	0.009	0.046						
	1.52	8.74						
Previously married (widowed, divorced, or separated)	0.024	0.009						
	3.21	1.37						

[a] Wage regressions also include controls for 13 occupations and 14 industries.
[b] t-Statistics are presented below the coefficient estimates.

1990s, married women earned 4.6 percent higher wages than other women, and the difference is statistically significant at the 0.01 level.

In columns 3–8 of Table 5, log-wage regressions are presented for married, never-married, and previously married women separately. Since the effect of children on exits has dropped most for married women, the negative effect of children on wages should have fallen most for married women. The results are consistent with this hypothesis. Among married women, the marginal effect of children on wages fell from 3.1 percent in the 1970s to 1.6 percent in the 1990s. For previously married women, there was no statistically significant change in the marginal effect of children on wages over time. Among single women, there was a statistically significant increase in the negative effect of children on wages.[9] Thus, the negative impact of children on wages has diminished only for married women. This is consistent with the fact that exit rates following childbirth fell most among married women.

Part of the reason that children should have a smaller negative effect on women's earnings in the 1990s than the 1970s is that childbearing is less likely to reduce women's labor market experience or sever ties with an employer. Another part of the explanation is that children should have a smaller effect on occupational and industrial choices. That is, if women are less likely to interrupt their careers when they have children, they should be more inclined to select into occupations and industries with training investments.

To the extent that the measured effect of children on wages is capturing tenure, occupation, and industry effects, the estimated coefficient on children should diminish as these variables are added to the wage equation. Moreover, given that the evidence from exit equations suggests that the link between children and these labor market characteristics has diminished over time, the addition of these variables to wage equations should reduce the estimated child effect more in the 1970s than the 1990s.

To investigate these issues, another data source is required since the March CPS has no information on employee tenure or experience. The May 1979 and April 1993 CPS have virtually the same wage and labor market information as the March surveys with additional information on employee tenure. Unfortunately, however, no information is available for total labor market experience.

Table 6   Effect of Number of Children on Wages[a]

Model	1979	1993
All women		
No tenure/no ind. & occ	−0.039 (−7.16)	−0.021 (−3.69)
With tenure/no ind. & occ.	−0.03 (−5.55)	−0.017 (−3.04)
No tenure/with ind. & occ.	−0.031 (−5.97)	−0.015 (−2.88)
With tenure/with ind. & occ.	−0.023 (−4.52)	−0.012 (−2.38)
Married women		
No tenure/no ind. & occ.	−0.037 (−5.40)	−0.018 (−2.55)
With tenure/no ind. & occ.	−0.027 (−4.10)	−0.015 (−2.18)
No tenure/with ind. & occ.	−0.029 (−4.55)	−0.015 (−2.22)
With tenure/with ind. & occ.	−0.022 (−3.41)	−0.013 (−1.96)
Previously married women		
No tenure/no ind. & occ.	−0.056 (−4.40)	−0.02 (−1.82)
With tenure/no ind. & occ.	−0.046 (−3.58)	−0.021 (−1.67)
No tenure/with ind. & occ.	−0.041 (−3.43)	−0.015 (−1.31)
With tenure/with ind. & occ.	−0.033 (−2.78)	−0.014 (−1.19)
Never-married women		
No tenure/no ind. & occ.	−0.015 (−1.01)	−0.03 −2.00)
With tenure/no ind. & occ.	−0.01 (−0.934)	−0.02 (−1.41)
No tenure/with ind. & occ.	−0.008 (−0.56)	−0.02 (−1.33)

Model	1979	1993
With tenure/with ind. & occ.	-0.007	-0.01
	(-0.5)	(-0.81)

NOTE: Data sources are the May 1979 and April 1993 Current Population Surveys. The sample is restricted to female wage and salary workers aged 21–40. The models also include controls for age and its square, part-time status, firm size (four dummies), plant size (two dummies), race (two dummies), union coverage, education (three dummies), and public sector status.
[a] t-statistics are in parentheses.

In Table 6, the estimated effect of children on wages is presented for four specifications. All four include numerous employer and employee characteristics and the number of children in the family. In the first specification, tenure, occupation, and industry controls are excluded from the regression. In the second through fourth specifications, these controls are added separately and then jointly to determine how much of the reduced children effect is due to the fact that children have a smaller effect on tenure and industrial or occupational choice. The regressions are estimated separately by marital status and by year.

Consistent with the results from the March CPS data, the effect of children on wages fell across time for all women, married and previously married women, regardless of whether tenure, industry, or occupation are controlled for. Also, as in the March CPS, the negative effect of children rose over time for never-married women.

Comparing the four specifications for a given sample reveals that part of the explanation for the declining effect of children on wages is their reduced correlation with tenure, occupation, and industry. For example, in the regression for all women, the coefficient on children dropped 0.018 between 1979 and 1993 when tenure, occupation, and industry are excluded from the model. When these additional controls are added, the coefficient on children drops only 0.011 between 1979 and 1993. Thus, the reduced effect of children on wages over time is partly because children have less effect on women's tenure and on their inclination to select into low-wage occupations or industries.

The results by marital status reveal a similar pattern for married and previously married women. Without controls for tenure, occupation, or industry, the coefficient on children drops 0.019 and 0.033

among married and previously married women. With these controls added, the coefficients drop 0.009 and 0.019. Thus, the changing relationship between number of children and these labor market characteristics (tenure, occupation, and industry) account for an important share of the declining effect of children on wages.

For never-married women, the negative wage effect of children has grown over time, but the increase in the coefficient is smaller when tenure, industry, and occupation are controlled for. This seems to suggest that, in contrast to the case for married and previously married women, the adverse effect of children on labor market characteristics has worsened over time among never-married women.

SUMMARY AND CONCLUSIONS

This study documents the dramatic decline in women's exit rates that has occurred since 1976 and shows that the declines have been most pronounced among married women with young children. A model of married women's exit behavior was estimated as a function of labor market characteristics and factors that could influence the value of time in the home. The model was used to determine how much of the change in married women's exit behavior occurring between the 1970s and 1990s could be accounted for by changes in observed characteristics. Less than one-fifth of the decline in exit rates can be accounted for by changes in observed characteristics. This is true for the exit behavior of all married women and for women with a child less than one year old.

The fact that changing labor market characteristics account for so little of the decline in exit rates leads to a natural question: What has caused the decline that is not included in the model? A simple response is that "social norms" have changed and women now find it more acceptable to work when they have young children. Testing this hypothesis is rather difficult, however. Before abandoning the neoclassical economic explanations, there are several additional avenues that might be explored. First, rising divorce rates may increase married women's desire to establish a career. In support of this argument, Johnson and Skinner (1986) find that higher divorce probabilities increase married women's labor supply. An advantage of this explanation is that it is consistent with a greater decline in married women's exit rates than single or previously married women's exits.

A second possible explanation for the rapid decline in married women's exit rates is that there may be a compounding effect of a decrease in exits. Namely, if married women's exit rates fall, statistical discrimination against women diminishes and women can move into jobs with greater training investments. As they move into such jobs, the cost of an exit is increased. The difficulty in empirically testing this hypothesis is that training investments are difficult to measure.

Given that the exit rates of married women fell more than never-married or previously married women, human capital and statistical discrimination theory predict that married women's wages should have risen relative to others. This prediction is supported in the wage analysis. Furthermore, since children have a much smaller effect on exit rates in the 1990s, theory also predicts that the effect of children on wages should diminish over time. This hypothesis was tested and supported with two separate data sources. In both cases, the negative effect of children on wages has diminished over time. The analysis also reveals that part of the reason that children have a smaller negative effect on married and previously married wages is that the negative relationship between children and "wage enhancing" labor market characteristics (as measured by tenure, occupation, and industry) has diminished over time.

In general, the predictions of human capital and statistical discrimination theory are borne out by the empirical analysis. As women's exits have fallen, their wages have grown. Moreover, as the effect of children on exits fell, their effect on wages dropped as well. Finally, the subgroups of women whose exit rates fell the most have generally experienced the greatest wage growth since the 1970s.

Notes

1. Statistical discrimination against women will also emerge in efficiency wage models if women have higher quit rates. The logic is that the efficiency wage premium serves as a smaller deterrent to shirking for women since the expected present value of the premium is reduced by a higher quit rate. (See Bulow and Summers 1986.)

2. Other studies of women's employment behavior surrounding childbirth include Leibowitz, Klerman, and Waite (1992, 1992a), Klerman and Leibowitz (1990), and Klerman (1990).
3. There are two reasons that we did not include years prior to 1976. First, the earlier data provide less information on household relationships and in many cases makes it difficult to match mothers with children. Second, the earlier data have categorical responses on weeks worked in the prior year, making it impossible to construct a realistic estimate of the hourly wage.
4. Numerous other data sets, including the U.S. and Canadian censuses, provide information about past and present employment status. The primary advantage with the March CPS is that such information is available on an annual basis for 20 consecutive years.
5. In a probit model of exit rates, among previously married women, there is no significant difference in intercepts for the 1976–1979 and 1992–1995 periods. Among previously married women, there is a statistically significant 2.7 percent lower exit rate in 1992–1995 than in 1976–1979. Among married women, the exit rate is estimated to be 7.0 percent lower in the later period.
6. The diminishing effect is reflected in the positive coefficient on the quadratic term. The marginal effect of higher real wage does not turn positive until wages rise to about $59.
7. The probit estimates for the 1970s and 1990s data are not presented for the sake of brevity. Generally speaking, the pattern of results is similar to that for all married women with two exceptions. First, the statistical significance of the control variables are lower when the sample is restricted to women with infants. This is undoubtedly partially due to the much smaller sample size. Second, children have a much smaller effect on exit rates when the sample is restricted to women with infants. The fact that a two-year-old is associated with a lower exit rate might reflect the fact that a woman working with a two-year-old has a strong attachment to the labor market. Support for such behavior is found in Nakamura and Nakamura (1992).
8. The t-statistics for equality of the coefficient on number of children is 2.99. Thus, there is a statistically significant difference in the effect of children on wage in the 1970s and 1990s.
9. The t-statistics for testing the null hypothesis of equal coefficients on number of children in the 1970s and 1990s is 2.09 for never married women. Thus, the null is rejected at the 0.05 level.

References

Bulow, Jeremy I., and Lawrence H. Summers. 1986. "A Theory of Dual Labor Markets with Application to Industrial Policy, Discrimination, and Keynesian Unemployment." *Journal of Labor Economics* 4(3): 376–414.

Even, William. 1987. "Career Interruptions Following Childbirth." *Journal of Labor Economics* 5: 255–277.

Even, William, and David Macpherson. 1990. "Plant Size and the Decline of Unionism." *Economics Letters.*

Goldin, Claudia. 1989. "Life-Cycle Labor-Force Participation of Married Women: Historical Evidence and Implications." *Journal of Labor Economics* 7(1): 20–47.

Hirsch, Barry T., and David A. Macpherson. 1995. "Wages and Gender Composition: Why Do Women's Jobs Pay Less?" *Journal of Labor Economics* 13(July): 426–471.

Johnson, William R., and Jonathan Skinner. 1986. "Labor Supply and Marital Separation." *American Economic Review* 76(June): 455–469.

Klerman, Jacob A. 1990. "Work around Childbirth." Unpublished paper, RAND, Santa Monica, California.

Klerman, Jacob, and Arleen Leibowitz. 1990. "Child Care and Women's Return to Work after Childbirth." *American Economic Review* 80(May): 284–288.

_____. 1994. "The Work-Employment Distinction among New Mothers." *Journal of Human Resources* 29 (Spring): 277–303.

Leibowitz, Arleen, Jacob Klerman, and Linda Waite. 1992. "Women's Employment during Pregnancy and following Childbirth." Report to the U.S. Department of Labor.

_____. 1992a. "Employment of New Mothers and Childcare Choice." *Journal of Human Resources* 27(Winter): 112–133.

Light, Audrey, and Ureta Manuelita. 1995. "Early-Career Work Experience and Gender Wage Differentials." *Journal of Labor Economics* 13(January): 121–154.

Mincer, Jacob, and Solomon Polachek. 1974. "Family Investments in Human Capital: Earnings of Women." *Journal of Political Economy* 82(March/April): 76–108.

Nakamura, Alice, and Masao Nakamura. 1992. "The Econometrics of Female Labor Supply and Children." *Econometric Reviews* 11(1): 1–71.

_____. 1994. "Predicting Female Labor Supply: Effects of Children and Recent Work Experience." *Journal of Human Resources* 29 (Spring): 304–327.

_____. 1996. "An Event Analysis of Female Labor Supply." In *Research in Labor Economics*, volume 15, Solomon Polachek, ed. Greenwich, Connecticut and London: JAI Press, pp. 353–378.

O'Neill, June. 1985. "The Trend in the Male–Female Wage Gap in the United States." *Journal of Labor Economics* 3(1): S91–116.

O'Neill, June, and Solomon Polachek. 1993. "Why the Gender Gap in Wages Narrowed in the 1980s." *Journal of Labor Economics* 11(January): 205–228.

Polachek, Solomon. 1981. "Occupational Self-Selection: A Human Capital Approach to Sex Differences in Occupational Structure." *The Review of Economics and Statistics* 63(February): 60–69.

Shapiro, David, and Frank Mott. 1994. "Long-Term Employment and Earnings of Women in Relation to Employment Behavior Surrounding the First Birth." *Journal of Human Resources* 29(Spring): 248–276.

Shaw, Kathryn. 1994. "The Persistence of Female Labor Supply: Empirical Evidence and Implications." *Journal of Human Resources* 29(Spring): 348–378.

5

U.S. Health Policy and Mothers of Children with Disabilities

Janet Hunt-McCool
Economics Consultant

In this chapter, the effects of tying health insurance coverage to employment are explored as they affect a potentially vulnerable segment of the U.S. population: mothers whose children suffer from disabilities or physical limitations. The U.S. insurance cannot be described by a single set of benefits or a simple set of regulations at the federal or state level. This system is largely voluntary and has evolved privately. Benefits, costs to workers, and regulation of insurers vary substantially by the firm-specific policy covering an employee and his/her family. In many ways, the U.S. health insurance system in which employers voluntarily bear the costs of health care provision is unique among developed countries.

The shortcomings of this system are well known: a large segment of population has no health insurance; many people risk loss of insurance through job change, retirement, or unemployment; and uncertainty exists about costs, benefits, and continued access to health insurance. The risk of adverse selection may preclude small firms from offering health insurance. Persons in worse than average health are more likely to demand insurance than others. Premiums, in turn, will rise above the level that would cover the average worker, reflecting the greater needs of those who elect coverage. In small firms, a large and diverse risk pool is not available to offset this potential selection problem. Further, because insurance is a per-person expenditure, part-time workers and low-wage workers may not be offered employment-based health insurance.

Not only does the voluntary nature of health insurance coverage have the potential to distort the price of insurance through adverse selection, but tax preferences further separate the value of insurance from their resource costs, creating demand pressures on a very expensive health care system. (See Newhouse [1994] on the relationships between medical care use and coverage, and between out-of-pocket costs and use of services.)

More and more U.S. workers and families are losing private insurance coverage as premiums increase. Medical care inflation has exceeded the average rate of inflation in most years of the last two decades. Employers are therefore reducing coverage or limiting benefits in response to higher health care costs. They may also be limiting pension benefits in response to health costs (Hunt-McCool, Hunt, and Gabel 1998).

Recently, attention has focused upon the indirect consequences of an insurance system that effectively ties coverage to full-time work. These consequences include job lock or limits on voluntary job change from insurance clauses that deny benefits for health conditions that existed prior to employment. Incentives for firms to discriminate against workers in poor health are also created because premiums reflect the average health experience of workers in a firm. Premium costs are not uniform; rather, they vary to the individual firm based on expected health risks, generosity of benefits, state mandates of covered benefits, and competition in the insurance market. (These issues are found in Woodbury [1983]; Madrian [1994]; Newhouse [1994], among others.)

In this analysis, I focus on the indirect effects of the U.S. health care system on the labor market: the case of female labor supply for mothers of children with disabilities and physical limitations. Two institutional constraints create special problems for this group. First, premiums per worker are indivisible regardless of the hours one works. Because workers must repay benefit costs indirectly through their productivity, full-time work is often a prerequisite for obtaining work-related health insurance. Secondly, because of scale economies, risk pooling, and the problems of adverse selection, a firm can generally offer health insurance at a premium substantially lower than the cost of an individually purchased health plan. Thus, full-time work is not only a prerequisite for employer-based coverage, it may also be associated with a substantial reduction in the premium.

It is also reasonable to assume that substantial demands are made on the nonmarket time of caregivers if family members suffer from special health problems. Therefore, if the individual has both a high value of nonmarket time and a high demand for health insurance, a tension is created between the competing uses of time. Full-time work is generally required to obtain health insurance. It may come at the expense of time needed for monitoring and caring for a child with special needs.

A test of the competing forces on the allocation of time is provided in this research. The labor supply of married mothers and single mothers of children with disabilities are contrasted using data from the U.S. National Medical Expenditure Survey (NMES). The health insurance options facing these mothers include 1) no insurance, 2) Medicaid, a state/federal program for very low income households, 3) employment-based insurance, often conditional on full-time work and relatively high wages, or, 4) if married, possible coverage by the spouse's employer-provided insurance policy. If the mother is not married and the child is not covered by the policy of the former spouse, then the extent to which time and paid medical care are substitutes determines whether these mothers work, how much they work, and the nature of their insurance coverage, if any.

In addition to the analysis of labor supply, this research employs data on the specific health conditions of children. The ICD9 (*International Classification of Disease*, 9th edition) codes attached to all children's physician visits and hospitalizations were reviewed. A public health pediatrician, Dr. Jennifer Mayfield, developed indicators of conditions that were considered sufficiently severe or chronic to require 1) substantial medical expenses, or 2) the need of additional monitoring of the child. Parental responses to a child health survey were also employed to identify other children with substantial physical limitations or mental disorders. These conditions were then grouped into categories based on chronicity and disease state.

In this way, the analysis attempts to study two questions regarding female work effort in the United States: the effects of various public and private health insurance offerings on labor supply given child health, and the effect of specific child-health problems on work effort.

The analysis proceeds along the following lines. In the next section I provide background material to illustrate the extent of this potential problem. The theory of labor supply under insurance and health care needs is then developed as an extension of the work of health production functions and the allocation of time.

The third section contains a description of the data and the empirical test: a multinomial logit model of work choices under alternative scenarios about insurance coverage. Previewing this evidence, insurance affects the labor supply of both single and married women in predictable ways. The final section concludes the analysis.

THE U.S. HEALTH INSURANCE SYSTEM

The U.S. health care system is a composite of producers, payers, and consumers in the private and public sector. Key features of the system are 1) near universal care for the elderly through Medicare, a federal program, 2) a limited state/federal Medicaid program for some poor, some poor children, and some elderly in need of long-term care, 3) and an employer-based system of health insurance provision for the majority of U.S. households that hold insurance.

Both for-profit and nonprofit providers (persons and institutions) compete for medical care dollars. As noted, private insurance coverage is voluntary, largely at the level of the employer. Regulations vary by type of coverage and by state. A consequence of rising health care costs has been limitations on insurance offerings by employers to their employees. The number of workers covered has declined over time. The probability of obtaining private coverage has been found to depend upon age, gender, income, geographic location, health status, marital status, and the distribution of firms by type and size within a geographic area. Nearly 90 percent of private insurance coverage is employment-based, with just under 60 percent of the U.S. population receiving coverage in this manner.

Still, three-quarters of persons without health insurance live in households with working family members. This is not a problem of poverty, per se. Most persons without insurance are in households in excess of the poverty threshold. Currently, some 18 percent of the U.S. population have no insurance coverage, either private or public. This number has increased over time with the rising cost of health. The loss of coverage has disproportionately occurred among persons outside the highest wage group.

Private insurance is often available for persons not covered by work or a spousal policy, or ineligible for public coverage. However, premiums vary a great deal between individuals and groups, making individual purchases out-of-reach for many. The asymmetry of information between insurers and individuals, or the adverse selection problem, is often considered to be the source of this differential.

Medicare is the federal program that covers most elderly and certain qualified younger disabled persons. All but one percent of older persons (65 and above) qualify for Medicare, insuring some basic coverage for 38 million persons in 1996. Like private insurance, Medicare beneficiaries generally pay a deductible and a co-payment for most services. Medicare does not cover all services; notably, for prescription drugs. Because hospital use and prescription drugs may result in substantial out-of-pocket costs, many older persons purchase private supplemental coverage as well.

The Medicaid program covers certain eligible groups: the blind, disabled, aged, pregnant women, and low-income families with children. The income and other criteria for eligibility vary by state once basic federal criteria are met. Services coverage is highly variable as well. Thus, it is extremely difficult to provide a proper description of the program.

In 1994, Medicaid covered 40 to 60 percent of the low-income population in each of the states, totaling 34 million persons. Spending by states ranged from around $1,000 per covered person to an average $4,800 at this time. Half of this spending was devoted to acute care, while long term care services accounted for one-third. The remainder was spent on hospitals serving a disproportionate share of low income and Medicaid persons. Most coverage applies to the poor or near-poor elderly, and to the very young. Medicaid is free and without user fees. Special provisions for children are found in a number of state Medicaid programs. For example, Medicaid is virtually the only program that covers in-home care for children with disabilities.

Historically, eligibility for Medicaid was tied to eligibility for assistance through either Aid to Families with Dependent Children (AFDC) or another means-based program, Supplemental Security Income. In recent years, however, Congress expanded Medicaid to poor children and pregnant women who do not qualify for cash assistance. Recently, the Temporary Assistance to Needy Families program replaced AFDC, but eligibility for Medicaid remains nearly the same (Liska 1998).

The result of living in households maintained solely by females is often poverty. In the United States, another consequence is being without health insurance coverage. Indeed, while more women in the United States are covered by health insurance than men, this is the result of public coverage and spousal benefits in private policies. Privately, fewer women than men are offered health insurance on the job (Schur and Taylor 1991). In the United States, one-half of approximately 75 million families have children. Twelve million of these families are maintained by women only, while 4 million are maintained by men. Policy to limit Medicaid growth by the states and the erosion of employee coverage suggests that more and more low-income women with children may lose coverage.

THE ALLOCATION OF TIME

At this time, stylized examples of health production, a nonmarket use of time, is discussed. Then, a formal model in which health insurance and full time work are explicitly linked is developed. The consequences for labor supply of women are developed under this constraint.

Examples of Insurance Offerings and the Allocation of Time

The basic model of health production (Grossman 1972) is an extension of the more general model of Becker's (1965) theory of the allocation of time. In the health production model, at least one of the home-produced goods is the stock of family health. Its inputs, like any other home goods, are time of family members and market-purchased goods—in this case, medical care. Allowing for substitution between time and goods (medical care), production isoquants can be developed that are associated with some indicators of health (e.g., absence of bed days per year, pain-free days, life years). Like any other home production, the family is constrained by income (earnings and asset income), time, and the production technology. These constraints apply to health production as well as any other home-produced good that generates utility for the family. Thus, health states are traded against other home-produced goods such as time in recreation, dining, and educating children. Crucially, money income is generated primarily through market work, so time in home production is purchased by a reduction of work hours (and therefore money earnings).

Figure 1 contains the production isoquant and budget constraint in the case where access to health care and labor supply are independent. This figure may be applicable in the United States for married women if the husband provides health insurance to the family or if earnings of the female are too low to qualify for health insurance on the job regardless of hours worked. In these cases, time in health production and medical care needs do not place undue constraints on labor supply.

In contrast, Figure 2 shows the effects of receiving health insurance on the job, effectively reducing the per-unit price of medical inputs. (Firm purchases of group health insurance are cheaper than privately purchased insurance due to such factors as scale economies, tax preferences, and bargaining power associated with size.) In this case, cheaper health inputs are revealed in a rotation of the budget constraint upward from T. However, nonmarket time per week is constrained. If the parent works 40 hours per week in order to obtain insurance, the maximum time remaining is 128 hours per week. The budget constraint is stepped accordingly.

In Figure 3, the budget constraint under Medicaid is shown. A substantial penalty for market work occurs in the form of loss of eligibility for Medicaid (via the underlying limits on the associated program Aid to Families with Dependent Children). In the figure, this constraint is noted as AFDC. The 100 percent tax on earnings occurs at very low levels of earnings for many women, given poverty-based eligibility rules. (These rules vary by state. Some states may require work for AFDC eligibility, and some allow women to maintain child care and Medicaid for up to two years after leaving the program. Mostly, rules are more restrictive and include lifetime and calendar month limitations on eligibility.)

Work, Marriage, and Insurance Coverage: The Evidence

Figure 1 shows the case where purchases of health care and labor supply are independent. Health production (H) is dependent upon mar-

Figure 1 Independence of Hours of Work and the Price of Purchased Health Services

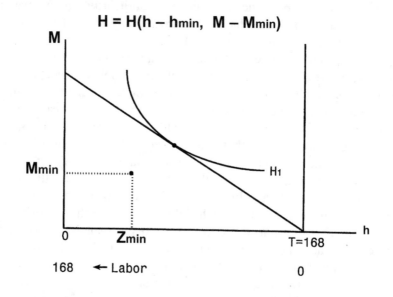

Figure 2 Health Insurance Provided by Employer, Health Care Costs, and Labor Supply

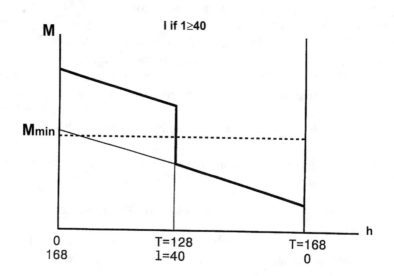

Figure 3 Health Services Costs, Labor Hours, and Medicaid

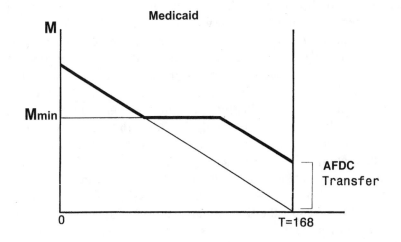

ket purchased health services (*M*) and time in health production (*h*). *T*, the maximum time in health production, is constrained by the number of hours in the week, 168 hours. Therefore, time used in health production is taken away from time in the labor market, so if *h* = 168, then labor supply must be 0. The biological/health specific minimum requirements imply a minimum number of hours in health production (Z_{min}) and purchased medical services (M_{min}). Independence of the two inputs implies only that their relative prices are constant and not dependent upon hours of work, so the budget line is straight. This budget allows the household to afford at most H_1 amount of health.

Figure 2 shows what happens to the budget constraint if the price of market-based medical services changes with employer-sponsored health insurance. The price of insured health benefits drops vis-à-vis the private price pushing the budget constraint upward on the *M* axis. But to receive insurance (*I*), full-time work is likely to be required. In the figure, this is the point where *I* = 40, denoting 40 hours of market work. Time for important home production activities such as time in child health is reduced to a maximum of 128 hours. The budget constraint becomes stepped accordingly.

Salkever (1980, 1982a, 1982b), Breslau, Salkever, and Staruch (1982), and Breslau (1983) have examined how disabled and chronically ill children affect maternal time allocation. Salkever found that children with disabling health conditions affected maternal labor supply by reducing annual hours of work, but that child health had only a small impact on the participation decisions. He defined children's health conditions through indicators such as mobility and sensory limitations, mental and nervous system disorders, heart problems, and circulatory or respiratory ailments. His data included only white, two-parent families. The availability of insurance, public or private, was not explicitly modeled in his analysis, although he did acknowledge their importance. Breslau, Salkever, and Staruch reported that having a disabled child reduced labor supply of married women but had little effect on single mothers. Breslau found that if a child in the household had cystic fibrosis, cerebral palsy, myelodysplasia, or other severe physical handicaps, the time a married mother spent in housework increased by more than three hours per week. No significant effect on the time in housework by single mothers was found. A theme common to these studies is that married women alter hours more so than single women in response to children's health problems.

A Formal Model of the Allocation of Time

Our model of parental time allocation in the presence of children with health problems draws upon the household production framework of Becker (1965) and Grossman (1972). The framework is extended to incorporate the availability of work-related health insurance and the required trade-off between benefits and wages in a competitive labor market. As such, it is a logical extension of Figures 1 and 2, in which the marginal exchanges of time in health production (L_h) offer market-purchased health. Services (M) are affected by health insurance.

Consider the case of one parent and one child with health capital H_0. Household utility is defined as $U(X, H)$ where X is a good purchased exclusively in the market and H is child health, produced with inputs of time and medical care. The child health production function is

(1) $H = H[M, L_h \mid H_0, r(e)]$,

where the productivity of inputs M (market-based medical services) and L_h (parental time in child health) is contingent on the initial stock of health, H_0, and the rate of depreciation of health capital, $r(e)$. The rate of depreciation is unknown but expected to follow a known probability distribution defined by e_1 or e_2. In good health (state 1), which occurs with probability p, depreciation is r_1, which is low. In state 2 with probability $(1 - p)$, depreciation is r_2, which is high. Specifically, we assume that the change in health in state 1 is too low to demand medical inputs in excess of the amount of the insurance deductible D.

The marginal productivity of M and L_h are presumed greater in the poor-health state. Hence there is a state-specific utility created by the inputs of time, market goods, and medical care. If the family has health insurance for the child, the price of medical care, P_m, is not constant. Instead, out-of-pocket medical care expenditures for the family are

(2) $\ D + \xi(P_m, M_2 - D),$

assuming that the poor-health state occurs so that spending on M exceeds the deductible, D.

Additional out-of-pocket spending beyond D is determined by ξ, the co-insurance rate, so that the family spends only ξM per unit of M. However, in the health state r_1, spending is not expected to exceed the deductible and is simply $P_m M_1$.

The household pays for health insurance from the employer indirectly in the form of reduced wages. This is a requirement of competitive labor markets in which no employer can afford to offer more total compensation than its rivals. Firms can, however, vary the distribution of total compensation between wages and benefits. If a worker earns total compensation equal to $\$S$ per hour and the worker holds health insurance, hourly compensation may be written as

(3) $\ S = w + p_i I,$

where $P_i I$ is the value of insurance purchased per hour of work by an equivalent reduction in hourly wages.

Labor supply is determined by maximizing expected utility,

(4) $\ \max E\{ U(X,H) = p_1(U^1, H^1) \} + 1 - p_1(U^2, H^2),$

subject to a time constraint that divides total weekly hours between home production and market labor:

(5) $T = L_h + L_m,$

an hourly compensation constraint expressed in Eq. 3, and the child health production function described by Eq. 1.

Let $G(M, I)$ describe the family cost of health care. The cost of health care is uncertain but has the expected value of the sum of spending in each state weighted by the state-specific odds:

(6) $E\{G(M,I \mid \xi, D, P_m M)\} = p P_m M + (1 - p)[D + \xi(p_m M - D)].$

Total income of the household is made up of unearned income, V, and total wage income $w L_m$. Because purchases of market goods (X) and spending on medical care cannot exceed total income, the budget constraint is defined by equating actual spending with actual income in each state as

(7) $X + G(M, I) = V + w L_h + V + w(T - L_h),$

or simply as

(8) $X = V + (S - P_i I)(T - L_h) - G(M, I),$

where X, I, and G are specific to the state of health that actually occurs.
This problem can be restated as

(9) $\max E\{U[V + (S - P_i I)(T - L_h) - G(M, I), H(I_h, M)]\}$

$= p U[V + S(T - L_h^1) - P_m M, H_1] + (1 - p)U[V + (S - P_i I)(T - L_h^2)$

$-(D + \xi(P_m M - D), H_2)]$

The first order conditions are

$E(U)_I = -p U_x P_i(T - L_h^1) - (1 - p)U_x[P_i(T - L_h^2) + G] = 0$

$E(U)_{L_h} = -p U_x(S - P_i I) - (U_h H L_h^1) - (1 - p)U_x[S - P_i I - H^2] = 0$

$E(U)_m = -p[U_x(G_m^1 - U_h H_m^1)] - (1 - p)U_x(G_m^2 - U_h H_m^2).$

They can be transformed into the familiar conditions for optimal insurance: an individual will transfer consumption of X between states of child health (through the purchase of insurance) in proportion to the odds of the poor health state occurring. As p increases, G_1 approaches zero and there are no cost savings from insurance. Similarly, if p is low, the benefits from insurance are great. An individual should be willing to trade wages (and hence consumption) in state 1 for this benefit. The equilibrium level of L_h is described in the remaining conditions so that the exchanges between market goods and child health and medical care and child health are optimal given the probabilities of each health state.

The first order conditions can be differentiated to develop I, L_h, and M, defined as functions of exogenous prices, income, and the variables in the utility and production functions. Maternal labor supply is obtained by solving the demand for time in home production. It too is state-specific and depends upon the state of health of the child that occurs. Maternal labor supply can be expressed as

$$(10) \quad L_m = T - L_h = L_m(w, P_i I, P_m V, \xi H_o, r(e)).$$

Constraints on Insurance Provision

In reality, time constraints can preclude market work entirely, or limits on work hours and limited earnings potential may preclude the offer of health insurance. A likely constraint facing female households is that their wages may be too low for the firm to offer any health insurance. For example, health insurance is unlikely to be offered to part-time or minimum or low-wage employees who earn too little to offset the costs of insurance. For persons affected by these constraints, $PI = 0$ and $w = S$, regardless of preferences.

Because full-time employment is usually a requirement for work-related coverage, the utility of employer-sponsored insurance depends upon the degree to which parental time in child health can be substituted for market-provided health care and the extent to which substitutes exist for private health insurance. Women with very low earnings are unlikely to be offered job-related health insurance. An alternative source of coverage is Medicaid for low-income persons. Eligibility requirements vary by state but are generally means-tested.

Both the availability of employment-based health insurance and of Medicaid eligibility are unknown *a priori*. Even full-time work may not guarantee that a worker will obtain employment-related coverage. Firm attributes including average preferences of workers, size of the work force, health risks, and the ability to achieve group purchase discounts will affect availability at the firm level. Similarly, a complex system of regulations by states and federal government determines Medicaid eligibility. Accordingly, the decision to participate in the labor market is conditioned on the likelihood of obtaining work-related or public insurance coverage. Such probabilities are explicitly included in the estimates of the maternal labor supply decision.

AN EMPIRICAL TEST

Data

To examine the relationships between maternal labor supply and child health, and between health insurance coverage and labor supply, we employ data from the 1987 National Medical Expenditure Survey (NMES). NMES was a year-long survey of the medical care use and expenditures, and health insurance coverage of the U.S. population based on about 15,000 households. A limited number of questions were also devoted to employment and hours of work. This analysis employs a subset of families with children between 1 and 17 years of age. These data consist of 3,069 two-parent and 1,590 single-parent families in which mothers are present. The sample of married mothers was further restricted to households in which husbands were employed full time as wage and salary workers.

A restriction of the data included the age of children. Mothers of children less than one year of age were excluded from the analysis because of complex institutional rules about parental leave time and difficulties discerning child illness or limitations at this early stage.

NMES contains two sources of child health information. First, the symptom, reason, or condition associated with any reported medical event (e.g., physician office visit, hospitalization, use of outpatient clinic) or disability day was coded into a specific disease category according to diagnostic classed established by the *International Classification of Diseases,* 9th edition. Secondly, information on parental responses to the NMES Health Questionnaire for children 4 and under and for children 5 to 17 was coded for the presence or absence of health problems. This information included the general health status of children, the presence of activity limitations, and the presence of acute or chronic health problems. We considered a child to be in need of special medical care or monitoring time if she or he had activity limitations, chronic health problems such as asthma, heart murmurs or other heart problems, or constant, long-lasting digestive problems.

Criteria for defining child health problems included physical disabilities and illnesses of a chronic, persistent, or recurrent nature. Three decision rules made up the classification scheme: the condition or diagnosis was potentially costly either in terms of time or medical care costs; the condition was associated with the risk of unanticipated child care demands that could interrupt routine schedules such as schooling or work; and the presence of the condition was likely to be independent of the time at which it was reported (e.g., the condition was chronic or recurrent).

The following classes of child health problems were extracted:

LIMITATIONS = sensory and ambulatory limitations.
INFECT = acute and chronic infectious diseases.
ALLERGY = allergies and asthma.
PSYCH = drug dependency, emotional problems, depression, and eating disorders classified as psychological.
TRAUMA = head trauma, fractures affecting mobility, and severe burns.
METADIG = disorders of the metabolism or digestive tract.
PULMCAR = disorders of the pulmonary and cardiovascular systems.

Infectious diseases and allergies, common among children, were included only when they were associated with an unusual event such as the loss of 10 or more days from school or an episode of hospitalization. They are denoted by

INF × BED = infectious disease resulting in a large number of bed days.

ALL × STAY = allergy or asthma resulting in one or more hospital episodes.

Table 1 contains a description of the distribution of children aged 1–17 in the data according to specific health conditions. Most commonly, these children experienced acute or chronic infectious diseases, allergies or asthma, or recurrent or episodic problems that do not always connote severity. Between 2 and 3 percent of children in the sample had relatively serious health problems of a physically or mentally disabling nature, as well as problems that required hospitalization.

Model Specification

Multinomial logit estimates (MLE) of the choice of usual hours of work per week are used to estimate the effects of child health states and the availability of private and public insurance on maternal labor supply. They are estimated separately for married and single mothers. The operational definitions of labor supply and health are found in Table 2.

The choices available include no work, part-time hours (less than 35 hours per week) or work at full-time hours (the omitted group). Because multinomial logit incorporates the restrictive IIA assumption, we tested for IIA using the Hausman-McFadden statistic. This test

Table 1 Distribution of Health Conditions among Children

Conditions	%
Limitations	3.0
Allergy and asthma	13.0
Infectious diseases	15.4
Trauma	2.9
Pulmonary and cardiovascular disorders	3.3
Metabolic and digestive disorders	2.5
Psychological disorders	2.3
Number of children	8,945

Table 2 Variable Symbols and Definitions

Labor supply	
No work	Index denoting that mother does not work for pay
Part-time work	Mother works part time
Full-time work	Mother works full time
Health conditions of children	
LIMIT	Sensory and ambulatory limitations in child
PULMCAR	Pulmonary or cardiac disorder in child
METADIG	Metabolic, digestive, or endocrine disorder in child
PSYCH	Psychological or mental disorder
TRAUMA	Head trauma, fracture limiting walking, or serious burns
INFECT	Acute or chronic infectious disease
ALLERGY	Allergy or asthma
Health status of children (events)	
BED10	Child lost 10 or more school days due to illness
HOSP	Child was hospitalized at least once
Health conditions (interaction of conditions and events)	
ALL × STAY	ALLERGY = 1 and one or more hospital stays
INF × BED	INFECT = 1 and BED10 = 1
Insurance probabilities (predicted by probit)	
PROB. MEDICAID	Odds that mother is eligible for Medicaid if not working
PROB. INSURANCE	Odds that mother would be offered insurance on the job if she worked full time

(continued)

Table 2 (continued)

Other health insurance	
FATHER INSURED	Father holds employment-related health insurance
Personal characteristics	
EDUC	Years of education
BLACK	Race is black
Income and wealth of household	
NONEARNED INCOME	All nontransfer and nonwage income
FATHER'S WAGE	Father's hourly earnings

involves a comparison between coefficients of a full-choice model inclusive of all alternatives and the coefficients of the restricted model. The addition of an alternative should not alter parameter estimates of the remaining choices if IIA holds. We did not find compelling evidence of IIA violation (Hausman and McFadden 1984).

The independent variables in the model are the six categories of health limitations/conditions described previously, and

PROB. INSURANCE = estimated odds of private coverage if woman with these human capital and experience characteristics were to work full time.

PROB. MEDICAID = estimated odds of Medicaid coverage if woman with these human capital and socioeconomic characteristics were not at work. This is estimated for single mothers only. Income of husbands in the sample generally precludes Medicaid coverage.

BLACK = race is black.

EDUCATION = years of education.

CHILDREN 1–2 = presence of children in household aged 2 or younger.

CHILDREN 3–5 = presence of children in household aged 3 through 5.

BEDUC = interaction term of race and education.

BCHILDREN–2 = interaction term of race and children 2 or under.

BCHILDREN–5 = interaction term of race and children 3 to 5.

NONEARNED INCOME = all nonwage income except transfer payments.
This variable is found in the test of married mothers' labor supply only.
FATHER'S WAGE = hourly wage of spouse if married only.
BINCOME = interaction between race and income.
BFATHER'S WAGE = interaction between race and father's wage.

Multinomial Logit Results

Estimates of employment decisions by single and married mothers are found in Tables 3 and 4, respectively. The main finding with regard to disease states is that potentially chronic illnesses in children deter both single and married mothers from full- or part-time employment. This result differs from many previous studies that find a response only among married women. Women who do work appear to choose limited hours or part-time work.

In terms of insurance offerings, conflicting labor force incentives are evident. Single mothers are responsive to the odds of Medicaid coverage, while married women are responsive to the odds of obtaining private health insurance on the job.

The final column in each of the tables shows the distributional characteristics of each sample. Married mothers and single mothers have children with similar disability and disease profiles. However, they differ somewhat in the distributions of ages of children and in race. Single mothers are more likely to have children between one and two years old than their married counterparts. They are also disproportionately black. Because the labor market experience of black women and other women may vary independent from socioeconomic household characteristics, we calculated interaction terms between race and children, between race and education, and between race and income in the sample of married mothers.

The coefficients and marginal probabilities from the logit models for single mothers are described in Table 3. Specifically, a child with activity limitations increases the odds of no work relative to full-time work by almost 9 percentage points and increases the probability of part-time versus full-time work by about 4 percentage points. Children

Table 3 Trichotomous Logit Results of the Labor Supply of Single Mothers[a]

	Part-time vs. full-time work	dp/dx	No work vs. full-time work	dp/dx	Mean
Constant	1.925		−0.538		
	(0.512)		(0.285)		
LIMIT	0.531	0.087	0.467	0.039	0.063
	(0.272)		(0.286)		
PULCAR	0.485	0.071	0.574	0.058	0.066
	(0.260)		(0.271)		
METADIG	0.065	0.015	−0.021	−0.007	0.042
	(0.329)		(0.344)		
PSYCH	0.128	0.028	−0.010		
	(0.302)		(0.316)	−0.009	0.047
ALL × STAY	0.683	0.142	0.102	−0.025	0.026
	(0.483)		(0.485)		
INF × BED	−0.177	−0.005	0.274	0.053	0.020
	(0.483)		(0.448)		
PROB. INSURANCE	−1.344	−0.184	−1.786	0.193	0.650
	(0.951)		(1.0420)		
PROB. MEDICAID	0.422	0.071	0.351	0.028	0.543
	(0.127)		(0.0136)		
BLACK	2.076	0.377	1.219	0.613	0.42
	(0.781)		(0.873)		
EDUC	−0.194	−0.045	0.048	0.019	11.91
	(0.043)		(0.0420)		
CHILDREN 1–2	1.173	−0.232	0.387	−0.002	0.223
	(0.181)		(0.213)		
CHILDREN 3–5	0.448	0.093	0.069	−0.016	0.324
	(0.161)		(0.273)		

	Part-time vs. full-time work	dp/dx	No work vs. full-time work	dp/dx	Mean
BEDUC	−0.149	−0.026	−0.101	−0.006	
	(0.066)		(0.070)		
BCHILDREN–2	−0.569	−0.114	−0.167	0.009	
	(0.253)		(0.304)		
BCHILDREN–5	0.122	0.023	0.055	0.001	
	(0.231)		(0.273)		
LOG L			−1,462		
NO WORK			N1 = 485		
PART-TIME			N2 = 301		
FULL-TIME			N3 = 788		

[a] Coefficients are shown with standard errors in parentheses.

Table 4   Trichotomous Logit Results of the Labor Supply of Married Mothers[a]

	Part-time work vs. full-time work	dp/dx	No work vs. full-time work	dp/dx	Mean
Constant	−0.0669		1.479		
	(0.501)		(0.471)		
LIMIT	−0.021	0.010	−0.205	−0.039	0.046
	(0.239)		(0.256)		
PULCAR	0.332	0.026	0.532	0.081	0.048
	(0.243)		(0.242)		
METADIG	0.774	0.082	0.950	0.133	0.039
	(0.282)		(0.281)		
PSYCH	−0.231	−0.53	0.119	0.039	0.038
	(0.275)		(0.268)		
ALL × STAY	−0.037	−0.031	0.341	0.069	0.020
	(0.398)		(0.363)		
INF × BED	0.349	0.023	0.617	0.097	0.025
	(0.339)		(0.327)		
PROB. INSURANCE	0.095	0.202	−2.627	−0.524	0.670
	(0.91)		(0.902)		
FATHER INSURED	0.251	0.008	0.565	0.093	0.690
	(0.115)		(0.124)		
BLACK	1.293	0.206	0.587	0.025	0.157
	(0.865)		(0.859		
EDUC	−0.024	0.006	−0.147	−0.027	12.49
	(0.027)		(0.027)		
CHILDREN 0–2	0.201	−0.007	0.652	0.114	0.373
	(0.099)		(0.097)		

	Part-time work vs. full-time work	dp/dx	No work vs. full-time work	dp/dx	Mean
CHILDREN 3–5	0.103	0.088	0.052	–0.151	0.365
	(0.098)		(0.096)		
NONEARNED INCOME	3.0E-05	–2.0E-06	2.0E-04	2.0E-06	2053.00
	(8.0E-05)		(8.0E-04)		
FATHER'S WAGE	0.019	–0.0002	0.056	0.010	11.13
	(0.012)		(0.011)		
BEDUC	–0.152	–0.026	–0.035	0.004	
	(0.075)		(0.073)		
BCHILDREN–2	0.023	0.032	–0.398	–0.081	
	(0.264)		(0.275)		
BCHILDREN–5	0.206	0.088	–0.693	–0.151	
	(0.264)		(0.317)		
BINCOME	–1.0E-04	–0.007	–5.0E-05	–2.0E-07	
	(0.037)		(3.0E-04)		
BFATHER'S WAGE	–0.054	–0.007	–0.054	–0.007	
	(0.037)		(0.036)		
LOG L			–2,447		
NO WORK			N1 = 649		
PART-TIME			N2 = 668		
FULL-TIME			N3 = 1,140		

[a] Standard errors are in parentheses.

with pulmonary or cardiovascular health problems reduce the probability of full-time employment relative to working part time by 7 percentage points but raise the likelihood of part-time relative to full-time employment by 6 percent.

As the probability of Medicaid eligibility at zero hours of work increases, single mothers are more likely to work part time relative to full time. Each percentage point increase in eligibility results in an increase of no employment by 0.3 percentage points and of part-time employment by 0.7 percentage points. Although only marginally significant, a one-point increase in the probability of employment-related health insurance exerts an18-percentage-point decrease in part-time work relative to full-time employment.

Education mitigates the reduction in labor supply from full-time to part-time hours, and its influence is greater for black women than for other single mothers. The same is true for young children where the effects on the interactive influence on part-time work and full-time work are again mitigated by race.

Chronic child health problems also affect employment decisions of married mothers, as shown in Table 4. The odds of not working increase by 8.1 percentage points relative to full-time work if children experience pulmonary or cardiac problems. For mothers of children with metabolic digestive disorders, the odds of part-time work over full-time increase by 8.2 percentage points, with the effects of no work versus full-time work even stronger at 13.3 percentage points. Infectious diseases in children leading to inordinate bed days raise the odds of no work by almost 10 percentage points.

Health insurance on the job matters as well. Women will opt for full-time work versus not working if their own chances of being offered insurance increase. This effect is on the order of a 50-percentage point reduction in the odds of no work. There are no discernible effects of insurance on full-time versus part-time work, however.

A working husband with insurance appears to substitute well for own insurance. When the husband holds insurance, the mother typically more often chooses part-time work over full-time work or no work. These marginal effects are 0.093 for no work versus full-time work, but less than 1 percentage point on the choice of part-time versus full-time employment.

Finally, education is a significant determinant of work; as years of schooling increase, the odds of either part-time or no work decrease relative to full-time work. Education and race interact significantly to reinforce the work decision in the case of full-time over part-time work. Interestingly, race and the presence of older children shows a significant interaction effect on the decision to work. Its coefficient in the model predicting no work versus full-time work is significantly negative. Black mothers of older children tend to work full time more often than their white counterparts.

SUMMARY AND CONCLUSIONS

The artifact of combining employment and health insurance in the United States has certain deleterious consequences, especially for women's employment. Madrian (1994) has found job lock, for example. Similarly, Moffitt and Wolfe (1990) found a relationship between health care needs, employment-based insurance, and Medicaid. Women would be likely to reduce their Medicaid attachment by 6 percent and increase their workforce attachment by 12 percent if one-third more jobs offered health insurance. Wolfe and Hill (1992) simulated the effects of mandated benefits under different health states and varying hours of work. Health insurance created a stronger effect on work than either child care or wages if either the woman or a dependent child was in poor health.

This chapter addressed a related phenomenon—the rigidity in the work schedule created when essential health benefits are tied to the job. Data on mothers of children with disabilities were used to test for the competing effects on time use: the need to work full time to obtain insurance versus the need for time caring for the child. The research considered two new areas of inquiry: the insurance-employment rigidities of the system and the effects of specific health conditions on single and married mothers. Unlike much previous research, we found a linkage between child disability and time allocation for single women as well as married women. With regard to insurance, husband's coverage, the odds of own employment-based coverage, and the odds of Medicaid coverage all affected labor supply predictably. Finally, the results confirmed racial effects on labor, even in the presence of insurance. These effects interacted with education and number/age of children to increase black female supply relative to other mothers. To the extent black women are either disproportionately low-wage workers or heads of households in on near poverty, they are subject to the double risks of the erosion of private health insurance from employers as well as restrictions imposed by states on Medicaid expenditure growth if they are currently eligible. Even if they maintain health insurance on the job because they tend to work longer hours than their white counterparts, they are in danger of robbing time that would otherwise be devoted to monitoring and caring for special health needs of their children.

There are many reasons why health insurance tied to jobs is inefficient or inequitable.

The zero-sum alternative of Medicaid, available primarily to low-income single parents, has its own set of disadvantages. Lifetime income and wealth must remain low to maintain health care coverage, and market skills may depreciate with limits on work. Women would appear to suffer worse from the problems created by the employment/insurance nexus because they routinely provide a large part of the non-market time to their families.

Note

My sincere thanks to Alice Nakamura, participants in the W.E. Upjohn/Statistics Canada Joint Conference on Changes in Working Time in Canada and the United States, and workshop participants of the Institute for Health Care Research and Policy, Georgetown University, for helpful comments. This paper arose from earlier research conducted jointly with Alan Monheit. At the time this paper was written, the author was Associate Professor, Georgetown Institute for Health Care Research and Policy. Errors, of course, belong solely to the author.

References

Becker, Gary S. 1965. "A Theory of the Allocation of Time." *Economic Journal* 75(4): 493–517.

Breslau, Naomi. 1983. "Care of Disabled Children and Women's Time Use." *Medical Care* 21(1): 620–629.

Breslau, Naomi, David Salkever, and Kenneth Staruch. 1982. "Women's Labor Force Activity and Responsibilities for Disabled Dependents: A Study of Families with Disabled Children." *Journal of Health and Social Behavior* 23(2): 169–183.

Grossman, Michael. 1972. *On the Concept of Human Capital and the Demand for Health*. New York: Columbia University Press.

Hausman, Jerry, and Daniel McFadden. 1984. "Specification Tests for the Multinomial Logit Model." *Econometrica* 47: 1219–1240.

Hunt-McCool, Janet, Kelly Hunt, and Jon Gabel. 1998. *Does Health Insurance Crowd Out Pension Benefits?* KPMG Special Report.

Liska, David. 1998. *Medicaid: Ten Basic Questions Answered.* The Urban Institute Fact Sheets, Urban Institute, Washington, D.C.

Madrian, Brigitte C. 1994. "Employment Based Health Insurance and Job Mobility: Is There Evidence of Job-Lock?" *Quarterly Journal of Economics* 8(2): 27–52.

Moffitt, Robert, and Barbara Wolfe. 1990. *The Effects of Medicaid on Welfare Dependency.* Special report no. 49, Institute for Research on Poverty, University of Wisconsin.

Newhouse, Joseph P. 1994. *Free for All?* Cambridge, Massachusetts: Harvard University Press.

Salkever, David. 1980. "Effects of Children's Health on Maternal Labor Supply: A Preliminary Analysis." *Southern Economic Journal* 57: 156–166.

———. 1982a. "Children's Health Problems and Maternal Work Status." *Journal of Human Resources* 17: 94–109.

_____. 1982b. "Children's Health Problems: Implications for Parental Labor Supply and Earnings." In *Economic Aspects of Health*, Victor R. Fuchs, ed. University of Chicago Press, pp. 221–251.

Schur, Claudia, and Amy Taylor. 1991. "Choice of Health Insurance and the Two-Worker Household." *Health Affairs* (Spring): 155–163.

Wolfe, Barbara and Steven Hill. 1992. "The Effect of Health on the Work Effort of Low-Income Single Mothers." Discussion paper no. 979, Institute for Research on Poverty, University of Wisconsin.

Woodbury, Stephen A. 1983. "Substitution between Wage and Nonwage Benefits." *American Economic Review* 73(3): 166–182.

6
Early Retirees of a Telecommunications Firm— Patterns of Employment and Working Time

Gangaram Singh
San Diego State University

Anil Verma
University of Toronto

The aging population is a common phenomenon in many countries (Henretta 1997). In Canada, for instance, the median age of the population has increased from 17.2 years in 1851 to 33.5 years in 1991. It is estimated to be 37.5 years in 2001 (Singh 1998). At the same time, though, Canadian men over 65 years old have participated in the labor force at lower rates. In 1921, 70 percent of men from the 65+ age group participated in the labor force; by 1996, only 10 percent of them were doing so. Women from the 65+ age group have also participated at lower rates (e.g., 19 percent in 1921 and 3.5 percent in 1991), but recently, older women (65+ years) have participated at slightly increasing rates, with 3.6 percent in 1992 and 3.7 percent in 1993 (Singh 1998).

Ruhm (1991) concluded that the aging population and lower participation rates among workers above 65 years old have resulted in an "explosion" of interest in later-life labor force behavior. Another trend that has attracted widespread attention is related to a period of employment between career employment and full retirement (Herz 1995), known as bridge employment (Ruhm 1990; Doeringer 1990). Initial research on bridge employment has shown that it is primarily part-time in nature, it is often in a different sector and industry than career employment, and it is frequently characterized by lower wages than career employment (Doeringer 1990). In addition, bridge employment has many implications for institutional and public policies. For example, a public-pension scheme which "clawbacks" benefits as a result of earned income is a clear deterrent to work after early retirement (Singh 1998). The implication is that bridge employment is increasingly becoming an important phenomenon which warrants further investigation (Doeringer 1990; Marshall 1995).

The purpose of this chapter is to propose and test a model of work after early retirement. In the next section, we review past research on the labor force behavior of older workers, bridge employment, and nonstandard employment. We then use the information provided by the literature to build a model of work after early retirement. The model consists of three basic elements. First, we propose that many individuals experience a period of bridge employment between career employment and full retirement. Second, those who return to work after early retirement are likely to accept nonstandard employment for both supply and demand reasons. And third, standard/nonstandard employment is hypothesized to be related to a multitude of factors, including health status, financial resources, work history, macroeconomic conditions, and individual and demographic characteristics. The next section outlines the research methods used to test the elements of the model. The last two sections provide the results and contain discussion and implications.

PAST RESEARCH

Labor Force Participation of Older Workers

The study of older workers' labor force behavior dates back to the 1940s, when descriptive studies were used to show a positive relationship between retirement and poor health (Wentworth 1945; Steckler 1955). In the late 1970s and early 1980s, economists examined work disincentives contained in Social Security (in the United States). Evidence indicated a positive relationship between retirement and the receipt of Social Security benefits (Boskin 1977; Boskin and Hurd 1978). At the same time, the emergence of private pension plans prompted investigations of the impact of the structure of such plans on retirement. It was found that private pension plans subsidized early retirement and penalized delayed retirement, and once the subsidies were removed, older workers tended to postpone the age at which they left the labor force (Mitchell and Fields 1984).

In addition to poor health and inadequate financial resources, other factors were also seen as driving the retirement decision. First, Beck (1985) found that workers in high-status occupations and those who were employed in core industries were more likely to retire at or near their expected age. In addition, Hayward and Grady (1986) and Hayward and Hardy (1985) reported that individuals in occupations that require low physical demands and are characterized by high growth rate and substantively complex work were more likely to participate in the labor force. Second, Peracchi and Welch (1994) and McDonald and Wanner (1984) showed that the probability of leaving the labor force was highest during a recession. Finally, a small number of studies have shown that the retirement behavior of women and minorities is different from that of white men (Gustman and Steinmeier 1986; Ward and Dale 1992; Pienta, Burr, and Matchler 1994). For example, Pienta, Burr, and Matchler (1994) found that women who were more "family-oriented" (i.e., took time off to raise a family) were less likely to participate in the labor force in their later lives than those who were "work-oriented" (i.e., continuous attachment to the labor force).

Bridge Employment

Research on retirement has assumed that the retirement decision is a permanent and complete withdrawal from the labor force (Marshall 1995). Contrary to this assumption, Doeringer (1990) argued that a small but significant number of older workers return to work after their initial retirement. In Canada, Monette (1996) reported that 13 percent of individuals over 50 years old returned to work after their initial retirement. In the United States, Ruhm (1991) showed that 60 percent of the respondents from the Retirement History Survey ended their career jobs before the age of 60 years, but fewer than 20 percent were retired before the age of 60 years. Herz (1995) used three waves of the Current Population Survey to confirm that the level of bridge employment has increased over time.

Research on work after early retirement parallels that on retirement in terms of the factors that were investigated. Health status and financial resources received detailed attention. In this regard, Parnes and Sommers (1994) showed that work after early retirement was deterred by poor health. Ruhm (1990) reported that individuals with higher earnings or those who were receiving a pension were less likely to participate in postretirement work than those with lower earnings or no pension. Similarly, Boaz (1987) argued that work during retirement by both men and women is a response to low and moderate levels of nonwage income at the beginning of retirement, and for men work is a response to a decrease in the real value of nonwage income during retirement.

In addition to good health and inadequate financial resources, occupational characteristics were shown to affect postretirement employment. Myers (1991) reported that managers were more likely to participate in work after retirement than nonmanagers. Similarly, Beck (1985) showed that professionals, managers, proprietors, and farmers were more likely to reject retirement than other occupational groups. In addition, Holden (1988) found that men who performed more physically demanding jobs were less likely to work in retirement than those who performed less physically demanding jobs.

Nonstandard Employment

On one hand, it is clearly shown that many older workers return to work after their initial retirement. They are likely to do so for a number of reasons: 1) health, 2) financial resources, 3) work history, 4) macroeconomic conditions, and 5) other individual characteristics. On the other hand, there is evidence to show that nonstandard forms of employment have increased over the years. While there is no precise definition for nonstandard employment, it is generally accepted to be any form of employment other than full-time, full-year employment with an employer (Polivka and Nardone 1989; Cordova 1986; Bronstein 1991). Within this boundary, it is reported that nonstandard forms of employment account for 30 percent of the Canadian labor force (Betcherman et al. 1994). It is also argued that nonstandard employment is likely to become the norm with the institutionalization of flexibility in the allocation of labor (Lerner 1994; Rifkin 1996; Smith

1994). This is supported by Betcherman et al. (1994), who showed that nonstandard employment has increased from 24 percent in 1975 to 30 percent in 1993.

MODEL OF WORK AFTER EARLY RETIREMENT

Based on the literature reviewed above, we propose a model of work after early retirement that comprises three basic elements (Figure 1). Element 1 of the model proposes that many individuals return to work after early retirement for a period of bridge employment (Marshall 1995; Herz 1995; Ruhm 1990; Doeringer 1990; Singh 1998).

Returnees are likely to face a different labor market than the one which existed at the time they initially entered a phase of career employment. The "new" labor market is characterized by less demand for workers on the whole (i.e., organizations seek to "do more with less"). More importantly, there exists a tendency against the employment of older workers (Hutchens 1988). This behavior may stem from negative stereotypes which employers entertain about older workers (Mazerolle and Singh 1999). For example, employers often assume that older workers are less likely to retrain, to remain for a long period of time in the labor market, to be regular, and to be productive (CARNET 1995). In fact, research has shown that bridge employment is characterized by part-time employment (Monette 1996; Iams 1987; Ruhm and Sum 1988; Ruhm 1991) and lower wages (Doeringer 1990; Ruhm 1991). Hence, Element 2 of the model proposes that as retirees return to the labor market, they are more likely to be found in nonstandard employment such as part-time employment and self-employment.

Element 3 of the model proposes that standard/nonstandard employment is related to 1) health status, 2) financial resources, 3) work history, 4) macroeconomic conditions, and 5) individual and demographic characteristics. Individuals in good health have stronger desire and ability to return to work (Quinn 1977; Anderson and Burkhauser 1985; Breslaw and Stelcner 1987; Parnes and Sommers 1994; Morrow-Howell and Leon 1988; Holden 1988), and those in good health, who return to work, are more likely to do so in standard

Figure 1 A Model of Work after Early Retirement

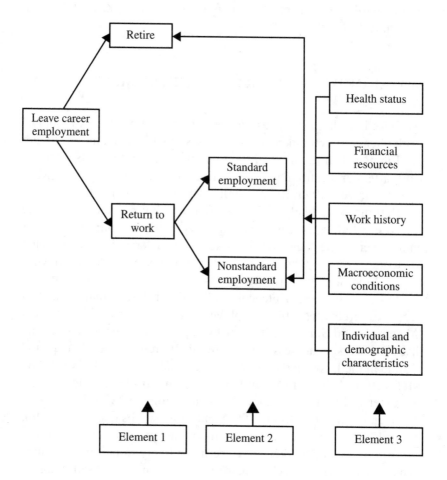

employment. The reservation wage for individuals who have fewer financial resources is likely to be lower than those who have greater financial resources. As such, those who have fewer financial resources are more likely to return to work. They are also more likely to do so in standard employment (Burtless and Moffitt 1985; McDonald 1994; Ruhm 1990). Life course theorists argue that it is important to examine later-life labor force behavior in terms of work history because of the interrelationship between the main life course events of school, work, and retirement (Marshall 1995). High levels of unemployment can reduce the likelihood of labor force participation (i.e., the discouraged-worker effect). Periods of high unemployment are also characterized by fewer standard employment opportunities. Individuals who left career jobs during periods of high unemployment are less likely to return to work, and if they do so they are more likely to occupy non-standard employment (Peracchi and Welch 1994; McDonald 1994). Individual and demographic characteristics can also affect the decision to return to work. For example, women follow different retirement patterns than those of men (Honig 1985).

In summary, we propose three basic elements of a work after early retirement (return-to-work) model.

1) For many early retirees, we expect a period of bridge employment between career employment and full retirement.

2) For those who return to work, we expect them to do so primarily in nonstandard employment (i.e., part-time employment and self-employment).

3) We expect the standard/nonstandard employment decision to be related to health status, financial resources, work history, macroeconomic conditions, and individual and demographic characteristics.

RESEARCH METHODS

Data

The data for this study are taken from the Survey of Work and Life-style Activities (SWLA), conducted among 6,846 Bell Canada employees who left the company between 1985 and 1995. Questionnaires were sent by mail to a sample of 3,614 of the 6,846 individuals in July 1995. This sample was arrived at by enumerating the 45–50 age group and randomly selecting 50 percent of the remaining group (above 50 years old).[1] Enumerating the 45–50 age group was done to ensure enough respondents from the "younger retirees" group. From the 3,614 potential respondents, 38 did not reply due to poor health, death, or relocation. Two thousand one hundred forty-seven individuals returned completed or partially completed questionnaires, resulting in a 60 percent response rate. Of the 2,147 respondents who returned the questionnaire, 1,772 provided complete information to examine their patterns of employment and working time after early retirement.

The SWLA has many advantages. It was conducted among retirees of Bell Canada, Canada's largest telecommunications firm. The sample includes respondents who voluntarily retired from a long-term career job. The majority of them left with a special financial settlement, and they were all entitled to a private pension from Bell Canada at the time of the Survey. The data allow us to distinguish standard from nonstandard forms of postretirement employment. The data also contain health, financial resources, work experience, and other individual and demographic characteristics. Macroeconomic conditions at the time of the transition were available from secondary sources, thus allowing for a comprehensive analysis of work after early retirement.

The SWLA also has some limitations. The respondents are not representative of the general Canadian population, in that SWLA respondents were generally more wealthy than the Canadian population (CARNET 1995). The data set does not contain important information on race and the size of private pensions, which are important explanations of older workers' labor force behavior. And it is not explicitly known whether the respondents prefer their chosen work patterns. Nevertheless, we conclude that the advantages far outweigh the disadvantages. Further, the data provide a good window to examine patterns of employment and working time among a selected set of early retirees.

Variables and Measures

Dependent variable

We created a nominal-category variable with three mutually exclusive groups as the dependent variable. The respondents were asked to state either "yes" or "no" to the following question: "Have you ever worked for pay since leaving Bell?" Those who returned to work were asked to report the following information on their four most recent postcareer jobs: 1) "Were you working for someone else or were you self-employed?", 2) "Was this job full-time or part-time work?", and 3) "Was this a full-year job or part of a year?", with one to six months being part year. We then used the information from these questions to allocate the respondents into three groups: 1) retired (i.e., did not work for pay since leaving Bell Canada); 2) returned to standard employment (i.e., full-time full-year); and 3) returned to nonstandard employment (i.e., part-time and self-employment).

Independent variables

Individuals were asked to report either "yes" or "no" to the following question: "Are you limited in the kind or amount of activity you can do because of a long-term condition or health problem; that is, one that is expected to last six months or more?" We consider those who responded "yes" to the question to be in "poor health."

Six financial-related variables were examined. Entitlement to a full and immediate pension, the receipt of public pension benefits (Canada/Quebec Pension Plan and Old Age Security), the ownership of investments, and a mortgage-free home all indicate greater financial resources. The ownership of a debt over $5,000, on the other hand, signifies fewer financial resources.

Six work-related variables were also investigated. Tenure at Bell Canada was measured in years. Occupations were separated into four groups based on union membership—managers, white-collar workers, blue-collar workers, and union members who were either from the white-collar or blue-collar group but did not provide information to categorize them into either group. Career mobility followed four different patterns: 1) upward, 2) upward and lateral, 3) lateral, and 4) downward. We used 10 questions to distinguish intrinsic job satisfaction from extrinsic job satisfaction.[2] And we created a measure for the centrality of work to individuals.[3]

The post-1990 period was characterized by higher levels of unemployment than the 1985–1990 period. As such, we created a dummy variable with 1 representing the post-1990 period and zero otherwise.

Seven individual and demographic variables were also examined. Gender, postcareer training, marital status, working status of spouse, and male with a working spouse were all defined by a dummy variable with one representing respectively female, undertook postcareer training, married, has a working spouse, and is a male with a working spouse. Education was divided into three categories: below high school, between high school and university, and university education. Age at leaving was measured in years.

Data Analysis Techniques

In order to test the first two elements of the model, we examined the frequency distribution for the sample to detect retirement, return to standard employment, or return to nonstandard employment. We then used multinomial logistic regression analysis to simultaneously control for the effect of health status, financial resources, work history, macroeconomic conditions, and individual and demographic characteristics on standard/nonstandard employment. Multinomial logistic regression analysis is the most appropriate technique given that the dependent variable is defined as a nominal-category outcome with three mutually exclusive categories (Singh 1998). This analysis shed light on the third element of the model.

RESULTS

Table 1 provides descriptive results. The first row of Table 1 shows the distribution of the sample in terms of retirement, returning to standard employment, or returning to nonstandard employment. It pro-

Table 1 Descriptive Statistics[a]

Dependent variable	Percentage of the sample
Retired	61
Returned to standard employment	7
Returned to nonstandard employment	32

Independent variables	Means
Health limitation	0.19
	(0.39)
[Full and immediate pension][b]	0.18
	(0.38)
Reduced pension	0.72
	(0.45)
Deferred pension	0.10
	(0.30)
Canada/Quebec pension plan	0.50
	(0.50)
Old age security	0.23
	(0.42)
Investments	0.66
	(0.45)
Mortgage-free home	0.73
	(0.44)
Debt over $5,000	0.20
	(0.40)
Tenure	32.1
	(6.22)
[Managers]	0.49
	(0.50)
White-collar workers	0.17
	(0.38)
Blue-collar workers	0.26
	(0.44)
Unknown union member	0.08
	(0.28)
[Upward career mobility]	0.15
	(0.36)
Upward and lateral career mobility	0.49
	(0.50)

(continued)

Table 1 (continued)

Independent variables	Means
Lateral career mobility	0.20
	(0.40)
Lateral and downward career mobility	0.16
	(0.37)
Intrinsic job satisfaction	21.17
	(3.96)
Extrinsic job satisfaction	8.91
	(1.56)
Work attachment	0.24
	(0.43)
Left after 1990	0.54
	(0.50)
Female	0.36
	(0.48)
Age at leaving	55.72
	(4.17)
[Below high school education]	0.64
	(0.48)
Between high school and university	0.28
	(0.45)
University education	0.08
	(0.27)
Postcareer training	0.15
	(0.36)
Married	0.83
	(0.38)
Working spouse	0.30
	(0.46)
Male with working spouse	0.22
	(0.41)
Number of observations	1,772

[a] Standard deviations are in parentheses.
[b] Square brackets represent reference category for subsequent multivariate analysis.

vides strong support for the first element of the model. The first element of the model proposes that, for many older workers, a period of bridge employment exists between career employment and full retirement (Herz 1995; Marshall 1995; Doeringer 1990). Thirty-nine percent of the respondents returned to either standard or nonstandard employment after early retirement.

The results also provide strong support for the second element of the model. The second element of the model proposes that postretirement employment is likely to be characterized by nonstandard employment (Hutchens 1988; Mazerolle and Singh 1999; CARNET 1995; Monette 1996; Iams 1987; Ruhm and Sum 1988; Ruhm 1991). Of the 39 percent who returned to work, 83 percent of that group returned to nonstandard employment. Retirement was the most likely choice (61 percent), followed by nonstandard employment (32 percent) and standard employment (7 percent).

Standard Employment

Multinomial logistic regression of standard employment, relative to retirement holding nonstandard employment constant, provides strong support for the third element of the model (Table 2). The third element of the model hypothesizes that standard/nonstandard employment significantly relates to health status, financial resources, work history, macroeconomic conditions, and individual and demographic characteristics. Individuals who reported a health limitation were less likely to return to standard employment than those who did not report a health limitation. Although this relationship is consistent with *a priori* expectation (Quinn 1977; Anderson and Burkhauser 1985; Breslaw and Stelcner 1987; Parnes and Sommers 1994; Morrow-Howell and Leon 1988; Holden 1988), it is not statistically significant at conventional levels.

But the results show strong associations between standard employment and the financial-related variables. Individuals who were entitled to a deferred pension relative to a full and immediate pension as well as those who owned a debt over $5,000 were more likely to become employed in standard employment. In contrast, the ownership of a mortgage-free home was associated with a lower probability of standard employment. Clearly, the results provide strong support for the

Table 2 Multinomial Logit Estimates of Standard and Nonstandard Employment[a]

Independent variables	Standard employment/ retirement	Nonstandard employment/ retirement
Health limitation	−0.23	−0.12
	(0.15)	(0.27)
[Full and immediate pension][b]		
Reduced pension	0.25	0.69
	(0.24)	(0.48)
Deferred pension	1.16	0.32
	(0.32)***	(0.60)
Canada/Quebec pension plan	−0.04	0.73
	(0.17)	(0.32)**
Old age security	0.21	0.38
	(0.22)	(0.46)
Investments	−0.21	−0.23
	(0.14)	(0.25)
Mortgage-free home	−0.34	0.22
	(0.15)***	(0.25)
Debt over $5,000	0.57	0.10
	(0.16)***	(0.25)
Tenure	0.02	−0.01
	(0.01)	(0.03)
[Managers]		
White-collar workers	−0.16	0.07
	(0.23)	(0.53)
Blue-collar workers	−0.58	0.38
	(0.18)***	(0.38)
Unknown union member	0.31	−0.03
	(0.24)	(0.41)
[Upward career mobility]		
Upward and lateral career mobility	−0.01	−0.60
	(0.17)	(0.36)*
Lateral career mobility	−0.26	−0.89
	(0.21)	(0.42)**

Independent variables	Standard employment/ retirement	Nonstandard employment/ retirement
Lateral and downward career mobility	−0.85 (0.25)***	−0.70 (0.56)
Intrinsic job satisfaction	−0.003 (0.02)	−0.04 (0.03)
Extrinsic job satisfaction	−0.02 (0.04)	−0.06 (0.08)
Work attachment	0.56 (0.15)***	−1.05 (0.23)***
Left after 1990	−0.63 (0.15)***	0.43 (0.26)*
Female	−1.10 (0.20)***	0.24 (0.42)
Age at leaving	−0.07 (0.02)***	−0.06 (0.04)
[Below high school education]		
Between high school and university	0.19 (0.14)	−0.10 (0.24)
University education	0.17 (0.23)	−0.15 (0.36)
Postcareer training	0.94 (0.17)***	0.12 (0.25)
Married	0.08 (0.19)	−0.35 (0.40)
Working spouse	0.31 (0.25)	0.87 (0.70)
Male with working spouse	0.03 (0.29)	−0.76 (0.73)
Constant	3.56 (1.53)**	5.22 (2.68)**
−2*Log likelihood ratio	2436.70***	
Number of observations	1,772	

[a]Standard deviations are in parentheses. ***= $p \leq 0.01$, **= $p \leq 0.05$, *= $p \leq 0.10$.
[b]Square brackets represent reference categories.

hypothesis that fewer financial resources induce standard employment after early retirement (Burtless and Moffitt 1985; McDonald 1994; Ruhm 1990).

The results also show clear associations between standard employment and various dimensions of work history. Blue-collar union members were less likely to return to standard employment (Beck 1983, 1985; Myers 1991; Morrow-Howell and Leon 1988; Hayward, Hardy, and Liu 1994). Blue-collar union members, it can be argued, have fewer skills that are applicable in the general labor market (Singh 1998). Lateral and downward career mobility is associated with a lower probability of standard employment than upward career mobility. Singh (1998) argued that lateral and downward career mobility reflect "blocked career goals." Lateral and downward career mobility recipients are less likely to return to standard employment because they may see no prospects for career growth. And the respondents who reported an above average attachment to work were more likely to become employed in standard employment (Parnes and Sommers 1994).

The macroeconomic environment at the time of the transition from career employment was also an important factor in the standard employment decision. The post-1990 period was characterized by higher levels of unemployment that translated into a lower probability of standard employment (Peracchi and Welch 1994; McDonald 1994).

And finally, the results show strong associations between standard employment and many individual and demographic characteristics. Females were clearly less likely to become employed in standard employment (Honig 1985). The older one left career employment, the less likely he or she was to become employed in standard employment (Hardy 1991). Postcareer training activities were positively correlated with standard employment after early retirement (Hill 1995; Myers 1991).

Nonstandard Employment

Multinomial logistic regression of nonstandard employment, relative to retirement holding standard employment constant, also provides support for the third element of the model (Table 2). Receiving Canada/Quebec Pension Plan benefits was associated with a higher probability of nonstandard employment. Canada/Quebec Pension Plan recipients are more likely to explore part-time employment (nonstandard employment) where they are allowed to earn approximately $7,000 before earned income is used to "clawback" Canada/Quebec Pension Plan benefits (Singh 1998). Respondents who experienced upward and lateral as well as lateral career mobility were less likely to return to nonstandard employment than those who experienced upward career mobility. According to Singh (1998), there is no room to explore "blocked career goals" in nonstandard employment. Interestingly, respondents who reported an above average attachment to work were less likely to become employed in nonstandard employment. For these workers, it was either standard employment or retirement, not nonstandard employment. And periods of high unemployment (post-1990) were clearly associated with a higher probability of nonstandard employment.

Summary of the Results

The results show strong support for all three elements of the work after early retirement model. Thirty-nine percent of the respondents returned to work after early retirement. A large majority (83 percent) of those who returned to work had done so in nonstandard employment. And the standard/nonstandard employment decision was affected by a number of factors that include financial resources, work history, macroeconomic conditions, and individual and demographic characteristics.

Perhaps the only surprising result is the relationship between the return-to-work decision and poor health. Although the sign on the health-limitation variable is negative as expected (Quinn 1977; Anderson and Burkhauser 1985; Breslaw and Stelcner 1987; Parnes and Sommers 1994; Morrow-Howell and Leon 1988; Holden 1988), the relationship is not statistically significant at conventional levels. Many reasons can account for this result. Potentially, poor health plays a less important role in the labor force participation decision among Canadian workers who do not have to "carry" the cost of health care. Also, the accommodation of health limitations engendered in Ontario's statute may work to diminish work disincentives. And finally, self-reported health status may contain biases. Stated differently, older workers may justify the retirement decision on poor health.

DISCUSSIONS AND IMPLICATIONS

In the traditional life course, individuals progressed through the main life course events of school, work, and retirement in an orderly sequence. Moreover, the transition from one event to another was often irreversible. For instance, an individual who made the transition from work to retirement did not go back to work. Retirement was construed as an event in which an individual made a complete and a permanent withdrawal from the labor force (Singh 1998). The model proposed and tested in this chapter provides an alternative to this widely conceived view. Our results clearly show that 39 percent of the respondents returned to a period of bridge employment after early retirement. Hence, the results of our chapter are consistent with an "emerging" view of the life course (Marshall 1995; Singh 1998). Individuals often "juggle" two or more of the life course events (e.g., school and work, work and retirement, or school, work, and retirement). Moreover, the orderly sequence of the traditional model is no longer applicable for many individuals.

Nonstandard employment has become increasingly important in the labor market (Polivka and Nardone 1989; Cordova 1986; Bronstein 1991; Betcherman et al. 1994), perhaps because of the institutionalization of the flexible allocation of labor (Lerner 1994; Rifkin 1996; Smith 1994). Our results show that 83 percent of the respondents who returned to work had done so in nonstandard employment. Two possible scenarios emerge from this relationship. If nonstandard employment accords with the preferences of early retirees, then they may become an invaluable source of labor in a market which "fosters flexibility." But if nonstandard employment does not match the preferences of early retirees, then the situation reflects a "suboptimum" use of older workers. Our results imply support for the second scenario. Individuals who were more "attached" to work were more likely to become employed in standard employment relative to retirement. At the same time, though, these same workers were less likely to become employed in nonstandard employment relative to retirement. In addition, periods of high unemployment were more likely to lead to nonstandard employment. Nevertheless, our evidence only implies that early retirees would prefer standard employment after career employment. This relationship clearly warrants further investigation.

Research on the labor force behavior of older workers has shown a clear link between the retirement decision and poor health as well as adequate financial resources. This perhaps relates to the assumption that retirement means a complete and a permanent withdrawal from the labor force. More importantly, the factors that surround the work-to-retirement transition (such as poor health and adequate financial resources) are most important. Our results indicate that in addition to the "conventional determinants" of later-life labor force behavior, there are other important factors. Work history clearly affected the decision to become employed on a standard/nonstandard basis. Blue-collar union membership and lateral and downward career mobility deterred standard employment, while above average work attachment promoted standard employment. An investigation of the relationship between later-life labor force behavior and work history must continue for one important reason—the world of work has undergone a significant transformation (Kochan, Katz, and McKerzie 1994). Changes such as the "end of the psychological contract," technological advancement, and diversity are likely to change work behavior. And changes in work behavior can subsequently affect the ways in which an individual decides to divide his or her time in terms of labor market activities and leisure (Singh 1998).

The return-to-work decision runs counter to the assumption that retirement means a permanent and complete withdrawal from the labor force. This assumption is the basis for many public and institutional policies. In Canada, for instance, an individual cannot accrue partial pension benefits for work after early retirement. Annuities are calculated at the "retirement time," and subsequent employment spells are not the basis for additional pension benefits (Singh 1998). In addition, our results show that nonstandard employment is positively related to the receipt of Canada/Quebec Pension Plan benefits. We argue that this relationship may be driven by the fact that an individual is allowed to simultaneously receive Canada/Quebec Pension Plan benefits and income from employment up to about $7,000. Unemployment rates are also directly related to standard/nonstandard employment. It is also noteworthy that postcareer training activities are positively related to standard employment. The implication is that the Canada/Quebec Pension Plan, macroeconomic policies, and training initiatives can all be used as policy instruments to promote either standard or nonstandard employment.

The results also have implications for human resource management. The decision to return to standard/nonstandard employment after early retirement is affected by both extrinsic and intrinsic reasons. Inadequate financial resources clearly underlie the standard employment decision, but so does work attachment. Compensation practices must reflect this reality. One of the most important challenges in terms of compensation is associated with the deferred compensation model. This model of compensation assumes that a worker is entitled to a lifetime income that is tied to his or her productivity. In the first half of the employment period, the individual is paid below his or her productivity level. In the latter half of the employment period, the individual is paid above his or her productivity level. The crucial question for employers is whether to treat returnees as "new" entrants and restart the deferred compensation model. Currently, work after early retirement is characterized by lower wages (Ruhm 1990; Doeringer 1990). This may be a powerful deterrent to a committed and motivated older workforce, but this is an untested assumption that warrants further investigation.

Beginning in the year 2011, the front end of the baby boom generation will approach the conventional age of retirement (65 years old). Issues of when and how they decide to make the work-to-retirement transition are likely to become increasingly important. Our results indicate that they do not have to follow the traditional model of a permanent and complete withdrawal from the labor force. Many of them are likely to gradually withdraw from the labor force. This means rethinking the issue of retirement and public and institutional policies, which are increasingly becoming outdated.

Notes

The authors are grateful to Human Resources Development Canada for financial assistance and the Centre for Studies of Aging, University of Toronto, for access to data collected in a survey financed by Human Resources Development Canada under the "Issues of an Aging Workforce" project.

1. The results presented in this study are based on weighted data which corrected for the initial stratification by age.

2. A factor analysis (extraction = principal component, number of factors = 2, and rotation = varimax) of the following 10 items—1) there was a lot of freedom to decide how I do my work; 2) I did the same thing over and over; 3) the pay was good; 4) my chances of promotion for career development were good; 5) I like my job; 6) I enjoyed the people I worked with; 7) the work I did was one of the most satisfying parts of my life; 8) some of my main interests and pleasures in life were connected with my work; 9) to me, my work was just a way of making money; and 10) the benefits were good. These resulted in the identification of two underlying factors: Items 1), 2), 5), 8), and 9) loaded onto one factor, and items 3), 4), and 5) onto the other. The first factor is interpreted as intrinsic job satisfaction, and the second factor as extrinsic job satisfaction. Scales using the respective items were subsequently constructed. The Cronback Alpha for intrinsic satisfaction was 0.75 and that for extrinsic satisfaction was 0.46.

3. Work attachment is measured with a multidimensional scale. Respondents were asked to indicate (on a four-point likert-type scale, with 1 being "never" and 4 being "often" how often did they: "miss the feeling of doing a good job"; "feel that [they] want to go back to work"; "worry about not having a job"; and "miss being with other people at work." The responses to these items were added (Cronback Alpha = 0.79).

References

Anderson, K., and R. Burkhauser. 1985. "The Retirement-Health Nexus: A New Measure of an Old Puzzle." *Journal of Human Resources* 20(3): 315–330.

Beck, S. 1983. "Position in the Economic Structure and Unexpected Retirement." *Research on Aging* 5(2): 197–216.

_____. 1985. "Determinants of Labor Force Activity among Retired Men." *Research on Aging* 7(2): 251–280.

Betcherman, G., K. McMullen, N. Leckie, and C. Caron. 1994. *The Canadian Workforce in Transition.* Kingston: IRC Press.

Boaz, R. 1987. "Work as a Response to Low and Decreasing Real Income During Retirement." *Research on Aging* 9(3): 428–440.

Boskin, M. 1977. "Social Security and Retirement Decisions." *Economic Enquiry* XV(1): 1–25.

Boskin, M., and M. Hurd. 1978. "The Effect of Social Security on Early Retirement." *Journal of Public Economics* 10(3): 361–377.

Breslaw, J., and M. Stelcner. 1987. "The Effect of Health on the Labor Force Behaviour of Elderly Men in Canada." *Journal of Human Resources* 22(4): 490–517.

Bronstein, A. 1991. "Temporary Work in Western Europe: Threat or Complement to Permanent Employment?" *International Labor Review* 130(3): 291–310.

Burtless, G., and R. Moffitt. 1985. "The Joint Choice of Retirement Age and Postretirement Hours of Work." *Journal of Labor Economics* 3(2): 209–236.

CARNET. 1995. *Issues of an Aging Workforce: A Case Study of Former Employees of Bell Canada.* Toronto: Center for Studies of Aging, University of Toronto.

Cordova, E. 1986. "From Full-Time Wage Employment to Atypical Employment: A Major Shift in the Evolution of Labour Relations." *International Labor Review* 125(6): 641–657.

Doeringer, P. 1990. "Economic Security, Labor Market Flexibility, and Bridges to Retirement." In *Bridges to Retirement*, P. Doeringer, ed. Ithaca: ILR Press.

Gustman, A., and T. Steinmeier. 1986. "A Disaggregated, Structural Analysis of Retirement by Race, Difficulty of Work and Health." *Review of Economics and Statistics* LXVIII(1): 509–513.

Hardy, M. 1991. "Employment after Retirement: Who Gets Back In?" *Research on Aging* 13(3): 267–288.

Hayward, M., and W. Grady. 1986. "The Occupational Retention and Recruitment of Older Men: The Influence of Structural Characteristics of Work." *Social Forces* 64(3): 644–666.

Hayward, M., and M. Hardy. 1985. "Early Retirement Process among Older Men: Occupational Differences." *Research on Aging* 7(4): 491–515.

Hayward, M., M. Hardy, and M. Liu. 1994. "Work after Retirement: The Experiences of Older Men in the United States." *Social Science Research* 23: 82–107.

Henretta, J. 1997. "Changing Perspectives on Retirement." *Journal of Gerontology* 52(1): 1–3.

Herz, D. 1995. "Work after Early Retirement: An Increasing Trend among Men." *Monthly Labor Review* 118(4): 21–27.

Hill, E. 1995. "Labor Market Effects of Women's Post-School-Age Training." *Industrial and Labor Relations Review* 49(1): 138–149.

Holden, K. 1988. "Physically Demanding Occupations, Health, and Work After Retirement: Findings from the New Beneficiary Survey." *Social Security Bulletin* 51(11): 3–15.

Honig, M. 1985. "Partial Retirement among Workers." *Journal of Human Resources* 20(4): 613–621.

Hutchens, R. 1988. "Do Job Opportunities Decline with Age." *Industrial and Labor Relations Review* 42(1): 89–99.

Iams, H. 1987. "Jobs of Persons Working after Receiving Retired-Worker Benefits." *Social Security Bulletin* 50(11): 4–18.

Kochan, T., H. Katz, and R. McKerzie. 1994. *The Transformation of American Industrial Relations.* New York: Basic Books.

Lerner, S. 1994. "The Future of Work in North America: Good Jobs, Bad Jobs, Beyond Jobs." *Futures* 26(2): 185–196.

Marshall, V. 1995. "Rethinking Retirement: Issues for the Twenty-First Century." In *Rethinking Retirement,* E. Gee and G. Gutman, eds. Vancouver: Gerontological Research Center, Simon Fraser University.

Mazerolle, M., and G. Singh. 1999. "Older Workers' Adjustments to Plant Closures." *Relations Industrielles* 54(2): 313–336.

McDonald, L. 1994. "Retirement Revisited: A Secondary Data Analysis." Working paper series, "Issues of an Aging Workforce: A Study to Inform Human Resources Policy Development." Centre for Studies of Aging Workforce, University of Toronto.

McDonald, L., and R. Wanner. 1984. "Socioeconomic Determinants of Early Retirement in Canada." *Canadian Journal of Aging* 3(3): 105–116.

Mitchell, O., and G. Fields. 1984. "The Economics of Retirement Behavior." *Journal of Labor Economics* 2(1): 84–105.

Monette, M. 1996. *Canada's Changing Retirement Patterns.* Ottawa: Ministry of Industry.

Morrow-Howell, N., and J. Leon. 1988. "Life-Span Determinants of Work in Retirement Years." *International Journal of Aging and Human Development* 27(2): 125–140.

Myers, D. 1991. "Work after Cessation of Career Job." *Journal of Gerontology* 46(2): 93–102.

Parnes, H., and D. Sommers. 1994. "Experience of Men in Their Seventies and Early Eighties." *Journal of Gerontology* 49(3): 117–124.

Peracchi, F., and F. Welch. 1994. "Trends in Labor Force Transitions of Older Men and Women." *Journal of Labor Economics* 12(2):210–242.

Pienta, A, J. Burr, and J. Matchler. 1994. "Women's Labor Force Participation in Later Life: The Effects of Early Work and Family Experiences." *Journal of Gerontology* 49(5): 231–293.

Polivka, A., and T. Nardone. 1989. "On the Definition of 'Contingent Work'." *Monthly Labor Review* 112(12): 9–16.

Quinn, J. 1977. "Microeconomic Determinants of Early Retirement: A Cross-Sectional View of White Married Men." *Journal of Human Resources* 12(3): 329–346.

Rifkin, J. 1996. "Vanishing Jobs." Accessed June 1996 at
http://www.mojones.com/MOTHER_JONES/SO95/rifkin.html.

Ruhm, C. 1990. "Bridge Jobs and Partial Retirement." *Journal of Labor Economics* 8(4): 482–501.

_____. 1991. "Career Employment and Job Stopping." *Industrial Relations* 30(2): 193–208.

Ruhm, C., and A. Sum. 1988. "Job Stopping: The Changing Employment Patterns of Older Workers." IRRA 41ST Annual Proceedings. Madison: Industrial Relations Research Association.

Singh, G. 1998. *Work after Early Retirement.* Unpublished Ph.D. Dissertation, Center for Industrial Relations, School of Graduate Studies, University of Toronto.

Smith, V. 1994. "Institutionalizing Flexibility in a Service Firm: Multiple Contingencies and Hidden Hierarchies." *Work and Occupations* 21(3): 284–307.

Steckler, M. 1955. "Why Do Beneficiaries Retire? Who among Them Return to Work?" *Social Security Bulletin* 18(5): 3–12,35–36.

Ward, C., and A. Dale. 1992. "Geographical Variation in Female Labor Force Participation: An Application of Multilevel Modeling." *Regional Studies* 26(3): 243–255.

Wentworth, E. 1945. "Why Beneficiaries Retire." *Social Security Bulletin* 8(1): 16–20.

7
Working Time over the Life Cycle
Do Public Pensions Matter?

Michael Baker
University of Toronto

Dwayne Benjamin
University of Toronto

The steady reduction of the labor force attachment of older workers is one of the most significant changes in working time in the past half century. Over the same time period, governments in Canada and the United States have enhanced their public pension programs. An obvious policy question is whether these two trends are causally related: Has the increased generosity of public pension programs led to rising retirement rates? This possibility is the topic of lively debate with few conclusions. While some researchers suggest it is no coincidence that retirement patterns mirror key features of public pension plans, others point out that the trend in retirement appears invariant to periodic reform of program parameters, and thus attribute only a minor role to public pensions. A resolution of this disagreement is important for a variety of reasons. First, some view the progress of the baby boom through the labor market as an emerging policy concern. As the "employment hierarchy" becomes increasingly top heavy, there is a perceived need to draw older workers into retirement to make room for younger cohorts. Public pension plans are potentially an important means through which the government could affect such a policy. Second, people are increasingly aware that the fiscal health of "pay-as-you-go" public pension plans is quickly deteriorating.[1] Again, information on the behavioral effects of system rules must be a building block of the therapy needed to restore financial stability. Finally, retirement behavior can potentially shed light on important questions of labor supply and life-cycle behavior. For example, part of the expanding literature on liquidity constraints focuses on the decision of many workers to exploit the "early retirement provisions" available in some pension plans.

The principal difficulty facing previous researchers is the lack of exogenous policy variation with which to identify the effect of pensions on labor supply. The greater part of these past studies focus on the U.S. Social Security system. This research has been spurred by the availability of (panel) data sets such as the Retirement History Survey that provide a good view of the labor market behavior, wealth, and Social Security entitlements of older Americans. Yet the very structure of Social Security is a hindrance to these efforts. It is a federally mandated program with rules that apply uniformly to all parts of the country. Therefore, evaluation of program changes must rely on time-series variation in retirement behavior, and it can be difficult to distinguish secular trends from the effects of a policy intervention. An alternative is to exploit cross-section variation in Social Security entitlements. While everyone faces the same program parameters at a point in time, differences in earnings histories, for example, will translate into different Social Security entitlements, and hence different potential retirement benefits. Unfortunately, because earnings histories are probably correlated with other important determinants of labor market outcomes, this source of variation may not be reliably exogenous to the retirement decision.

Short of a pure natural, or real, experiment, the next best alternative would be cross-jurisdictional/time-series variation in program parameters that provide a number of "natural" control groups for any policy given variation. As long as differences in the timing of changes can be treated as exogenous, we could use the cross-jurisdictional variation to identify possible behavioral effects. One strategy would be to pursue a cross-national, comparative approach, for example, comparing Canada with the United States. Unfortunately, there are too many differences in the pension plans in the two countries to isolate the effect of a specific program parameter. An alternative exists within Canada. While it is a curse in many other dimensions, a benefit of constitutional wrangling to social scientists is that it has led to two distinct pension programs. The Quebec Pension Plan (QPP) covers those working in the province of Quebec, while the Canada Pension Plan (CPP) covers workers in the rest of the country. These plans are virtually identical in most respects, but there have been significant differences in the timing of reforms of certain key parameters. These reforms can be used to isolate the effect of the policy change by comparing the behavior of older workers in the two otherwise identical jurisdictions, before and after the policy change in each jurisdiction.

For example, in 1975 the CPP eliminated the earnings test (or retirement test), whereby CPP benefits were reduced in proportion to a pensioner's employment income. The QPP did not eliminate its earnings test until 1977. Thus, for two years there was a divergence of this pension parameter in the two jurisdictions. Another episode occurred in 1984, when the QPP introduced early retirement provisions, permitting workers to initiate their (actuarially reduced) pensions at age 60 instead of 65. It was not until 1987 that the CPP allowed early retirement. Again, there is a three-year window through which one can compare retirement behavior in the two jurisdictions under different rules.

The cross-jurisdictional variation has recently drawn the attention of researchers. For example, in Baker and Benjamin (1999a) we examined the possible consequences of the removal of the earnings test on the labor force attachment of men over 65. In Baker and Benjamin (1999b) we investigated the impact of early retirement provisions on the labor force decisions of men between 60 and 64 years old. Finally, Gruber (1996) exploits a CPP/QPP divergence in disability pensions. In 1987, the CPP increased its disability insurance (DI) benefits (not retirement benefits) to match those in the QPP. Gruber estimates whether this relative increase in DI benefits affected the labor force behavior of men younger than 60 outside Quebec.

In this chapter we focus on the divergence of early retirement provisions between 1984 and 1987, extending the results in Baker and Benjamin (1999b). Here we use time-series Labour Force Survey (LFS) data to determine whether the change in pension policy was associated with a change in retirement behavior: Did Canadians take advantage of the new early retirement provisions? In fact, we find little evidence that retirement age was affected by this significant policy change. While many men between the ages of 60 and 64 certainly began collecting public pensions, few appear to have changed their labor force behavior in order to do so; most of the new pensioners had weak labor force attachment, or would probably have retired anyway.

To follow up on this hypothesis, we employ the Labour Market Activity Survey (LMAS) individual-level panel data to examine the previous labor force attachment of the 1987 retirees. The results from this exercise provide some confirmation of the evidence provided by the time-series data.

TRENDS IN RETIREMENT

In this section we review trends in the labor force attachment of older workers in Canada using census data from 1970, 1980, and 1990. Sample sizes are large enough to allow relatively precise estimation of the association between age and work over the life cycle. Our main objective is to document the change in employment rates for men and women over this 20-year period. Since "working time" has many dimensions, however, we also investigate the degree to which older men and women appear to be moving into part-time work.

In Figure 1 we plot age profiles of employment–population ratios for men and women. Looking first at the results for men, we can see a strong association between age and the probability of working. In 1970, for example, the probability of working begins to fall slightly at age 55, then declines much more steeply at age 65. Most significantly, the position of this profile has shifted over time, with the drop in employment rates beginning much sooner, falling most steeply between ages 60 and 65. In terms of timing, 1970 to 1980 saw an especially large drop in employment for those men older than 65, while between 1980 and 1990, the greatest drop was for men between 60 and 65, precisely the age group affected by the introduction of early retirement to the CPP/QPP. The results for women are more ambiguous, mostly because of the secular increase in women's labor force attachment at all ages. Thus, there has only been a small net decrease in the number of 60- to 65-year-old women working over this period. Clearly, disentangling the secular increase in women's employment from possible changes in their retirement behavior would require a careful accounting of age and cohort effects—something that would be difficult to do with available data.

Figure 1 Age/Employment Profiles for Men and Women

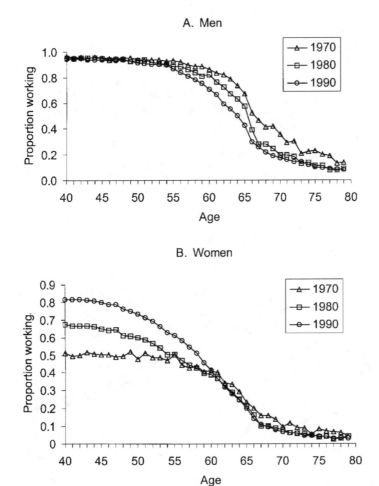

NOTE: The graphs are plots of the average proportions of the population employed (reporting positive weeks worked) in the previous (reference) year, calculated for single age groups. The data are from the Public Use Microdata Files (individual level) of the Censuses of Canada, 1971, 1981, and 1991.

Figure 2   Age/Part-Time Employment Profiles for Men and Women

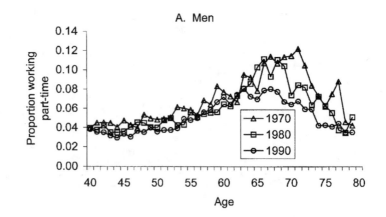

A. Men

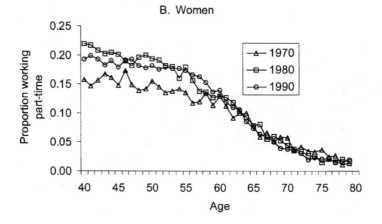

B. Women

NOTE: The graphs are plots of the average proportions of the population employed mostly part-time in the previous (reference) year, calculated for single age groups. The data are from the Public Use Microdata Files (individual level) of the Censuses of Canada, 1971, 1981, and 1991.

An important question in the retirement literature is whether withdrawal from the labor force is gradual or is characterized by a transition through part-time work. We attempt to look at this question indirectly in Figure 2. Without panel data that track individuals, the transition from full- to part-time work cannot be identified; however, the census data still permit a snapshot of the relationship between age and the propensity to work part time. For men, we can see that while part-time work is rare, it is most prevalent among the elderly. The probability in 1990 of working part time increases from around 0.04 for 45-year-olds and peaks at about 0.08 for 65-year-olds. Over time, however, the probability of part-time work has fallen, moving in the same direction as the probability of working at all. In the next panel, we see that women are much more likely than men to work part time and that this probability tracks the participation/age profile, so that women are less likely to work part time as they get older. As with their overall employment patterns, women are more likely to work part time in 1990 than they were in 1970.

In summary, these figures suggest that the most important change in the working time of Canadian men has been the steady decrease in retirement age. Furthermore, there is no evidence that men are more likely to work part time along the way from full-time work to complete retirement. The retirement picture for women is complicated by the dominant trend toward greater participation over the past 20 years. Given this additional complication, the remainder of our work addresses the retirement behavior of men.

THE CANADIAN PUBLIC PENSION SYSTEM

Here we provide a brief overview of the Canadian public pension system as it is currently constituted. At this point, however, we do not distinguish between the CPP and QPP because they are virtually identical. Instead we highlight comparisons with U.S. Social Security, postponing discussion of the 1984 policy divergence to a later section. The first distinguishing feature of the Canadian system is that income support for the elderly is comprised of three distinct programs. First is the CPP/QPP, which are typical public pensions, much like Social Security. Benefits are based on individual earnings histories.[2] The other two programs are age-based transfers. Old Age Security (OAS) is paid to all Canadians over the age of 65.[3] For most of its history, OAS has been a pure lump-sum transfer; however, OAS benefits are now reduced through the income tax system if income exceeds a threshold. The Guaranteed Income Supplement (GIS) is an income-tested transfer program for individuals over 65. These transfers are directed at relatively poor seniors, and the means test has an implicit 50 percent tax-back rate for all earnings, including CPP.

In Figure 3, we show the value of monthly benefits for these three programs for the period corresponding to the census data reported in Figures 1 and 2. The upward trend in generosity is quite clear: The maximum monthly CPP and GIS benefits increased significantly between 1970 and 1990, while OAS benefits remained virtually constant (in real terms). The secular increase in real monthly benefits from the public pension system has been offered as a possible explanation for the retirement trends evident in Figure 1.

Figure 3 Real Monthly Benefits of Canadian Social Security Programs, 1967–1991

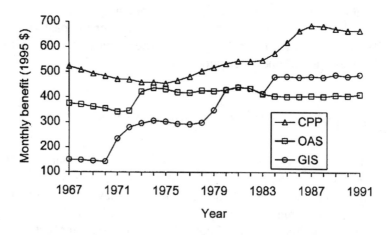

NOTE: The Social Security programs are CPP (Canada/Quebec Pension Plan); OAS (Old Age Security); and GIS (Guaranteed Income Supplement). CPP and GIS are reported as the maximum monthly benefit. Data are from CCH Canadian Limited (1996).

The Canadian and U.S. systems differ slightly in terms of the age at which individuals can begin collecting benefits. In both programs the normal retirement age is 65, when an individual can collect his full entitlement of benefits. In the United States, early retirement is an option for individuals between the ages of 62 and 64, with an actuarial reduction in benefits of seven percent per year by which the individual is younger than 65. While collecting Social Security, the usual earnings test (retirement test) applies, whereby benefits are reduced by one-third for every dollar earned above a cut-off. In Canada, the early retirement age is lower, as CPP benefits can be initiated by individuals between 60 and 64. The actuarial reduction is similar to that in the United States, at 0.5 percent per month that the person is under age 65. For early retirement there is a weak retirement test, and earnings must be less than the maximum CPP benefit in the month prior to retirement. After eligibility has been so "established," no further earnings test is applied. For the other two old-age transfer programs, early retirement is not possible, and an individual must be at least 65 years old to collect benefits.

HOW PUBLIC PENSIONS MIGHT AFFECT RETIREMENT DECISIONS

Our focus in this section is an evaluation of the likely effects of the introduction of early retirement provisions on retirement behavior. Why should the retirement age in a pension plan matter for work decisions?

Theoretical Possibilities

In most circumstances, early retirement provisions should have no effect on retirement behavior. Consider an individual at age 59 who is deciding what age to retire. For each year he works, he increases his lifetime earnings by W (his salary, ignoring discounting). At age 65, he can retire (if he wishes) and begin collecting his public pension (plus whatever private pension he has). Given this budget constraint, he decides how much he wants to work. In the absence of early retirement provisions he could still retire at, say, age 62—he merely has to wait until age 65 to begin collecting his pension. If capital markets are perfect, he could just borrow against this future income stream. The date he begins receiving a check from the government should not constrain his labor supply choice. Whether the introduction of early retirement affects his retirement decision will depend on whether the provision changes his budget constraint.

There are a few possibilities. If the adjustment of the pension is actuarially fair—fully adjusting for the implied reduction in pension contributions of the early retiree, as well as the value of the advancement of pension payments and longer payout period—then, by definition, the average person's budget constraint should not change. Of course, for some individuals with private information about shorter life expectancies, or for those with high discount rates relative to the average in the population, early retirement may now represent a bargain. Let's assume that the actuaries can take care (in principle) of these adverse selection problems on average (which, of course, they cannot). Our interest is in the effect of early retirement on the "average" person. The only way that early retirement provision will matter is if the budget constraint changed. One way this can happen is if the actuarial adjustment is unfair on average. In Baker and Benjamin (1999b), we showed that the actuarial adjustment in the CPP/QPP was unfair, so that there is a small subsidy to early retirement, i.e., the penalty for early initiation of the CPP is too small. This subsidy changes the budget constraint, unambiguously tilting an individual toward earlier retirement. While the subsidy is small on average (about $3,000 in present value terms for retiring at age 60 compared to age 65), it is almost double for lower-income men, since the reduction in CPP benefits is made up in part by higher GIS benefits at age 65. So for poorer men, the implicit subsidy received from early retirement may represent a large fraction of household wealth and thus exert a large retirement-inducing income and substitution effect.

Another way that early retirement can change the budget constraint is if there are liquidity constraints, i.e., if individuals cannot borrow against their social security wealth at the same interest rate that is used in the actuarial reduction of benefits. For such individuals whose early retirement is constrained by lack of credit, allowing them to collect retirement benefits sooner may relax this constraint, facilitating their retirement. To the extent that these constraints are important, as might be the case with lower-income men, then we might see an increase in retirement as early retirement is permitted.

Previous Evidence

As suggested earlier, there is considerable disagreement in the literature over the link between Social Security and the behavior of older workers. The most obvious evidence in favor is the spike in the retirement hazard at age 62, the earliest age when individuals can initiate Social Security benefits. This point is emphasized in Hurd (1990). Hurd and Boskin (1984) also pointed out that retirement at age 62 is positively related to individual peaks in social security wealth. Kahn (1988) emphasized the role of liquidity constraints by showing that low-wealth individuals are more likely to retire at age 62 than high-wealth individuals, though it is difficult to fully control for the fact that high-wealth individuals also have a greater opportunity cost of retirement. Finally, Ruhm (1995) focused on the change in the spike at age 62 over time. By the process of elimination, he shows that it is difficult to explain the increased probability of retirement at age 62 with changes in individuals' characteristics (such as education) that are associated with individuals' opportunity costs. This leaves Social Security as the remaining explanation.

Counterarguments are based on two types of evidence. First, it is difficult to formally link changes in Social Security provisions to changes in retirement behavior. For example, Krueger and Pischke (1992) examined the retirement behavior of the so-called "notch" generation. The 1977 revisions to Social Security permanently lowered the social security wealth of all successive birth cohorts relative to previous cohorts. If social security wealth is an important determinant of retirement patterns, one would expect the "notch" cohorts to exhibit different behavior. The authors find virtually no effect of these revisions. The second type of evidence points to deteriorating labor market conditions for older men as a driving force toward early retirement. Peracchi and Welch (1994), for example, emphasized that characteristics associated with poor labor market outcomes are becoming increasingly important predictors of retirement. In a Canadian context, Osberg (1993) showed that early retirement decisions bear striking similarity to constrained labor supply decisions. An extreme interpretation of these findings would suggest it is thus a pure coincidence that early retirement has increased while pensions have become more attractive. Of course, a fairer summary of both perspectives would recognize that both factors may be at play.

Exploiting a Policy Divergence

It is difficult to identify the effects of early retirement provisions on individual behavior when everyone faces the same program parameters, or when people differ in systematic ways that may cloud the social security aspects of their labor force decisions. This difficulty is common to countries that have national plans. Policy interventions or reforms tend to be universal in application and so are perfectly correlated with time. In these cases the effects of any coincident temporal shock to the labor market can be easily mistaken for the effects of the reform itself. Ideally, what is sought is a reform that affects only a randomly selected subgroup of the eligible population. In this case, those individuals who are not affected by the reform serve as a comparison group to control for any secular trends in and/or shocks to labor market behavior.

Of course, the strict requirements of a random experiment are unlikely to be satisfied by the reforms that we observe of national pension plans around the world. These conditions can be approximated, however, in so-called "natural experiments." We now turn to a description of the divergence in early retirement provisions in the CPP and QPP, why we think it can reasonably be viewed as an "experiment," and our empirical analysis of the apparent responses of Canadians to the policy change.

The Introduction of Early Retirement Provisions

The original provisions of both the CPP and QPP allowed public pensions to be collected starting at age 65. The issue of introducing more flexible age provisions was debated in the late 1970s, partly in response to calls for rules that were consistent with those observed in the pension plans of other countries. The QPP took the lead for reform in 1984. Starting in January of this year, individuals were allowed to initiate pension receipt at any time between the ages of 60 and 70. An individual's "full pension," based on his or her employment and earnings history, continued to be available at age 65 only. Application at an earlier age led to an actuarially adjustment of a 0.5 percent reduction in the full pension for each month the age of application preceded 65 (e.g., 6 percent per year). Symmetrically, pensions were increased 0.5 percent for each month the age of application exceeded age 65. A final provision was that individuals initiating a pension before age 65 had to have substantially ceased working, as evidenced by a low earnings requirement in the year of application. There was no further retirement test for future years, however, so an individual could resume paid employment at a "regular" salary after the year of application.

These early retirement provisions of the QPP were in effect for three years before an identical reform was enacted in the CPP. Part of the reason for the delay appears to be that the province of Ontario was initially very cool to extending the benefits to individuals younger than age 65, and this province has effective veto over changes to CPP parameters. Nevertheless, starting in January 1987 individuals covered by the CPP had choice over the age at which they initiated benefit receipt, subject to the same restrictions present in the QPP.[4] Because the reforms of the programs are sequential, for each reform we have access to a control group to account for any trends in labor market behavior that might be unrelated to the pension changes. For the QPP reform in 1984, for example, we can compare the retirement decisions of Quebecers before and after the introduction the new provisions, relative to the behavior of individuals in other parts of Canada. For the reform of the CPP in 1987, the two groups trade roles: it is now individuals in the rest of Canada who are subject to the reform and those in Quebec who serve as the comparison group.

The legitimacy of this strategy is founded on assumptions that any secular trends in retirement behavior or shocks coincident with the reforms, are common to individuals in the group affected by the policy intervention and those in the comparison group. Our confidence in these assumptions is strengthened by the fact that the variation in the incidence of the reform in each case is geographical. While geographic-specific shocks are certainly a possibility, this sort of variation is arguably less problematic than variation based on age or some other demographic characteristic that is clearly a factor in labor market activity. As explained below, we attempt to control explicitly for region-specific labor market shocks. Furthermore, we observe the reform twice, so its effects are overidentified. Consistency of our estimates of the impact of the changes across the two reforms serves as a check that we are not erroneously attributing the effects of the introduction of early retirement provisions to a shock.

A Graphical Overview

We begin by examining CPP and QPP benefit expenditures and "savings" over the period of the reforms. This should provide a direct view of the popularity of the early retirement provisions. In Panel A of Figure 4, we plot the 1971–1994 time series of QPP and CPP benefit expenditures using the population 65 years of age and older as a nor-malization.[5] The series for the two programs follow each other quite closely until 1983. Entering the period when the early retirement rules differed between the two programs (1984–1986), a wide gap opens up between the QPP and CPP series: QPP benefits significantly increase relative to those in the CPP. The gap then closes in 1987 when early retirement became possible in the CPP. This symmetric opening and closing of a gap in the benefits paid out by public pension plans is strongly suggestive of a policy response. In Panel B, we examine pension program "savings," defined as the difference between program expenditures and contributions. As is well-known, both the CPP and QPP moved from running an annual surplus to an annual deficit over the 1980s and early 1990s. We can also see some effect of the intro-duction of the early retirement rules, as the relative rate of decrease in savings accelerates in the QPP beginning in 1984, and in the CPP in 1987.

While the preceding evidence suggests that the policy intervention had implications for program finances, it is not yet clear that there is a labor supply dimension. There are a number of ways to measure retire-ment, and we adopt a variety of approaches to provide a comprehensive view of changes in individuals' labor market attachment over the period. We focus on the 60–64 age group. Our data are annual aver-ages for the years 1980–1994, taken from the monthly LFS. In panel A of Figure 5 we plot the employment rates for this age group in the two jurisdictions. A distinctive secular decline in employment is evident in

Figure 4 CPP and QPP Benefits Paid Out and Savings

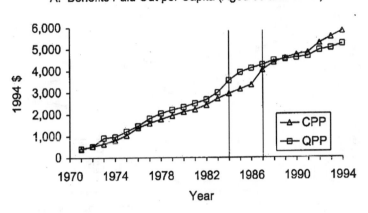

A. Benefits Paid Out per Capita (Aged 65 and Older)

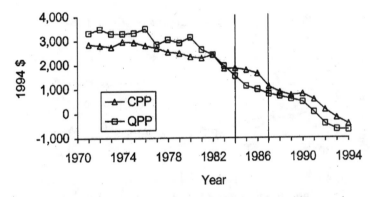

B. Savings per Capita (Aged 65 and Older)

NOTE: The graphs show the average CPP and QPP benefits paid per capita, calculated as the ratio of total benefits to the population aged 65 and older. CPP/QPP savings are the difference between revenue and expenses for the CPP and QPP, again normalized the population 65 and older. Data are from the CANSIM, Statistics Canada.

Figure 5 Employed Population Rate

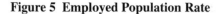

A. Age 60–64 Group

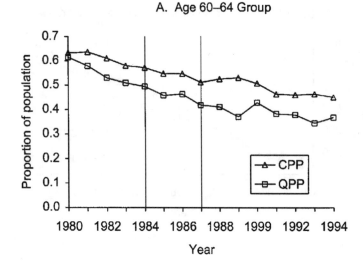

B. Difference between Age Groups 60–64 and 55–59

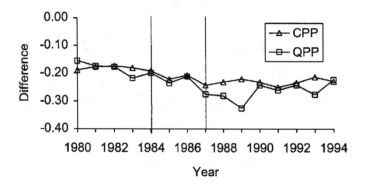

NOTE: The graphs show the average proportion of the population employed in the reference week. The proportions are calculated as annual averages from monthly tabulations of the Labour Force Survey. The CPP average is calculated over all provinces except Quebec, while the QPP average is calculated from Quebec only.

both series, as suggested by the census data. Also, in the early 1980s a gap emerges between the rates in Quebec and the rest of the country. It appears to widen in the middle and particularly the end of the decade, before narrowing somewhat in the early 1990s. There is no obvious evidence in this figure, however, that the introduction of early retirement to the QPP leads to an excess decrease in Quebec employment in 1984–1986, nor that there is a complementary effect in the rest of Canada after 1987. In fact, the only prominent deviation in the rates is the fall in Quebec's employment in 1989, but this has no simple correlation with the policy reform.

In panel B we plot the difference in the employment rates between those aged 60–64 and 55–59 to control for any jurisdiction specific business cycle effects that might be influencing employment. This should reduce the possibility that differential business cycle conditions between Quebec and the rest of Canada will lead to spurious differences in labor market outcomes over the window of the policy divergence. In fact, this picture reveals that the emergence of the Quebec/rest of Canada (ROC) gap in panel A appears to be due to some wider influence on the Quebec labor market that affected younger workers as well. Again, there is no evidence of an effect of the two policy interventions.

Figure 6 contains complementary series of "not in labor force" (NILF) rates. In panel A we see that there is a distinct increase in the rates over the period, and a Quebec/ROC gap emerges in 1981 coincident with the gap in employment rates. Also, there is little evidence of an excess decrease in labor market participation when the QPP early retirement policy is introduced, although it is not trivial to infer differences in slopes from these figures. In panel B we again use age group differences, and again the most significant Quebec/ROC deviation occurs in the late 1980s after the policy intervention has occurred in both jurisdictions.

In Figure 7 we examine the time-series variation in retirement; the data are from self-reported activity when not in the labor force. It is clear that retirement rates in this age group grew over the period. Starting at roughly 11 percent in the early 1980s, they almost double in all parts of the country over the period. Also, it appears that the rates move from one plateau to another, with most of the growth occurring over the period of policy reform. It is also clear, however, that the

Figure 6 Population Not in Labor Force

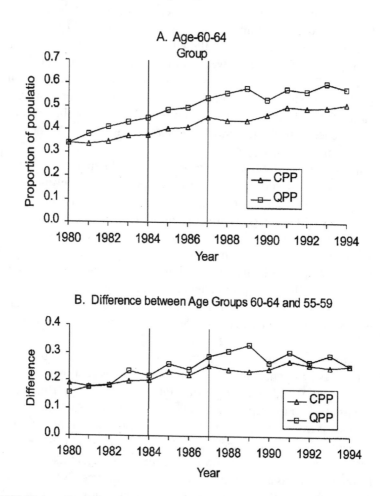

NOTE: The graphs show the average proportion of the population out of the labor force in the reference week. The proportions are calculated as annual averages from monthly tabulations of the Labour Force Survey. The CPP average is calculated over all provinces except Quebec, while the QPP average is calculated from Quebec only.

Figure 7 Retired Population Rate

A. Age 60–64 Group

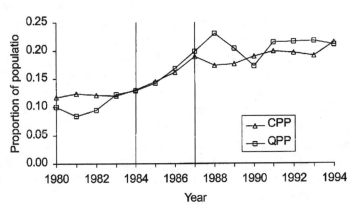

B. Difference between Age Groups 60–64 and 55–59

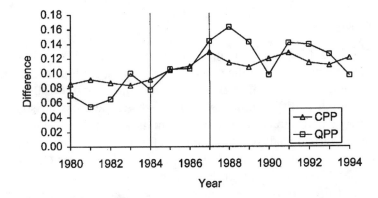

NOTE: The graphs show the average proportion of the population reporting their main activity out of the labor force as "retired" in the reference week. The proportions are calculated as annual averages from monthly tabulations of the Labour Force Survey. The CPP average is calculated over all provinces except Quebec, while the QPP average is calculated for Quebec only.

growth occurs simultaneously in Quebec and the ROC. This result is confirmed in the age 60–64/56–59 differences, again suggesting no obvious effect of the policy interventions.

A possible indirect effect of the policy intervention is that it led to a "relabeling" phenomenon; individuals who are not employed may be drawn out of the labor force as the support of pension benefits becomes available. They may prefer to report themselves retired instead of unemployed, or to collect pension benefits when UI benefits are exhausted. To investigate this possibility, in Figure 8 we graph the incidence of unemployed among the not employed over the period. At the beginning of the period the rate is higher in Quebec, but it falls below the ROC level as the QPP reforms are introduced in 1984. Furthermore, a marginally higher rate is restored in Quebec once the complementary reform of the CPP is completed. In the differenced data this effect is even clearer, as in Quebec the relative rate falls well below the ROC level starting in 1984.

Finally, in Figure 9 we examine hours worked in the reference week, conditional on working. Here again there is little evidence of an effect of the policy and the series for Quebec display quite erratic swings.

Regression Results

The graphical analysis documents the effect of the QPP/CPP reform on the finances of the public pension plans, but it provides little evidence of corresponding effects on the labor supply of 60- to 64-year-olds. It is difficult, however, to construct the cross jurisdiction "difference in differences" estimates from these pictures. We next turn to a more formal analysis of the policy reform, which provides a direct view of these estimates and allows us to control for other factors that may affect the behavior of this age group.

The LFS data provide quarterly observations on labor market · attachment by province, while the data on CPP/QPP expenditures and contributions are provided annually. Using annual observations from both data sets, we estimate the model as

$$y_{it} = \beta_1 + \beta_2 QUE_{it} + \beta_3 t + \beta_4 Y84_{it} + \beta_5 QUE_{it} \times Y84_{it} + \beta_6 Y87_{it} + \beta_7 QUE_{it} \times Y87_{it} + \varepsilon_{it},$$

Figure 8 Unemployed Category

A. Age 60–64 Group

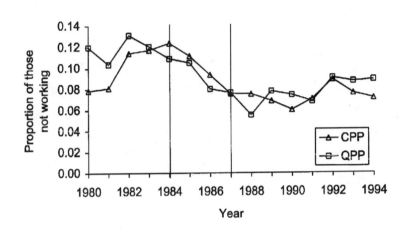

B. Difference between Age Groups 60–64 and 55–59

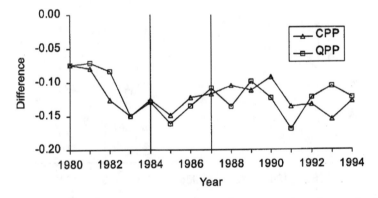

NOTE: The graphs show the average proportion of those not working who are classified as unemployed. The proportions are calculated as annual averages from monthly tabulations of the Labour Force Survey. The CPP average is calculated over all provinces except Quebec, while the QPP average is calculated from Quebec only.

Figure 9 Average Hours Worked (if Working)

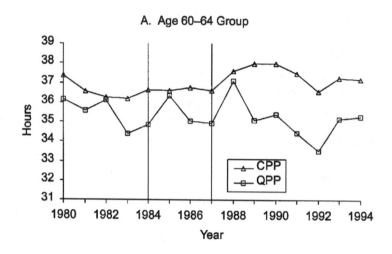

A. Age 60–64 Group

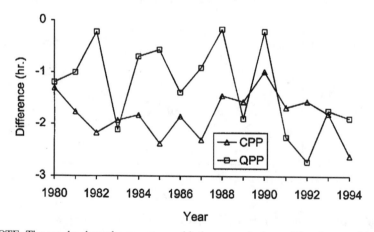

B. Difference between Age Groups 60–64 and 55–59

NOTE: The graphs show the average weekly hours worked, conditional on working at least one hour per week. The means are calculated as annual averages from monthly tabulations of the Labour Force Survey. The CPP average is calculated over all provinces except Quebec, while the QPP is calculated from Quebec only.

where QUE_{it} is a Quebec effect, $Y84_{it} = 1$ if $t \geq 1984$ and 0 otherwise, and $Y87_{it} = 1$ if $t > 1987$, and 0 otherwise. Therefore, β_5 is an estimate of the Quebec/ROC difference of a "trend break" in the dependent from 1984 onward, when the QPP reforms were put in place. β_7 provides a complementary estimate for the years from 1987 onward, when the reforms were introduced to the CPP.

Aggregating within years and across provinces (other than Quebec) has the effect of smoothing out much of the seasonal noise in the data, as is evident in Figures 4–9. To more fully account for this source of variation, both genuine and sampling-based, we estimate a slightly different specification, using the quarterly averages of the data, as well as exploiting variation across provinces in the rest of Canada. In this specification we add quarterly dummy variables to the equation as well as a full set of province effects.[6]

In the first two rows of Tables 1 and 2, we use our measures of CPP/QPP pension benefits and savings from Figure 4 as dependent variables. The key coefficients are the Quebec interaction terms. In both the annual and quarterly data, Quebec experiences a significant positive trend break (relative to the ROC) in benefit expenditures in 1984 with the advent of the QPP reforms. This confirms the suggestion in Figure 4 that an additional Quebec/ROC gap in benefit expenditure emerged with this policy intervention. The ROC makes a complementary shift in 1987, closing the gap with Quebec that opened in 1984. Again the timing is coincident with the reform of the CPP in this year. The estimates for savings provide a mirror image on these results. QPP savings shift downward relative to their CPP counterpart starting in 1984, but there is a corresponding relative decline in CPP savings starting in 1987. Together, these results point to significant effects of the policy change on the use of public pensions, and a resulting deterioration of program finances.

In rows 3 and 4 of Tables 1 and 2 we examine the employment rates of 60- to 64-year-olds to see whether there is a corresponding movement out of the labor force. The point estimate of $QUE_{it} \times Y84_{it}$ suggests Quebec did experience a (relative) negative trend break in 1984. This result is insignificant in the annual data but significant in the quarterly data. On the other hand, there is no corresponding relative shift in employment in the ROC in 1987. In the next row we use the 60–64/55–59 difference in employment rates as the dependent vari-

Table 1 Difference-in-Difference Estimates, Annual Data (Rest of Canada versus Quebec)[a]

Dependent variable	Y84[b]	Y87[b]	Que × Y84[c]	Que × Y87[c]
CPP benefits (per 65+)	54.23	519.50	375.35	−684.33
	(73.00)	(72.18)	(87.58)	(88.94)
CPP savings (per 65+)	240.34	−277.89	−707.93	149.38
	(128.97)	(127.53)	(154.73)	(157.14)
Employment rate, 60–64	−0.017	0.001	−0.026	−0.019
	(0.017)	(0.017)	(0.021)	(0.019)
Difference in employment rates (60–64 minus 55–59)	−0.036	−0.039	−0.007	−0.026
	(0.018)	(0.019)	(0.023)	(0.020)
Retirement rate, 60–64	0.014	0.028	0.021	0.015
	(0.011)	(0.012)	(0.015)	(0.013)
Difference in retirement rates (60–64 minus 55–59)	0.021	0.026	0.009	0.019
	(0.013)	(0.014)	(0.017)	(0.015)
Unemployment category, 60–64	0.005	−0.047	−0.033	0.016
	(0.011)	(0.011)	(0.014)	(0.012)
Difference in unemployment category (60–64 minus 55–59)	−0.007	0.038	−0.022	0.008
	(0.020)	(0.021)	(0.025)	(0.022)
NILF, 60–64	0.014	0.022	0.038	0.012
	(0.015)	(0.015)	(0.019)	(0.017)
Difference in NILF rate (60–64 minus 55–59)	0.030	0.033	0.023	0.016
	(0.108)	(0.019)	(0.023)	(0.020)
Hours worked (if working) 60–64	0.484	1.309	−0.216	−0.963
	(0.605)	(0.629)	(0.776)	(0.688)
Difference in hours worked (if working), (60–64 minus 55–59)	0.301	1.102	0.476	−0.867
	(0.514)	(0.535)	(0.660)	(0.585)

[a] Annual data for labor market variables are annual averages of quarterly tabulations of the Labour Force Survey, for Quebec and the "Rest of Canada" (ROC), provided by Statistics Canada, 1980–1994. For the CPP/QPP measures, the data are annual totals of benefits paid out, or "savings" (revenue less expenses), deflated by the CPI (1994 dollars), expressed on a per capita basis (for population 65 years and older). The CPP

results compare aggregate payouts to CPP and QPP. The data are based on adminis-trative reports, from Canadian Socio-Economic Information Management System (CANSIM). The sample covered by the CPP/QPP data is 1975–1993. The labor force variables are relatively standard: a) employment rate is the employment–popu-lation ratio; b) retirement rate is the percentage of the population reporting that they are retired; c) unemployed category is the share of those not working who are unem-ployed; d) not in labor force is the percentage of the population not in the labor force; e) hours worked (if working) are mean weekly hours, conditional on working. The levels rows show the estimated effects for the 60–64 age group, while the difference rows are the difference in these rates from a "base" group of the 55–59 age group.

[b] Y84 and Y87 are coefficients on variables indicating year $\geq$ 1984 and year $\geq$ 1987.

[c] Que_Y84 and Que_Y87 are the interactions of these variables with a Quebec dummy. Other controls include a linear trend and a Quebec dummy.

206   Baker and Benjamin

Table 2 Difference-in-Difference Estimates, Provincial Level Data[a]

Dependent variable	Y84[b]	Y87[b]	Que × Y84[c]	Que × Y87[c]
CPP benefits (per 65+)	36.20	475.06	375.78	−639.13
	(30.89)	(29.49)	(47.09)	(48.10)
CPP savings (per 65+)	152.08	−331.54	−713.13	143.41
	(60.92)	(58.15)	(92.84)	(94.84)
Employment rate, 60–64	−0.017	0.001	−0.025	−0.019
	(0.007)	(0.007)	(0.011)	(0.010)
Difference in employment rates (60–64 minus 55–59)	−0.035	−0.037	−0.005	−0.024
	(0.006)	(0.006)	(0.010)	(0.008)
Retirement rate, 60–64	0.013	0.025	0.021	0.015
	(0.004)	(0.004)	(0.006)	(0.005)
Difference in retirement rates (60–64 minus 55–59)	0.019	0.022	0.009	0.018
	(0.004)	(0.004)	(0.007)	(0.006)
Unemployment category, 60–64	0.004	−0.047	−0.031	0.017
	(0.004)	(0.005)	(0.008)	(0.007)
Difference in unemployment category (60–64 minus 55–59)	0.001	0.043	−0.025	0.012
	(0.007)	(0.008)	(0.013)	(0.010)
NILF, 60–64	0.013	0.020	0.037	0.012
	(0.006)	(0.007)	(0.011)	(0.010)
Difference in NILF rate (60–64 minus 55–59)	0.028	0.029	0.022	0.015
	(0.005)	(0.006)	(0.010)	(0.008)
Hours worked (if working), 60–64	0.389	1.104	−0.210	−0.926
	(0.333)	(0.357)	(0.587)	(0.502)
Difference in hours worked (if working), (60–64 minus 55–59)	0.127	0.824	0.496	−0.796
	(0.242)	(0.259)	(0.426)	(0.364)

[a] Labor market variables are quarterly province-level averages based on tabulations of the Labour Force Survey, provided by Statistics Canada, 1980–1994. For the CPP/QPP measures, the data are province-level annual totals of benefits paid out, or "sav-

ings" (revenue less expenses), deflated by the CPI (1994 dollars), expressed on a per capita basis (for population 65 years and older). The data are based on administrative reports, from CANSIM. The sample covered by the CPP/QPP data is 1975–1993. The labor force variables are relatively standard: a) employment rate is the employment-population ratio; b) retirement rate is the percentage of the population reporting that they are retired; c) unemployed category is the share of those not working who are unemployed; d) not in labor force is the percentage of the population not in the labor force; e) hours worked (if working) are mean weekly hours, conditional on working. The levels rows show the estimated effects for the 60–64 age group, while the difference rows are the difference in these rates from a "base" group of the 55–59 age group.
[b] Y84 and Y87 are coefficients on variables indicating year $\geq$ 1984 and year $\geq$ 1987.
[c] Que $\times$ Y84 and Que $\times$ Y87 are the interactions of these variables with a Quebec dummy. Other controls include a linear trend, province and quarter dummies. Regressions are weighted by the provincial population (60–64 for labor market variables, total population for CPP/QPP).

able. Here we try to partial out any region specific business cycle effects that may be simultaneously affecting employment. In both data sets, the estimates suggest that any trend breaks experienced in 1984 were shared equally by individuals in Quebec and the ROC. Furthermore, in 1987 Quebec experiences the relative decrease in employment, that has no correlation with our policy experiment. Overall, consistent with Figure 5, there is little evidence of a policy effect in these data.

In rows 5 and 6 we conduct a similar analysis of self-reported retirement rates. In the "simple" results we see a relative upward shift in retirement rates in Quebec starting in 1984. This effect is accentuated in 1987, however, as the estimate of $QUE_{it} \times Y87_{it}$ is both positive and significant. In the "difference" results there is little evidence that the different timing of CPP/QPP reform had any affect on the retirement trends.

The next two rows contain the results for unemployment rates among the population who are not working. The simple results reveal a coherency with the policy reform. There is a negative (relative) trend break in Quebec starting in 1984 and in the ROC starting in 1987.

Once we turn to the differenced data, however, the results are not as clear, and we now observe a positive trend break in the ROC starting in 1987. This may reflect the fact that as the economic expansion in the latter part of the 1980s takes hold, the proportion of the unemployed among those not working for most age groups falls. To the extent that the old (like the young) are among the last to experience the benefits of the expansion, the fall in their proportion will lag that of other groups.

An analysis of NILF is presented in rows 9 and 10. In the simple results (quarterly data) we again find some evidence of a policy effect. There is a significant positive trend break in Quebec starting in 1984. We also see an upward shift in the ROC in 1987, although this appears to be shared by individuals in Quebec. As has been the case for most of the other variables, however, once we compare 60- to 65-year-olds to 55- to 59-years-olds (who should be unaffected by the policy change) there is little evidence of a policy effect.

Finally, in the last two rows we examine hours among those who worked in the reference week. It is not obvious how the policy change should affect hours. One possibility is that early retirement leads to marginal reductions in hours; for example, by a move to part-time work. However, if the availability of pensions draws workers with marginal attachment out of employment, we might expect to see average hours actually increase among those who continue working due to a selection effect. The results, however, display little consistent evidence of either possibility.

These data, therefore, provide little evidence that the policy intervention had a labor supply effect. Moreover, many of the changes in labor force attachment for the 60–64 age group appear to be common to all parts of the country, or part of larger trends that affected younger individuals as well. The strongest evidence is of a relabeling effect, as individuals who are not working moved out of the labor force (from unemployment to retirement) in tandem with the policy reforms. Our results thus suggest that while many Canadians took advantage of the opportunity to collect early retirement benefits, few changed their labor supply in order to do so. Whatever forces were driving Canadians to retire earlier continued to do so, in equal measure, in Quebec and the rest of Canada. The only difference was that instead of waiting to receive benefits at age 65, benefits could be started right away.

A Closer Look at the Elderly

To follow this hypothesis more closely, our final exercise is to use a panel data set, the 1986–1987 LMAS, to examine the labor market activity of individuals in the years surrounding the reform of the CPP. The LMAS has a single variable capturing the receipt of "pension income" in the calendar year. Cross checking this variable with the incidence of different types of pensions in the 1987 and 1988 SCFs, the LMAS variable appears to capture both public and private pension income. Therefore, we do not obtain a clean measure of individuals collecting CPP or QPP pension income from this survey. The 1988 SCF data indicate that roughly one-third of individuals, aged 60–64, collecting private or public pensions in 1987, collected a private pension but not CPP or QPP.

We examine the labor market activity of males in the rest of Canada between the ages of 59 and 63 as of January 1987.[7] Summary means for 1986 and 1987 are presented in Table 3. We focus on two types of individuals: males who started receiving pension income in 1987 and thus presumably took advantage of the early retirement provisions of the CPP as they became available, and males who had no pension income in either 1986 or 1987.[8] The first three rows indicate that males who initiated pension receipt in 1987 are much more dependent on transfer income in 1986 than males in the no pension group. The incidence of UI is seven percentage points higher, and they have twice the rate of Social Assistance receipt. The higher rate of UI receipt continues in 1987 as pension benefits are initiated. The picture here is that some of these individuals are cycling through UI (and presumably unemployment) into a pension.

In the next four rows we examine labor market activity. By weeks worked, total hours, and the incidence of no weeks, males who initiated pension receipt in 1987 had less labor market attachment in 1986 than those who didn't. By 1987 the difference is more dramatic, as nearly one-half of these new pensioners are not employed for the entire year.

These results suggest that individuals who took advantage of the early retirement provisions in the public pension plans had a relatively loose attachment to the labor market. The differences are perhaps less striking than they might be, but we identify the individuals who initiate

Table 3 Selected Characteristics of Males in the Rest of Canada Initiating Pension Receipt in 1987[a]

	1986		1987	
Sample	Started receiving pension income in 1987	No pension income in 1986 or 1987	Started receiving pension income in 1987	No pension income in 1986 or 1987
UI	0.16	0.09	0.16	0.09
Social assistance	0.07	0.04	0.03	0.04
Workers' compensation benefits	0.08	0.02	0.07	0.04
Total hours	907.5	1320.0	502.6	1294.7
Weeks worked if employed	44.5	49.6	37.4	50.0
Weeks worked = 0	0.31	0.08	0.47	0.10
Retired from a job	0.34	0.04	—	—
Primary school education or less	0.39	0.33	—	—

SOURCE: 1986–1987 Labour Market Activity Survey.

[a] Sample sizes: males with no pension income in 1986 or 1987, 916; males who started to receive pension income in 1987, 215. Sample includes males aged 59–63.

CPP receipt in 1987 with error. Furthermore, the contamination comes from individuals who only collect private pension income. This group is likely to have higher skills and resources than average. For example, in the 1988 SCF, 19 percent of this group, aged 60–64, has a university education compared to just 4 percent of individuals who receive public pension income. They also have twice the employment rate (51 percent versus 25 percent), work more if employed (44 weeks versus 29 weeks), and have a higher rate of labor market participation (55 percent versus 28 percent; all figures for the reference year). Therefore, the inclusion of this group in sample implies that the statistics in Table 3 likely overstate the labor market attachment of individuals who initiated CPP receipt in 1987.

Thus, these results show that a good number of the "early retirees" in 1987 were not simply part of the trend toward early retirement sweeping North America, but they were also workers who weren't working anyway. Their behavior is not the kind envisioned by those who designed the early retirement provisions. It appears instead that the new CPP and QPP recipients that initiated their benefits before age 65 either weren't working or wouldn't have worked anyway.

CONCLUSION

In 1980, over 60 percent of men between the ages of 60 and 64 were working; by 1994, this had fallen to 50 percent. In the intervening years, the Canadian government had introduced early retirement provisions to its public pension plan, making it easier for 60- to 64-year-olds to receive pension benefits. Was there any causal relationship between the change in pension policy and the increase in retirement rates? In this chapter we exploit a difference in the timing of the introduction of early retirement provisions in the two public pension programs in Canada, the CPP and the QPP. Our results suggest that there is no obvious link in the timing of these changes and changes in men's labor market behavior. However, we find that there was a strongly associated increase in the collection of pension benefits in each jurisdiction that lines up perfectly with the staggered introduction of early retirement. Early receipt of pensions was clearly popular. Why don't we observe any corresponding change in working time, given the increase in pension receipt? Our results suggest two explanations. First, there was a steady downward trend in employment probabilities that was unaffected by early retirement. The only difference was that the new retirees could collect pension benefits, whereas their predecessors had to wait until they were 65. Second, many of the new pension recipients were men who wouldn't have been working anyway—men who had only weak labor force attachment. In this dimension, at least, and looking only at the short-run response to the policy change, it does not appear that public pensions had much of an impact on working time over the life cycle.

Notes

We thank Miles Corak, James Pesando and seminar participants at Princeton, Toronto, the CERF conference "Changes in Working Time in Canada and the U.S.," and the NBER Summer Institute for helpful comments. We also thank Steve Roller at Statistics Canada for assistance with unpublished LMAS files. Finally, we gratefully acknowledge the research support of CERF and SSHRC.

1. For a summary of the public finance issues associated with retirement and Canadian public pension plans, see Baker and Benjamin (2000).
2. The details of how benefits are computed and the historical evolution of these plans are described in Baker and Benjamin (1999), Burbidge (1987), and CCH Limited (1996).
3. Baker (forthcoming) provides an overview of the provisions of this, and the associated Spouse's Allowance (SPA), as well as an analysis of their effects on retirement behavior.
4. Some of the legislative and political details of this divergence in opinion are documented in Baker and Benjamin (2000).
5. CPP/QPP benefit expenditures and contributions are available through CANSIM.
6. CPP/QPP expenditures and contributions are only available on an annual basis. Therefore, for these series we use the annual specification with the addition of the province effects.
7. We do not use the data for Quebec. The cross check with the Survey of Consumer Finance (SCF) data suggests that in 1986 the LMAS pension variable for this province captures public pensions or private pensions, but not both. On the other hand in 1987 it appears that the variable does capture both types of pensions. We have tried to find an explanation for these inconsistencies such as differences in the wording of the French and English questionnaires, or any changes in the French survey over the period. So far our attempts, as well as the efforts of Statistics Canada officials, have failed to uncover an explanation.
8. In our sample, 54.6 percent of males have no pension income in either year, 27.8 percent have pension income in each year, 11.9 percent start to receive pension income in 1987, and 5.8 percent stop receiving pension income in 1987.

References

Baker, Michael. Forthcoming. "The Retirement Behavior of Married Couples: Evidence from the Spouse's Allowance." *Journal of Human Resources*.

Baker, Michael, and Dwayne Benjamin. 1999a. "How Do Retirement Tests Affect the Labor Supply of Older Men?" *Journal of Public Economics* 71(1): 27–51.

_____. 1999b. "Early Retirement Provisions and the Labor Force Behavior of Older Men: Evidence from Canada." *Journal of Labor Economics* 17(4): 724–756.

_____. 2000. "Public Pension Programs and Labor Force Attachment." In *Public Policy to a Labor Market in Transition,* France St-Hilaire and W. Craig Riddell, eds. Montreal: Institute for Research on Public Policy, pp. 287–315.

Burbidge, John. 1987. *Social Security in Canada.* Canadian Tax Paper No. 79, Canadian Tax Foundation, Toronto.

CCH Canadian Limited. 1996. *Canadian Employment Benefits and Pension Guide Reports.* North York, Ontario, CCH Canadian Limited.

Gruber, Jonathan. 1996. "Disability Insurance Benefits and Labor Supply." Working paper no. 5866. Cambridge Massachusetts: National Bureau of Economic Research.

Hurd, Michael. 1990. "Research on the Elderly: Economic Status, Retirement, and Consumption and Saving." *Journal of Economic Literature* 28(6): 565–637.

Hurd, Michael, and Michael Boskin. 1984. "The Effect of Social Security on Retirement in the Early 1970s." *Quarterly Journal of Economics* 99(11): 767–790.

Kahn, James. 1988. "Social Security, Liquidity, and Early Retirement." *Journal of Public Economics* 35(2): 97–117.

Krueger, Alan, and Jorn-Steffen Pischke. 1992. "The Effect of Social Security on Labor Supply: A Cohort Analysis of the Notch Generation." *Journal of Labor Economics* 10(10): 412–437.

Peracchi, Franco, and Finis Welch. 1994. "Trends in Labor Force Transitions of Older Men and Women." *Journal of Labor Economics* 12(4): 210–242.

Osberg, Lars. 1993. "Is It Retirement or Unemployment? Induced Retirement and Constrained Labor Supply among Older Workers." *Applied Economics* 25(4): 505–519.

Ruhm, Christopher. 1995. "Secular Changes in the Work and Retirement Patterns of Older Men." *Journal of Human Resources* 30(Spring): 362–385.

Part III

8

Self-Employment and Schedule Flexibility for Married Females
Evidence for the United States from SIPP

Theresa J. Devine
Office of the Public Advocate for New York City

As the employment rate for prime-age married women in the United States rose through the 1980s, their self-employment rate rose by more. As shown in Figure 1, 9.4 percent of employed married women aged 25–55 were self-employed in their primary jobs in 1990, up from 5.7 percent in 1975.[1] Self-employment rates for previously married and never-married women also rose but stayed relatively low.

Figure 1 Self-Employment of Employed Married Women in the United States, 1975–1990

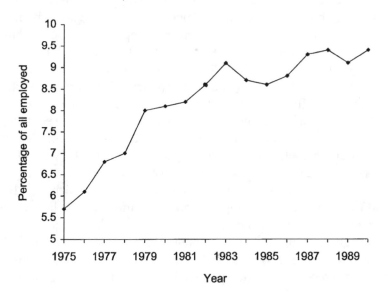

In 1990, married women represented three out of four self-employed women, versus just over half of all wage-and-salary women.

Self-employed married women report substantially lower earnings on average than their wage-and-salary counterparts (Devine 1990, 1994). They are also more likely than their wage-and-salary counterparts to work a lot of hours, and they are even more likely to work relatively few hours (Devine 1990, 1994). There is evidence of limited availability of jobs with either very high hours or very low hours in the wage-and-salary sector (Altonji and Paxson 1988, 1992; Lang and Kahn 2001; Blank 1994). Taken together, these findings suggest that married women's self-employment could be a way to exercise more control over work schedules than typically possible in the wage-and-salary sector.

This chapter presents new evidence on this work schedule hypothesis from the Survey of Income and Program Participation (SIPP).[2] The SIPP data are useful for this purpose for several reasons. Each SIPP interview collects relatively detailed information on job characteristics and work schedules (weeks worked, usual hours, and deviations from usual schedules). SIPP is longitudinal, so changes in usual schedules and self-employment status can be measured, and SIPP interviews are just four months apart, which means that short-term change may be measured quite accurately. SIPP also collects detailed information on business characteristics (including husband/wife business ownership, legal status, and number of employees). The combination of labor market activity, business characteristics, and household characteristics data makes SIPP a relatively rich data source for the study of self-employment in the United States. The following section describes the SIPP data and sample used here. Since these data are complex, subject to misinterpretation, and have not been used widely, this discussion is relatively detailed. The next sections present a summary of the characteristics of self-employed women, relative to wage-and-salary women and nonworking women, followed by evidence on schedules and self-employment. Included here is the evidence on husband/wife business ownership and reported earnings. The last section concludes with some final thoughts.

Several findings point to a potential relationship between self-employment and scheduling. First, self-employed and wage-and-salary women report very different usual hours of work. In comparison to the distribution of hours for wage-and-salary women, the distribution of hours for self-employed women exhibits greater mass in the upper tail and particularly the lower tail. Second, self-employed women tend to deviate from their usual schedules more frequently. Relative to full-time wage-and-salary women, full-time self-employed women are more likely to temporarily cut back their hours to part-time. Third, both full-time and part-time self-employed women tend to change their usual schedules more often during a single year. Fourth, self-employed women are more likely to attribute their part-time hours and schedule variability to choice, as opposed to insufficient work. Fifth, the data suggest that self-employment decisions of married women are not independent of their husbands' employment and self-employment status. Finally, usual hours of self-employed women exhibit greater correlation with usual hours of their husbands, particularly when their husbands are also self-employed. All of these findings, while preliminary, provide a basis for future research.

DATA

SIPP is a longitudinal multipanel survey conducted by the U.S. Bureau of the Census since 1984. Each SIPP panel is a large representative sample of the noninstitutionalized resident U.S. population, with the household as the basic sampling unit and interviews conducted for all household members ages 15 and over; the initial 1986 panel consisted of more than 30,000 persons in over 11,500 households. Approximately one-third of all SIPP interviews are conducted with proxy respondents, but the likelihood of a proxy interview varies with demographic characteristics; just 19 percent of the wives studied here had proxy interviews. SIPP has a relatively short four-month reference period for each round of interviews (also called a *wave*), which should improve respondents' recall of the incidence, timing, and duration of events. The detailed SIPP core questionnaire also generates relatively detailed information about labor market activity, income, personal characteristics, and household characteristics for each reference period.

Most important for the present study are SIPP's detailed data on work schedules, self-employment activity, and business characteristics.

These data, however, are not perfect, and using them accurately takes a lot of time and care. Most important among limits of the self-employment data is the lack of dates for self-employment within four-month reference periods. Self-employment status can be measured accurately only for an entire four-month reference period. In this chapter, a person is categorized as only self-employed or self-employed with wage-and-salary employment during the reference period, but the latter does not mean simultaneous activity.[3] In some cases, characteristics are also reported for a woman's *main job*, defined as the job with the maximum hours reported for the reference period, but uncertainty about the timing of jobs means that the main job label must be interpreted cautiously. In general, one cannot distinguish sequential jobs and coincident jobs within a four-month SIPP reference period.

A second major limit of the SIPP data is the way that business information is collected and reported. Information on the legal form of ownership (corporation, sole-proprietorship, partnership), number of employees, and other business characteristics is available for up to two businesses in each wave for each self-employed person—but only if a respondent expects gross business earnings to be at least $1,000 over the 12 months following an interview. This might seem like an effective screen for "casual" businesses, but it is problematic in practice. Expectations change between interviews, leaving gaps in longitudinal records for some businesses. Even if the $1,000 threshold is passed, data on business characteristics may not appear on a business owner's record. Business characteristics are collected just once per household business, even if there are multiple owners in a household, and these data appear only on the record of the person who reports the information.[4] The reporting owner's record has person numbers for up to three other owners in the household, as reported by this owner, but there is no pointer on the records of other owners.

If a person is self-employed, his or her record may indicate that business data have been collected but not from whom, and several factors complicate attempts to find this missing information. There can be differences in opinion within a household about business ownership versus work (with or without "pay") in the family business. Ownership without self-employment is possible. Self-employed household members can also work in different businesses, even with coownership, so exact matches of person numbers can be confusing. Industries can be used for verification, but this is not foolproof. A single business can operate in different industries, different businesses can operate in the same industry, and different descriptions can result in different industry codes (even at the two-digit level). The data set used below has been constructed using owner identification information from each interview, additional owner identification information from adjacent interviews (as necessary and available), and industry checks.[5]

Detailed income information represents one of SIPP's most attractive features. The most recent hourly wage is collected for each hourly wage-and-salary job, and total gross earnings in each month is collected for each wage-and-salary job, whether salaried or hourly. Income data collected for the self-employed depend on expected gross business earnings. If expected gross earnings are at least $1,000, total income received from the business as regular salary or other income for personal purposes is reported by month, accompanied by flags for receipt of regular salary and receipt of other income. For those expecting low revenue, business earnings net of expenses are collected for the entire four-month reference period, bounded below by zero.[6] Losses are not reported.

Comparisons of self-employed earnings data and wage-and-salary earnings data must be made cautiously when using SIPP, like any other survey. Wage-and-salary earnings may include money that workers invest, while earnings of the self-employed may exclude business investment. Wage-and-salary earnings do not include investment returns, while self-employment earnings may include investment returns. Nonwage compensation (such as health care and deferred compensation) differ systematically between wage-and-salary employment and self-employment. The timing of income receipt versus job performance is yet another issue. Particularly important for the present study is the distribution of reported earnings among individual family business owners. A couple may report all business income in one spouse's name, for example, which will bias the spouses' reported individual earnings in opposite directions.

Notwithstanding all of these limitations, the SIPP data have the advantage of a relatively low nonresponse rate. In the sample used here, earnings are imputed for just 3.8 percent of wives who report only self-employment, 3.7 percent of wives who report only wage-and-salary employment, and 5.7 percent of wives who report both.[7] Due to these low nonresponse rates and the use of reported earnings values for imputation in the SIPP data set, including or excluding imputed earnings values has essentially no significant effect on earnings distributions. Women for whom imputations were made are excluded only when earnings data are examined.[8]

This chapter uses data for a sample of 3,058 women who were aged 25–55 at the start of 1986, not enrolled in school, not in the armed forces, married, and living with the same spouse for the first 16 months of the survey reference period. Much of this chapter focuses on the wave 1 reference period, which covers four-month intervals spanning October 1985 to March 1986. The 16 months for waves 1 to 4 extend through April 1987.[9] As needed, additional variables are defined below.

CHARACTERISTICS OF MARRIED WOMEN BY SELF-EMPLOYMENT STATUS

To set the stage for evidence on work schedules, this section first presents a summary of employment and self-employment activity for our sample, and then turns to the characteristics of these women, their jobs, their husbands, and their households.

Self-Employment, Employment, and Work

The first pair of columns in Table 1 summarize employment, self-employment, and casual work for pay during wave 1 for the entire sample of married women and the subsample with regular employment. *Regular employment* is defined in SIPP as an arrangement for "regular" work for an employer or in a self-owned or family business, but there are no hours or schedule restrictions in the definition. Overall, two-thirds of the women had regular jobs (including a few who reported unpaid work), and another 2 percent did some casual work for pay in wave 1.[10] Of the women with regular jobs, 1 in 10 reported only self-employment, more than 1 in 8 reported both self-employment and wage-and-salary employment, and 1 out of 9 was self-employed in her main job (using maximum usual hours to assign this label). The sec-

Table 1 Employment, Self-Employment, and Work of Married Women

	Wave 1		Year 1 (waves 1 to 3)	
Activity	% of sample	% of employed	% of sample	% of employed
Regular job	66.6	100.0	72.7	100.0
Only wage and salary	58.0	87.1	61.4	84.5
Self-employed in any job	8.6	12.9	11.3	15.5
Only self-employed	6.8	10.3	6.9	9.5
Self-employed and wage and salary	1.7	2.6	4.4	6.0
Self-employed in main job[a] (based on usual hours)	7.2	10.8		
Casual work for pay when no regular job	2.4	0.4	4.8	2.7
Some self-employed or casual work	11.0	13.3	15.7	17.7
Regular job or casual work	68.7	100.0	75.5	100.0
Number of observations	3,058	2,036	3,058	2,223

[a] Measured only for wave 1 because main job can change.

ond pair of columns in Table 1 presents a comparable summary for the full first year. More than 1 out of 7 employed wives reported some self-employment during the year, and nearly 1 out of 10 reported only self-employment.[11] In short, these data indicate that self-employment represents an important part of married women's market work activity.

Demographic Characteristics

Table 2 presents demographic characteristics for married women by wave 1 regular employment, wage-and-salary, and self-employment status. The age distribution for the women without regular employment (column 1) is bimodal within the 25 to 55 bounds; relatively few are ages 35 to 44. Relative to employed women, the non-employed also tend to be less educated, more likely to be Hispanic, more likely to be immigrants, less likely to be citizens, more likely to be parents or guardians, and more likely to report a disability. These findings are generally consistent with previous findings on labor force participation.

Table 2 Demographic Characteristics of Married Women, by Self-Employment Status[a,b]

Characteristics	No regular job	Only wage and salary	Self-employed	
			Only	With wage and salary
Age (%)				
25–34	38.5	39.1	33.5	34.0
34–44	27.5	34.7	38.3	43.4
45–55	34.1	26.2	28.2	22.6
Mean age	39.25 (9.17)	38.21 (8.50)	39.08 (8.28)	38.13 (7.73)
Education credentials (%)				
None	20.3	12.3	12.9	11.3
H.S. diploma/GED	48.0	44.8	47.4	35.9
Some college (no degree)	13.8	14.7	16.8	17.0
Vocational/technical certification	1.5	3.5	1.4	1.9
Associate's degree	3.1	5.3	3.8	11.3
Bachelor's degree	10.7	13.6	13.4	17.0
Professional degree	0.0	0.6	1.0	1.9
Master's degree	1.9	4.7	1.9	3.8
Doctorate	0.3	0.5	0.5	0.0
Mean years of school completed	12.19 (2.68)	12.92 (2.55)	12.90 (2.29)	13.40 (2.38)
Race/ethnicity (%)				
White – non-Hispanic	84.9	85.2	93.8	96.2
Black – non-Hispanic	4.0	5.6		0.0
Other race – non-Hispanic	3.5	3.0	3.8	1.9
Hispanic – any race	7.5	6.1	2.4	1.9
Immigrant	10.6	6.9	9.6	3.8
U.S. citizen	93.9	96.7	97.1	96.2

Characteristics	No regular job	Only wage and salary	Self-employed	
			Only	With wage and salary
Parent/guardian of children (%)				
Under age 1	10.1	4.5	4.3	3.8
Ages 1–5	34.1	23.0	24.9	15.1
Ages 6–14	44.9	41.9	42.6	41.5
Ages 15–17	17.4	21.3	21.5	32.1
Mean number of children	1.5 (1.3)	1.2 (1.2)	1.3 (1.3)	1.4 (1.2)
Work limiting disability during survey (%)	12.5	5.7	7.7	18.9
Health care coverage (%)				
Some coverage	87.1	94.6	89.5	92.5
Private health insurance	80.2	93.0	84.7	88.7
Plan through own job	1.4	49.4	8.1	26.4
Covered by another person's plan	78.5	65.5	72.2	73.6
Military plan (CHAMPUS or CHAMPVA)	4.9	3.4	5.3	3.8
Government plan (Medicaid or Medicare)	4.3	0.6	1.0	0.0
Covered for 12 months	79.0	92.0	84.2	88.7
Number of observations	1,022	1,744	209	53

[a] Characteristics in wave 1 reference period unless noted otherwise.
[b] Standard deviations are in parentheses.

Turning our focus to women who report only wage-and-salary employment versus those who report only self-employment, we observe that the self-employed women tend to be slightly older, similar in terms of years of education but less credentialed beyond a high school diploma, much less likely to be black or Hispanic, more likely to be immigrants but not less likely to be citizens, and more likely to report work-limiting disabilities. The self-employed also appear slightly more likely than wage-and-salary women to be parents or guardians of children under 15.[12] These data are also consistent with findings from the Current Population Survey (Devine 1990, 1994). The small sample size for women who report both wage-and-salary employment and self-employment limits what we can say about women in this group. But the differences between the figures for this group and those for the other groups of women are notable. The data suggest that these women are more likely to be between the ages 35 and 44, highly educated, white,

Table 3 Occupations, by Self-Employment Status, Wave 1 (%)

Occupation	Wage and salary	Self-employed	
		Only	With wage and salary
Executive, administrative, and managerial	11.4	17.7	7.5
Professional specialty	14.6	5.3	17.0
Technical and related support	4.0	1.0	0.0
Sales	10.7	24.9	18.9
Administrative support, including clerical	32.1	11.5	18.9
Household service	1.2	3.8	0.0
Protective services	0.3	0.0	0.0
Other services	12.8	23.4	18.9
Farm operators and managers	0.1	3.8	1.9
Other agriculture	0.7	2.4	3.8
Mechanics and repair	0.4	0.0	0.0
Construction trades	2.1	3.3	3.8
Machine operators, assemblers, and inspectors	7.0	1.9	7.5
Transportation and material moving	0.7	0.5	0.0
Handlers, helpers, and laborers	1.7	0.5	1.9

non-Hispanic, nonimmigrant, parents and guardians of older children, and to report a work-limiting disability.

Occupations for wave 1 main jobs are shown in Table 3, and these data exhibit sharp differences by self-employment status. Relatively large numbers of women who report only self-employment have sales and service occupations, and relatively few have technical and administrative support occupations. Perhaps most noticeable is the relatively low percentage of only self-employed women in professional specialty occupations, but this category includes teachers and nurses in addition to lawyers and physicians. Women who report only self-employment are more likely than other women to describe themselves as executives, administrators, and managers, but it should be borne in mind that these occupation labels may not have the same meaning for self-employed and wage-and-salary women. The main job occupations of women with both wage-and-salary employment and self-employment are professional specialty, nonfarmer agricultural, construction trade, and operator occupations. These women are also more likely than wage-and-salary women to report sales and other services, and they are more likely than only self-employed women to report administrative support occupations. In general, the occupation data suggest that self-employment and reported occupation are not independent.

Industries are reported in Table 4. Not surprisingly, relatively more self-employed women are in agriculture, but the overall percentage is well under 10 percent; agricultural employment is actually most likely for women who report both self-employment and wage-and-salary employment. A large percentage of wage-and-salary women work in retail trade, but the percentage is even greater for women who are only self-employed. The same holds for services when considered as a group, although the distributions over alternative service industries are quite different. More wage-and-salary women are in professional services, as found in the occupation data. Women who are only self-employed are more concentrated in personal and business repair services. Women with both self-employment and wage-and-salary employment are much more likely than wage-and-salary women to be in personal services, and they are more likely than self-employed women to be in professional services and finance, insurance, and real estate. They are also the most likely to be in business and repair ser-

Table 4 Industry, by Self-Employment Status, Wave 1 (%)

| | | Self-employed | |
Industry	Wage and salary	Only	With wage and salary
Agriculture, farming, fishing, and mining	1.2	6.7	9.4
Construction	1.3	1.4	1.9
Nondurable manufacturing	7.7	1.0	3.8
Durable manufacturing	7.4	1.4	1.9
Transportation, communication, and utilities	4.2	1.4	3.8
Wholesale trade – durables	1.7	1.4	0.0
Wholesale trade – nondurables	1.4	1.0	0.0
Retail trade	16.0	31.1	13.2
Finance, insurance, and real estate	9.1	4.3	9.4
Business repair services	4.8	12.9	17.0
Personal services	3.9	26.3	13.2
Entertainment services	0.6	1.4	1.9
Professional services	37.4	9.6	22.6
Public administration	3.2	0.0	1.9

vices. As with occupation, the SIPP data suggest that self-employment and industry are linked, but causality is unclear.

Household and Husband Characteristics

Household and husband characteristics are summarized in Table 5. On average, non-employed women live in the households with the lowest total household incomes, which is no surprise. The average reported income for the household of women who are only self-employed is the next lowest.

Turning to household income net of wife's income, however, we see a different picture. Household income net of the wife's earnings is larger, on average, for the self-employed women, particularly those who are only self-employed. This is consistent with the hypothesis that

Table 5 Household and Husband's Characteristics, by Wife's Self-Employment Status[a,b]

| | | | Self-employed | |
| | No regular | Only wage | | With wage |
Characteristic	job	and salary	Only	and salary
Household income	11,017	14,501	14,076	16,101
($US 1986)	(8,977)	(8,421)	(11,065)	(12,770)
Net of wife's earnings–	11,017	10,081	11,515	10,740
regular jobs ($US	(8,977)	(7,359)	(9,307)	(9,815)
1986)				
Home ownership (%)				
Homeowner in month 1	75.6	78.6	86.6	83.0
Switch to non-owner	4.7	3.8	5.3	1.9
over year				
Switch to owner over	4.6	5.4	3.3	3.8
year				
Husband's demographics				
Mean age	42.3	40.8	42.6	40.2
	(10.4)	(10.0)	(10.0)	(8.9)
Mean years of	12.7	13.2	13.6	13.3
completed education	(3.3)	(3.0)	(2.8)	(2.5)
Husband's health care				
coverage (%)				
Some coverage	87.4	93.2	86.1	86.8
Private plan	82.0	91.7	83.7	86.8
Plan in own name	81.5	76.8	80.9	75.5
Plan through own job	74.5	72.1	64.1	66.0
Covered by another	1.6	31.7	5.7	17.0
person's plan				
Military plan	2.1	1.5	2.9	0.0
(CHAMPVA or				
CHAMPUS)				
Government plan	6.0	2.5	1.9	0.0
(Medicaid or				
Medicare)				

(continued)

Table 5 (continued)

Characteristic	No regular job	Only wage and salary	Self-employed Only	Self-employed With wage and salary
Plan through employment for 12 months	64.9	63.2	54.5	58.5
Plan in own name for 12 months	73.4	68.4	72.2	69.8
Husband's employment status (%)				
Employed in regular job	90.1	93.5	96.7	96.2
Only wage and salary	74.3	78.8	45.9	50.9
Only self-employed	11.6	11.2	40.2	18.9
Wage and salary/self-employed	4.3	3.6	11.0	26.4

[a] Characteristics measured for wave 1 reference period unless noted.
[b] Standard deviations are in parentheses.

the wives of higher earners are more likely to choose self-employment, since the earnings of their husbands can be used to smooth consumption and provide financial capital for their businesses. The relatively high level of home ownership and greater age, education, and employment of husbands of self-employed women are also consistent with this hypothesis. These data suggest that husbands of self-employed women are relatively secure.

At the same time, however, self-employed women also have relatively greater dispersion in the distribution of their net household incomes, and their husbands have relatively low health insurance coverage rates (particularly coverage through employment). Moving to the bottom of Table 5, we find the most striking numbers in the table and, therewith, a potential explanation for the variation in household income. More than half of the women who are only self-employed have spouses who are also self-employed, and four out of five of these self-employed husbands are only self-employed. In contrast, just about one out of seven of the husbands of non-employed and wage-and-salary women report any self-employment. The self-employment status of women's husbands is seen to be, by far, the most notable difference between self-employed women and their wage-and-salary and non-employed counterparts. This issue is taken up again below.

SELF-EMPLOYMENT AND WORK SCHEDULES

This section focuses on the relationship between self-employment and work schedules. Several forms of descriptive evidence are considered.

Usual Hours

Usual hours worked per week on all jobs—collected without reference to specific jobs—are summarized by self-employment status in Table 6. Perhaps most striking is the similarity in mean hours across

Table 6 Usual Weekly Work Hours, by Self-Employment Status, Wave 1[a]

| | Only wage and salary | Self-employed | |
		Only	With wage and salary
Mean hours	34.86	34.15	35.83
	(11.40)	(17.97)	(16.82)
Usual schedule (%)			
Under 20 hr.	10.5	19.1	11.3
20–34 hr.	21.1	28.7	37.7
Less than 35 hr.	31.6	47.8	49.1
35 or more hr.	68.5	52.2	50.9
Exactly 35 hr.	5.6	3.3	0.0
35–40 hr.	56.3	25.4	24.5
Exactly 40 hr.	43.1	18.2	17.0
More than 40 hr.	12.1	26.8	26.4
41–59 hr.	10.1	17.7	17.0
60 hours or more	2.0	9.1	9.4
Usually 35+ hours but some part-time	5.4	6.7	5.7
Any part-time	37.0	54.5	54.8
Number of observations	1,744	209	53

[a] Standard deviations are in parentheses.

classifications, but nearly as striking are the contrasts in every other aspect of these hours distributions. Self-employed women are much more likely than wage-and-salary women to report a lot of hours. More than 1 in 4 self-employed women report usual hours above 40, versus less than 1 out of 8 wage-and-salary women. Nearly 1 out of 10 self-employed women reports at least 60 hours, versus just 1 out of 50 of wage-and-salary women. Differences at the low end of the hours distribution are also large. Nearly 1 out of 5 of the only self-employed women reports under 20 hours, versus 1 out of 9 wage-and-salary women. Also note that just 17 to 18 percent of self-employed women report exactly 40 hours, versus 43 percent of their wage-and-salary counterparts.

Perhaps most important is the distinction between part-time and full-time usual hours, because fringe benefits in the wage-and-salary sector generally hinge on full-time status and evidence of a full-time wage differential also exists (e.g., Blank 1990; Nakamura and Nakamura 1983). Using the conventional threshold of 35 hours for full-time status, nearly half of the self-employed women report part-time usual hours, versus less than one-third of the wage-and-salary women.

SIPP also asks workers with full-time usual hours about cutbacks to part-time weeks each month. As shown, similar percentages of the three worker groups report such deviations (about 5 to 7 percent), but these numbers represent very different percentages of full-time workers. More than 1 out of 8 of the self-employed full-time workers report such a deviation, versus 1 out of 12 wage-and-salary full-time workers. Adding these numbers to the percentages with usual part-time hours add yet another perspective. Nearly 55 percent of the self-employed worked part time at least part of the reference period, versus 37 percent of the wage-and-salary women. Women's explanations for their part-time work (not shown here) also differ by self-employment status. While 1 out of 10 wage-and-salary part-timers attributes her part-time hours to insufficient work, just 3 percent of the self-employed part-timers provide this explanation. Reports of part-time work due to insufficient work are actually highest for women with both wage-and-salary employment and self-employment, suggesting that their self-employment could serve primarily as work between wage-and-salary jobs, or vice versa. These women also report more time absent without pay from all jobs.

In sum, the hours data for wave 1 suggest that self-employed and wage-and-salary women have very different usual weekly schedules, that the self-employed are more likely to deviate downward from their usual schedules, and that the self-employed who work part-time on a regular or irregular basis are more likely to work these lower hours by choice.

Self-Employment Dynamics and Usual Hours

Of particular interest is the extent that changes in self-employment status involves changes in hours, and vice versa. Table 7 presents a summary of changes in employment and self-employment status between waves 1 and 2.

Most striking in these transition data is the high level of turnover in self-employment. More than 1 out of 7 of the women who only report self-employment in wave 1 changes status in wave 2, versus just 1 out of 16 wage-and-salary women. Also striking is the incidence of movement in and out of the labor force. Relative to transitions between wage-and-salary employment and self-employment, direct movement in both directions between nonparticipation and self-employment and between nonparticipation and wage-and-salary employment is high.

The right-hand columns of Table 7 present hours changes as shifts between part-time and full-time status. Sample sizes for most transitions severely limit what we can conclude from these data, but several patterns are striking and could be used as a start for further research. First, women who stay self-employed are twice as likely to change part-time status as women who stay in wage-and-salary employment. Nearly 17 percent of the women who stay only self-employed report a change in status between waves 1 and 2, versus 8.4 percent of the women who stay only wage-and-salary employed. Women who move from self-employment to wage-and-salary employment also tend to be either full-time initially and then stay full-time or shift up from part-time status, while women who move in the reverse direction from wage-and-salary employment tend to be part-time and stay part-time. Note, also, that more than three-fourths of self-employed women who leave employment report part-time usual hours in wave 1, versus half of the wage-and-salary women who leave employment, although about

Table 7 Self-Employment and Hours Transitions

Employment class			Hours class		Wave 1 and 2 employment class (%)
Wave 1	Wave 2	Wave 1 employment class (%)	Wave 1	Wave 2	
Only SE[a]	Only SE	85.7			
			PT	PT	36.9
			PT	FT	10.1
			FT	FT	46.4
			FT	PT	6.7
Only SE	Only WS[b]	6.2			
			PT	PT	23.1
			PT	FT	15.4
			FT	FT	53.8
			FT	PT	7.7
Only SE	SE/WS	1.4			
			PT	PT	–
			PT	FT	–
			FT	FT	100.0
			FT	PT	–
Only SE	No job	6.7			
			PT	–	78.6
			FT	–	21.4
Only WS	Only WS	93.6			
			PT	PT	25.6
			PT	FT	4.5
			FT	FT	65.9
			FT	PT	3.9
Only WS	Only SE	0.6			
			PT	PT	72.7
			PT	FT	18.2
			FT	FT	9.1
			FT	PT	0.0
Only WS	WS/SE	0.9			
			PT	PT	12.5
			PT	FT	18.8
			FT	FT	62.5
			FT	PT	6.3

Employment class		Wave 1 employment class (%)	Hours class		Wave 1 and 2 employment class (%)
Wave 1	Wave 2		Wave 1	Wave 2	
Only WS	No job	4.9			
			PT	–	51.2
			PT	–	48.8
SE/W	SSE/WS	73.6			
			PT	PT	30.8
			PT	FT	15.4
			FT	FT	46.2
			FT	PT	7.7
SE/WS	Only SE	9.4			
			PT	PT	42.9
			PT	FT	0.0
			FT	FT	42.9
			FT	PT	14.3
SE/WS	Only WS	13.2			
			PT	PT	40.0
			PT	FT	40.0
			FT	FT	20.0
			FT	PT	0.0
SE/WS	No job	3.8			
			PT	–	50.0
			FT	–	50.0
No job	No job	89.3			
No job	SE	2.2			
			–	PT	54.5
			–	FT	45.5
No job	WS	8.5			
			–	PT	51.7
			–	FT	48.3
No job	WS/SE	0.0			

[a] Self-employed.
[b] Wage and salary.

half of the newly employed report part-time hours, regardless of self-employment status.

A similar hours pattern appears when one measures self-employment status for the year.[13] On average, women who report any self-employment have much greater variation in their hours during the year than women who report only wage-and-salary employment. As found in wave 1, women who report only self-employment are also less likely than wage-and-salary women to report any full-time employment during the year. The full-time women who are only self-employed are also more likely to report part-time deviations than full-time women who are only wage-and-salary employed but are less likely than women who report both types of employment. Most noticeable, however, is the incidence of spells of four-plus months without regular employment—27 percent of the women who only report self-employment, versus 14 to 17 percent of the women who report wage-and-salary employment. The self-employed are much more likely to shift their hours to zero.

In sum, SIPP data suggest that transitions into and out of self-employment are often transitions into and out of part-time employment. This relationship appears whether the origin state (for transitions in) or the destination state (for transitions out) is wage-and-salary employment or no employment. The data indicate that women who stay self-employed change their usual hours more frequently, sometimes by small amounts and sometimes by large amounts. The self-employed also appear more likely to take extended leaves from market work—the biggest kind of schedule change.

Wives' Work Schedules and Husbands' Employment, Self-Employment, and Work

Table 8 presents a summary of husbands' employment and work activity during the first year of the reference period, grouped by wives' employment and self-employment status for the year. As in the wave 1 data, husband activity data for the year indicate that the husbands of self-employed women have more stable employment and work activity than other husbands, but their self-employment status and its relationship to wives' status is even more striking. More than half of the

Table 8 Husband's Self-Employment Status and Labor Market Activity, Year 1[a]

| | Wife's employment status for year 1 | | | |
| | | | Self-employed | |
	No regular job	Only wage and salary	Only	With wage and salary
No regular job (%)	8.6	5.0	2.8	3.0
Regular job (%)	91.4	95.0	97.2	97.0
Husband's labor market time in year 1 (mean % of weeks in activity)	86.7 (31.2)	90.9 (25.3)	95.1 (18.8)	93.4 (20.9)
Regular job (including paid/ unpaid absence)				
Unpaid absence during regular employment	1.2 (5.5)	1.3 (5.6)	0.8 (4.2)	1.3 (5.0)
Looking or layoff when not employed	3.2 (12.6)	3.6 (13.5)	1.9 (10.2)	3.2 (12.5)
No regular labor market activity	10.1 (27.9)	5.6 (20.9)	3.1 (16.1)	3.4 (16.4)
Casual work if not in regular employment	0.6 (5.1)	0.5 (4.2)	0.0 (0.0)	0.9 (6.6)
Total weeks in paid regular employment	85.5	89.6		92.1
Husband's self-employment status (%)				
Only wage and salary	73.7	78.6	45.0	47.8
Only self-employed	9.5	9.7	33.2	23.9
Wage and salary/self-employed	8.3	6.7	19.0	25.4
Number of observations	835	1,878	211	134

[a] Standard deviations are in parentheses.

women who report self-employment during the year have self-employed husbands.

On the one hand, this finding on husband self-employment is surprising. We might expect couples to maintain one relatively steady source of income. On the other hand, self-employed husbands and wives might be able to coordinate their work schedules more easily and more effectively. Self-employment of both spouses might represent a substitution of their time in both market and nonmarket production, and joint ownership and operation of a single business could further enhance such opportunities. Of course, husband and wife time could also be complements in production in business, the home, or both.

Table 9 presents data on the characteristics of self-employed women's main businesses in wave 1. As discussed above, we observe most business characteristics only for women who expect their businesses to gross $1,000 in the following year. As shown, 89.5 percent of the women who report only self-employment and 71.7 percent of the women who also report wage-and-salary employment expect to reach this threshold. All other values in Table 9 pertain to the women with the $1,000-plus expected earnings. The first two columns present data for all of the self-employed women who satisfy the expected earnings criterion. The second pair of columns present data for the husband/wife businesses. The third pair of columns present data for women who do not list their husbands as co-owners of their businesses, or vice versa.

Focusing first on the data for all self-employed women, we observe that not quite one out of four of their businesses is incorporated, just over half are sole proprietorships, and about one-fifth are either described as partnerships or described by husbands as sole proprietorships. The women who also report wage-and-salary employment appear less likely to have incorporated businesses and more likely to be in partnerships. These numbers are roughly consistent with the March Current Population Survey (CPS) data for legal status of longest jobs. Also shown is information on the number of employees for the business, information that is not collected in the CPS or other household surveys for the United States. Here we see substantial heterogeneity. Nearly one-half of the women who are only self-employed employ only themselves, but about one-sixth have five or more employees other than themselves.

Table 9 Business Characteristics, Husband-Wife Ownership, and Husband's Employment, Main Business in Wave 1

Characteristic	All self-employed		Husband/wife business		Wife-owned business	
	Only self	Self/wage and salary	Only self	Self/wage and salary	Only self	Self/wage and salary
Total number of observations	209	53				
Expect revenues for next 12 months above $1,000 (%)	89.5	71.7				
Number of observations for business characteristics	187	38	65	10	122	28
Incorporated (%)	23.0	10.5	49.2	20.0	9.0	7.1
Unincorporated (%)	77.0	89.5	50.8	80.0	91.0	92.9
Sole proprietorship	55.6	50.0	0.0	0.0	85.3	67.9
Partnership	17.7	39.5	40.0	80.0	5.7	25.0
Ownership mix-up by husband	3.7	0.0	10.8	0.0	0.0	0.0
Number of employees (including respondent)						
1	47.6	42.1	1.5	0.0	72.1	57.1
2	16.0	29.0	33.9	60.0	6.6	17.9
3 to 5	19.8	18.4	33.9	20.0	12.3	17.9
6 or more	16.6	10.5	30.8	20.0	9.0	7.1
Co-owned by husband	34.8	26.3	100.0	100.0	0.0	0.0
Husband's employment (%)						
Wage and salary	42.3	44.7	6.2	10.0	61.5	57.1
Only self-employed	42.8	21.1	81.5	30.0	22.1	17.9
Self-employed/ wage and salary	12.3	29.0	12.3	60.0	12.3	17.9
No regular job	2.7	5.3	0.0	0.0	4.1	7.1

Fifty-five percent of the women who are only self-employed and 50 percent of those who also report wage-and-salary employment have self-employed spouses, but not all of these women operate businesses that are co-owned by their husbands. Just over one-third of the women who are only self-employed are self-employed in a husband/wife co-owned business. Some of the husband co-owners are not self-employed at all. Only four out of five of the co-owner husbands report only self-employment. Thus, although most of the joint ownership probably involves some joint operation of a single business, as least some of the joint ownership is simply joint asset ownership. Similar patterns appear for women in husband/wife businesses who also report wage-and-salary employment, but this evidence should be regarded as extremely tentative due to the sample size of 10 observations.

Business characteristics differ dramatically by husband/wife co-ownership. Among women who are only self-employed, 72 percent in wife-owned businesses employ only themselves, while 65 percent of the women in husband/wife owned businesses have three or more employees. Half of the jointly-owned businesses are incorporated, versus just 9 percent of the wife-owned businesses, and very few of the wife-owned businesses are described as partnerships with other persons. Overall, the co-owned businesses appear to be more serious enterprises.

These business characteristics data suggest that we might find differences in work schedules by husband/wife business ownership. Here, in particular, small samples preclude firm conclusions, but some patterns may still be worth noting. On average, wives of self-employed men report more usual hours than either their wage-and-salary counterparts or their self-employed counterparts with wage-and-salary husbands. The latter contrast reflects the very low hours of women in wife-owned businesses with wage-and-salary husbands; the very small number of self-employed women with wage-and-salary husband co-owners actually report a lot of hours, on average. Women who report both wage-and-salary and self-employment also tend to report high hours if their husbands do not have the same status. Employed wives of non-employed men report higher usual hours than wives of wage-and-salary men, but not all wives of self-employed men.

Husbands in nearly every employment category report more hours, on average, than their wives. The one exception is wage-and-salary husbands who co-own businesses operated by their wives. Self-employed men also tend to report more hours than wage-and-salary men, and self-employed husbands of self-employed women who co-own their wives' businesses report the most hours, on average, although one should also note the high variance of hours among the latter group of men in this sample.

Table 10 presents simple correlation coefficients for husband hours and wife hours by self-employment status. The finding of essentially no correlation for the hours of self-employed wives and wage-and-salary husbands reflects the contrast in hours between the wife-owned and husband-wife-owned businesses noted above. In general, these numbers suggest that there is greater correlation between the usual hours of self-employed women and the usual hours of their husbands, particularly when the husbands are also self-employed.

Earnings and Hours

Tables 11 and 12 present earnings for self-employed and wage-and-salary women, respectively. Data on total earnings for the full four-month wave 1 reference period are presented, due to the lack of SIPP data on the timing of work on specific jobs. Women are grouped by expected gross earnings of at least $1,000 versus less, and women with imputed earnings are excluded.

On average, women who are only self-employed tend to report much lower earnings than women who work in the wage-and-salary sector, while women who report both types of employment report the highest total earnings. Among the self-employed, women in incorpo-

Table 10 Correlation of Husband and Wife Usual Hours, by Husband and Wife Self-Employment Status, Wave 1

		Self-employed	
Husband's employment status	Only wage and salary	Only	With wage and salary
Only wage and salary	0.004	−0.046	−0.342
Only self-employed	0.130	0.313	0.474
Self-employed/wage and salary	0.049	0.165	−0.315
Number of observations	1,774	209	53

Table 11 Earnings in Wave 1: Self-Employed Wives[a,b]

	Self-employed	
	Only	With wage and salary
Expect revenues for next 12 months under $1,000		
Mean business earnings net of expenses ($)	131	480
	(151)	(806)
Mean earnings (including net business expenses) ($)	131	2,475
	(151)	(2,212)
Median earnings (net business expenses) ($)	87.5	1,629
Household income (%)	1.7	20.5
Number of observations	22	15
Expect revenues for next 12 months $1,000		
Collect a regular salary (%)	33.0	11.4
Other income for personal use (%)	39.1	45.7
No income for personal use (%)	27.9	42.9
Mean earnings ($)	2,828	6,814
	(4,850)	(9,823)
Median earnings ($)	1,090	4,400
Household income (%)	17.3	38.7
Number of observations	179	35
Incorporated		
Mean earnings ($)	3,625	8,873
	(4,531)	(8,353)
Household income (%)	17.4	57.7
Number of observations	41	4
Unincorporated		
Mean earnings ($)	2,591	6,548
	(4,932)	(10,087)
Household income (%)	17.2	36.3
Number of observations	138	31
Husband/wife owned		
Mean earnings ($)	2,146	4,923
	(3,687)	(2,436}

Table 11 (continued)

	Self-employed	
	Only	With wage and salary
Household income (%)	13.13	51.8
Number of observations	63	9

[a] Reported earnings sample.
[b] Standard deviations are in parentheses.

Table 12 Earnings in Wave 1: Wage-and-Salary Wives[a,b]

	Wage and salary
Mean earnings ($)	4,375
	(3,333)
Median earnings ($)	3,840
Household income (%)	33.2
Number of observations	1,709

[a] Reported earnings sample.
[b] Standard deviations are in parentheses.

rated businesses report the highest earnings, although some part of this differential is probably due to accounting practices.

Particularly striking in Tables 11 and 12 are women's contributions to household income. The earnings of wage-and-salary women represent one-third of their household incomes, on average, and the earnings of women who report both wage-and-salary and self-employment represent nearly two-fifths, on average. In contrast, earnings of the women who are only self-employed represent less than one-fifth, on average. A key factor here is probably the way that earnings are reported in husband/wife-owned businesses. On average, women in husband/wife businesses report earning just 13 percent of total reported household earnings, while inspection of the data reveals that the husbands of these women are often credited with total business income for the period.

Table 13 presents these earnings data grouped by self-employment status and hours. Given all of the issues raised above, interpretation of

Table 13 Earnings in Wave 1, by Self-Employment Status and Hours Status[a,b]

	Wage and salary	Self-employed	
		Only	With wage and salary
All employed women	4,375	2,532	5,512
	(3,333)[b]	(4,653)	(8,508)
Hours class			
Less than 20 hr.	1,193	989	2,626
	(1,065)	(1,947)	(2,105)
20 to 34 hr.	2,530	1,672	3,677
	(2,117)	(2,154)	(4,932)
35 to 40 hr.	5,089	4,614	4,054
	(2,880)	(7,241)	(3,952)
41 to 59 hr.	6,728	2,309	7,891
	(3,531)	(3,991)	(5,296)
60+ hr.	8,536	3,037	14,799
	(7,545)	(4,661)	(22,895)
Usual hours 35+ and some part-time weeks	3,574	2,536	2,273
	(2,135)	(4,074)	(1,502)
Usual hours 35+ and no part-time weeks	5,599	3,703	8,124
	(3,345)	(6,162)	(11,297)
Number of observations	1,709	201	50

[a] Reported earnings sample.
[b] Standard deviations are in parentheses.

these data must be guarded, but a few points stand out. First, women who are only self-employed have mean earnings below their wage-and-salary counterparts in every hours class, but the reverse holds for earnings dispersion for women with less than 60 hours. Second, mean earnings of women who are only self-employed versus only wage-and-salary employed tend to be most similar for those who work low hours (under 20) or standard full-time hours (35–40 per week), but earnings of the self-employed again exhibit much greater variation. Third, women who report both self-employment and wage-and-salary employment tend to earn a lot more than other women. Fourth, mean earnings of full-time self-employed and wage-and-salary women who report some part-time weeks are closer than mean earnings of their counterparts who report no deviations, although earnings of the self-employed are again much lower.

On the one hand, these earnings data suggest that self-employed women may pay a lower part-time penalty than wage-and-salary women. On the other hand, these earnings data seem to suggest that self-employed women who work a lot do not earn a premium. These tentative findings merit further analysis using larger samples than considered here.

CONCLUSION

This analysis of SIPP data stops short of providing direct evidence on the relationship between desires for work schedule flexibility and self-employment decisions. But the evidence presented on usual schedules, deviations from such schedules, changes in schedules, and general reasons for hours and absences exhibits sharp contrasts between self-employed and wage-and-salary women.

Self-employed and wage-and-salary women report very different usual hours of work. Self-employed women rarely report 40 hours as their usual per week, while 40 is the number reported most often by wage-and-salary women. Usual hours of the self-employed are more likely to be very high and even more likely to be very low. Half the self-employed report part-time usual hours, versus less than one-third of the wage-and-salary women. Self-employed women also deviate from their usual schedules somewhat more frequently than wage-and-salary women, either with reduced hours during a workweek or an absence of at least a week, and they change their usual schedules much more often during a single year.

SIPP provides little direct evidence on women's motivation for low usual hours or breaks from regular employment, but the available evidence tends to suggest that choice plays a more important role for self-employed women. Women who are only self-employed are less likely than wage-and-salary women to attribute their part-time hours and schedule variability to insufficient work. It also appears that self-employment may serve a role as work between wage-and-salary jobs for women who report both types of employment; these women are the most likely to attribute short hours to lack of work. All in all, these findings appear consistent with the hypothesis that self-employment gives women more control over their work schedules than wage-and-salary employment.

The data also suggest that self-employment decisions of married women are not independent of their husbands' employment and self-employment decisions. Usual hours of self-employed women are more correlated with the usual hours of their husbands, particularly when their husbands are also self-employed. This correlation suggests that self-employment of one or both spouses improve coordination of work schedules within families. Knowledge of business co-ownership within couples also appears to be important for analysis of schedule data, and even more important for the interpretation of reported earnings within families, relative to time worked. In general, the data suggest that a household framework should be used to study self-employment decisions of both married women and married men.

Notes

The author thanks Alice Nakamura for her many detailed comments on earlier drafts. The research for this paper was conducted primarily while the author was an NIH Fellow at the Population Research Institute of University of Chicago and NORC (1993–95) and a Visiting Scholar at the American Bar Foundation (1995–96). Support from the National Science Foundation (90-23-776, 90-103-07), U.S. Bureau of the Census, American Bar Foundation, Canadian Employment Research Forum, and W.E. Upjohn Institute is gratefully acknowledged. The content of this paper is the responsibility of the author and should not be attributed to the Office for the Public Advocate of New York City or to any funding source.

1. Self-employment rates are based on what workers report for their longest jobs in the reference years for the 1976–1991 March Current Population Surveys. The self-employment rate is defined here as the percentage of employed persons who are self-employed, counting both those with the incorporated and unincorporated businesses. Note also that this chapter focuses exclusively on activity during prime-age, which is defined here as ages 25 to 55. The self-employment rate for prime-age married men also increased during the 1975–1990 period, but only from 14.1 to 15.3 percent. An increase in the male nonagricultural self-employment rate from 12.1 to 14.8 percent was offset by a large drop in the agricultural self-employment rate from 62.4 to 51.3 percent. Among prime-age married women, the agricultural self-employment rate actually rose from 9.8 percent to 33.5 percent, and the nonagricultural rate rose from 5.6 to 9.1. The large increase

in female agricultural self-employment may partially reflect a change in farm women's perception of their contribution to farm production. See Devine (1990, 1994) for discussion of nonagricultural self-employment trends and characteristics of the self-employed. Aronson (1991) also provided a survey of the topic of self-employment.

2. See Devine (1992) for a simple but more formal model of household self-employment choice based on this reasoning. Lombard (1996) and Rettenmaier (1996) presented similar models of individual self-employment decisions.

3. Dates for wage-and-salary work are also incomplete. In general, side jobs and sequential jobs, whether or not they involve self-employment, cannot be distinguished for any of the SIPP panels. Like all longitudinal data sets, SIPP also has "seam" problems—a disproportionate incidence of changes in status between the last and first days of consecutive reference periods.

4. The fact that these data may be missing is not clear in either the data documentation or the raw data. If unfamiliar with the interview skip patterns, a user could easily misinterpret zeros that appear in the data file.

5. Not too many cases are affected this way, but they represent a significant portion of the available sample of household businesses and an important part of female self-employment.

6. The public use data files include self-employment monthly earnings for these respondents based on census calculations, as opposed to respondents' reports.

7. Imputation rates are much higher in the March CPS. Problems with imputation flags prevent exact measurement, but a reasonable estimate is about one-third of self-employment earnings observations and about 20 percent of the wage-and-salary observations (Devine 1995).

8. SIPP also collects information on profits (as a business characteristic), but only for unincorporated businesses, only if expected revenues are at least $1,000, only once per household business, only if the respondent describing the business "can" provide the information, and only if the respondent wants to report it. These profit data are not used here.

9. The present discussion pertains to self-employment data in the public-use rectangular Microdata files. The Full Panel Longitudinal File is used here only for the measurement of demographic and household characteristics; data on labor market activity in the Longitudinal File are problematic due to time aggregation and disaggregation, editing, and omitted variables. See Devine (1991, 1993) for additional discussion.

10. Women who report casual work are not counted as employed if this is their only work. The distinction between regular work and casual work for pay (as it is called in the documentation, but not interview) is not clear from the questionnaires or interviewer manuals. We only know that respondents do not mention it when they are asked if they had "a job or business, either full-time or part-time, even for only a few days" (Question 1 in the Labor Force and Recipiency section of the interview). For our purposes, the most important difference is information.

We know which months casual work is performed, but nothing more about this work. Casual work is ignored beyond this point in the present study.

11. These self-employment rates are quite close to the self-employment rates from the March CPS that are presented in Figure 1. The greater amount of labor market activity data collected in SIPP could be the source of the slightly higher rates in SIPP.

12. The children variables used here are not the standard measures based on children in the household. Parent identification numbers were first used to match children to their designated parents or guardians, and these family units were then united with the spouses of the designated parents and guardians. It is possible that some spouses are not guardians of the children. The assumption here is that these spouses have at least as much responsibility for the children as the level of responsibility implicitly assumed for standard measures of children in the family or household.

13. These tables are available on request.

14. When preparing tax returns in the United States, most corporation owners treat their own salaries as explicit expenses for their businesses, while owners of unincorporated businesses generally do not distinguish salaries paid to themselves from business earnings net of other business expenses. So, for example, business losses would be reported by a corporation owner as losses for the corporation, but as negative income for the unincorporated business owner. See Devine (1995) for additional discussion.

References

Altonji, Joseph G., and Christina Paxson. 1988. "Labor Supply, Preferences, Hours Constraints, and Hours-Wage Trade-Offs." *Journal of Labor Economics* 6(2): 254–276.

———. 1992. "Labor Supply, Hours Constraints, and Job Mobility." *Journal of Human Resources* 27(2): 256–278.

Aronson, Robert L. 1991. *Self-Employment.* Ithaca, New York: ILR Press.

Blank, Rebecca M. 1990. "Are Part-Time Jobs Bad Jobs?" In *A Future of Lousy Jobs? The Changing Structure of U.S. Wages,* Gary Burtless, ed. Washington, D.C.: The Brookings Institution: pp. 123–164.

———, 1994. "The Dynamics of Part-Time Work." Working paper no. 4911, National Bureau of Economic Research, Washington, D.C.

Devine, Theresa J. 1990. "The Recent Rise in Female Self-Employment." Working paper, Pennsylvania State University, University Park, Pennsylvania.

———. 1991. "Job Exits and Job-to-Job Transitions: The Potential of SIPP for Empirical Analysis." 1991 Annual Research Conference Proceedings, U.S. Bureau of the Census.

———. 1992. "Compensation Composition and Household Self-Employment Decisions." Working paper, Pennsylvania State University, University Park, Pennsylvania.

———. 1993. "Measurement of Job Exits: What Difference Does Ambiguity Make?" In *Labour Market Dynamics*, Niels Westergaard-Nielsen, Henning Bunzel, and Peter Jensen, eds. London: North-Holland.

———. 1994. "Characteristics of Self-Employed Women in the United States." *Monthly Labor Review* 117(3): 20.

———. 1995. "CPS Earnings Data for the Self-Employed: Words of Caution on Use and Interpretation." *Journal of Economic and Social Measurement* 21(3): 213–248.

Lang, Kevin, and Shulamit Kahn. 2001. "Hours Constraints: Theory, Evidence, and Policy Implications." In *Working Time in Comparative Perspective*, Vol. I, Ging Wong and Garnett Picot, eds. Kalamazoo, Michigan: W.E. Upjohn Institute for Employment Research, pp. xx.

Lombard, Karen V. 1996. "Female Self-Employment and the Demand for Flexible, Non-Standard Work Schedules." Working paper, University of Miami, Coral Gables, Florida.

Nakamura, Alice, and Masao Nakamura. 1983. "Part-Time and Full-Time Work Behavior of Married Women." *Canadian Journal of Economics* 16(May): 229–257.

Rettenmaier, Andrew J. 1996. "A Little or a Lot: Self-Employment and Hours of Work." Working paper, Private Enterprise Center, Texas A&M University, College Station, Texas.

9
Work Site and Work Hours
The Labor Force Flexibility of
Home-Based Female Workers

Linda N. Edwards
The Graduate Center, City University of New York

Elizabeth Field-Hendrey
Queens College and *The Graduate Center,*
City University of New York

The postwar period has seen a steady, almost inexorable rise in the labor force participation rates of women, from 32.7 percent in 1948 to 58.9 percent in 1995 (U.S. President 1996, Table B-35). Nonetheless, women are still largely responsible for the care of family and home. This "second shift" adds about 20 hours to the total weekly work hours of women who are in the labor force, in contrast to just seven hours for comparable men (Hersch and Stratton 1994). The multiple responsibilities of employed women translate into a need for greater flexibility in all aspects of the employment arrangement. Indeed, in a recent survey of employees concerning their child and elder care responsibilities, work flexibility was a factor that significantly reduced the stress associated with performing their dual roles of earner and caretaker (Neal et al. 1993).

One way women achieve flexibility is by choosing to work shorter than usual weekly hours (part-time) or fewer than usual weeks per year (part-year). There are a number of papers that focus on women's part-time work and on variations in weeks worked (for example, Blank 1988, 1990; Sundt 1989; and Averett and Hotchkiss 1996, 1997). However, there is another important dimension of flexibility in the employment arrangement that has not been extensively explored—work location. Women have the option of choosing to work at home rather than at another location. In this chapter we analyze the determinants of a woman's work site and explore the relationship between her choice of work site and work hours. In particular, we explore how labor force choices, work hours, and workweeks differ between women whose primary place of work is their own home—home-based workers—and women who work at an office or other place of business outside of the home—on-site workers—using data from the 1990 Public Use Microdata Samples (PUMS) of the Census of Population.

Although there are not at present a large number of people engaged primarily in home-based work, this type of work organization has been on the rise and is likely to continue to increase. Contributing to this trend are the steady improvements in both communication and computing technology, the continued rise in women's labor force participation and in two-career families, and the increased popularity of small business entrepreneurship. Data from the U.S. Censuses of Population show that the declining trend in the number of home-based workers from 1960 to 1980 was reversed in 1990, from 4.7 million in 1960, to 2.2 million in 1980, to 3.4 million in 1990. This represents an increase from 2.4 percent of the labor force in 1980 to 3.0 percent in 1990.[1]

An important reason why this type of work organization is attractive to women who desire greater flexibility is that the fixed costs of working, such as the time and out-of-pocket costs of commuting to work, are lower for home-based work than for on-site work. In addition, to the extent that female home-based workers provide their own child care, the marginal costs of home-based work may also be lower. These factors imply that both the reservation wage and the reservation hours for home-based and on-site work will differ, and also that the responsiveness of women's labor supply to wage changes and to variations in other socioeconomic factors will differ between home-based and on-site workers.[2]

In fact, our estimates of the effects of such fixed costs on the probability of labor force participation do differ dramatically between home-based and on-site workers. In particular, factors that are associated with higher fixed costs of working on site tend to have a smaller deterrent effect on home-based labor force participation than on on-site participation, confirming the importance of these costs. When we examine equations predicting weekly hours and annual weeks worked for each work site, we also find significant differences. The net effect of these differences is that home-based workers are predicted to work on average fewer annual hours (both average weeks worked and average weekly hours are reduced) and that the dispersion of their predicted work hours is greater as compared to what they would be for on-site workers. This greater dispersion of predicted work hours for home-based workers indicates that they are better able to adapt their work schedules in response to variations in family circumstances. Overall, our results affirm the proposition that home-based work is an attractive and viable alternative for women who need a flexible employment arrangement to overcome their high fixed-costs of labor force entry.

HOW DO HOME-BASED FEMALE WORKERS DIFFER FROM OTHERS?

Table 1 presents the demographic and socioeconomic characteristics of home-based and on-site female workers and of women out of the labor force as computed from the 5 percent Public Use Microdata Sample (PUMS) of housing units from the 1990 Census of Population of the United States.[3] Included in our analysis are all women aged 25 to 55 years who were either employed or out of the labor force, who did not live in group quarters, who were not in the Armed Forces, and who were not in school.[4] Identification of home-based workers is derived from answers to the journey to work question (no. 23A), which asks, "How did this person usually get to work last week?"[5] Persons who responded that they "worked at home" are regarded as home-based workers. This means that our sample of home-based workers includes only those who worked primarily at home; women who work mainly on-site but do some work at home (like teachers, for example) are not classified in this study as home-based workers. We focus on workers in the prime working years, 25 to 55, so as not to confuse the work site decision with decisions regarding schooling and retirement. The majority of those in the 25- to 55-year age-group will have completed their schooling and will not yet have entered retirement. To obtain approximately equal sample sizes for all three groups, we include in our analysis all observations of home-based female workers from the 5 percent PUMS, while for women who are on-site workers or

Table 1 Socioeconomic Characteristics of Women Aged 25–55, by Work Status and Work Site[a,b]

Variable	Home-based workers	On-site workers	Out of labor force
Age distribution			
25–34 yr.	34.5	38.2	38.3
35–44 yr.	37.4	36.1	31.2
45–55 yr.	28.1	25.7	30.4
Mean age	39.01	38.25	38.90
	(8.19)	(8.37)	(8.95)
Married, spouse present	80.4	63.5	75.9
With children under 6 yr.	29.9	15.1	29.7
With children 6–17 yr.	43.10	30.0	38.6
Not married or married without spouse present	19.60	36.5	24.1
With children under 6 yr.	1.60	2.9	5.2
With children 6–17 yr.	4.10	8.9	8.6
White, non-Hispanic	88.40	78.4	73.7
Black, non-Hispanic	3.50	11.7	11.5
Other race	2.90	3.6	4.4
Hispanic origin	5.30	6.3	10.4
Disabled	5.00	2.8	16.5
Urban residence	68.00	76.7	72.8
Rural residence	32.00	23.3	27.2
Farm	6.00	1.1	1.6
Nonfarm	26.00	22.2	25.6
Immigrant	8.00	9.3	14.1
Highest level of education completed			
Eighth grade or less	3.30	2.8	10.0
Some high school	8.30	8.9	19.6
High school degree	32.90	33.7	36.2
Some college	31.50	30.5	22.0
Bachelor's degree	17.70	16.1	9.4

Variable	Home-based workers	On-site workers	Out of labor force
More than Bachelor's degree	4.80	6.1	2.2
Mean years of schooling completed	13.38 (2.46)	13.40 (2.45)	12.01 (3.03)
Presence of person(s) over 65 in household	5.00	5.2	6.2
Mean family income ($)	50,787 (45,623)	46,222 (33,234)	38,804 (39,626)
Self-employed (%)	62.9	3.3	—
Mean annual earnings, 1989 ($)	10,273 (14,234)	18,469 (13,970)	—
Weekly hours worked			
Fewer than 35 hr.	42.0	20.8	—
35–45 hr.	36.0	69.2	—
More than 45 hr.	22.1	10.1	—
Mean hours worked per week, 1989	35.12 (17.34)	37.93 (10.52)	—
Mean weeks worked, 1989	43.53 (13.23)	46.59 (10.62)	—
Mean hourly wage, 1989[c] ($)	7.91 (13.38)	10.57 (9.03)	—
Spouse is a home-based worker (%)	11.3	1.0	1.6
Spouse has mobility or personal care limitations (%)	1.6	2.0	3.5
Number in sample	48,181 (100%)	60,983 (100%)	25,763 (100%)

[a] The information in this table is computed from the 5% PUMS sample of the 1990 Census of Population and Housing. Workers in group quarters or institutions are excluded, as are those who report themselves as home-based during the Census week, but did not work in 1989. In addition, workers whose earnings information for 1989 was not consistent with their reported class-of-worker status (self-employed v. employee) in 1990 are excluded. The data for home-based workers are from the full 5% sample; the data for on-site workers are based on 0.04 sub-sample of the 5% sample (yielding a 0.002 sample of the on-site worker population).

[b] Standard deviations are in parentheses.

[c] Computed from annual earnings, weeks, and hours worked for 1989.

who are out of the labor force, we take a 0.04 subsample of the 5 percent PUMS, yielding a 0.2 percent sample of the population of on-site female workers and women out of the labor force.

Home-based female workers differ from on-site workers in critical ways. The two most striking differences are with respect to self-employment and work intensity (hours and weeks worked). Home-based workers are much more likely to be self-employed than are their on-site counterparts: 62.9 percent of the former are self-employed, whereas the corresponding value for the latter is 3.3 percent. Home-based workers are also much more likely to choose unusual work schedules, both with respect to weekly hours worked and weeks worked per year. The mean weekly hours worked by home-based workers is about three hours less than for on-site workers, but the distribution of hours differs much more dramatically, as can be seen by comparing the standard deviations of work hours: 17.34 for home-based workers versus 10.52 for on-site workers. Put differently, about two-thirds of on-site workers work between 35 and 45 hours per week, while only about one-third of home-based workers follow this common full-time schedule. Indeed, our data indicate that over 50 percent of on-site workers worked a standard 40-hour week, while only about one-quarter of home-based workers did so. Thus, it is clear that there is a much greater degree of hours flexibility for women who work at home as compared to those who work on-site. Home-based workers also exhibit greater flexibility with regard to weeks worked per year. As was the case for weekly hours worked, mean weeks worked per year is lower and the variance is greater for home-based workers as compared to on-site workers. For example, both on-site and home-based women specify 52 weeks per year as their most frequent choice, but only 48 percent of home-based workers choose 52 weeks, as compared to 64 percent of on-site workers.

Home-based female workers differ from their on-site counterparts in other significant ways. Home-based workers are much more likely to have a spouse who is also a home-based worker and to live in rural and rural-farm areas. Further, home-based female workers are more likely than are on-site workers to be married with a spouse present, to have children under the age of 18 years, and to be disabled. The family income of home-based workers is higher than that of on-site workers (whether or not their own earnings are included), though the average hourly earnings of home-based workers are lower. Finally, the representation of nonwhites and Hispanics among home-based workers is less than their representation in the labor force at large.[6]

MODELING THE LABOR FORCE PARTICIPATION DECISION

Theoretical Issues

The most important difference between home-based work and on-site work is that the fixed costs associated with working (time costs associated with commuting, out-of-pocket commuting expenditures, clothing costs, and, to some extent, the costs of child [or other dependent] care[7]) are greatly reduced for home-based workers.[8] The model developed by Cogan (1981), which focuses on the role of fixed costs in labor force decisions, provides an appropriate starting point. Cogan shows that the existence of time fixed costs and money fixed costs of working raise the reservation wage relative to what it would be in the absence of these costs. The lower fixed costs of home-based work, therefore, imply that workers will have a lower reservation wage for home-based work than for on-site work.

Applying this model directly to the case of home-based work, however, has one important drawback. The model implies that at any given wage rate, a worker's utility will be higher in home-based work than in on-site work, suggesting that most workers would choose home-based work over on-site work. However, we know from the census data that most workers are not home-based. The likely explanation for this apparent contradiction is that the demand for home-based workers is low relative to the demand for on-site workers and relative to the supply of people who would like to do home-based work, so that rather than the wage offer for such work being the same as for on-site work, it is substantially below.

There are several reasons why employers will make lower wage offers for home-based jobs. First, home-based jobs may simply not be available in certain types of industries—those that require large amounts of fixed capital or require workers to be on-site, for example.

Heavy manufacturing, retail trade, and elementary and secondary schooling are examples. Second, a worker's marginal product may be lower in home-based work because of synergies between workers. Third, a worker's marginal product may be lower at home because of a lack of monitoring or supervision. Finally, employers may simply hold a belief (or suspicion) that a worker's marginal product is lower when she is at home than when she is on site, possibly because of the difficulty in monitoring home-based employees.

Thus, a more appropriate model assumes a lower wage for home-based work than for on-site work, as is illustrated in Figure 1. In this diagram, V represents unearned income, T represents the total time available, M represents the monetary fixed cost of working on-site (e.g., commuting costs), and K represents the time costs of working on-site (e.g., commuting time). The (monetary and time) fixed costs of

Figure 1 Diagrammatic Model of Work Site Choice

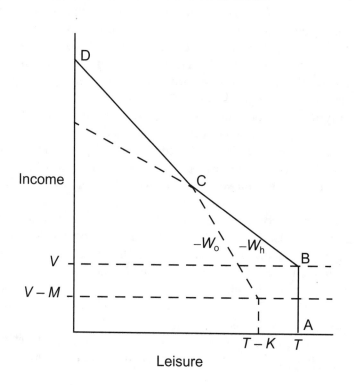

home-based work are assumed to be zero. W_h and W_o represent the offering wages for home-based and on-site work, respectively, and the budget constraint is ABCD. Depending on the woman's indifference map, she may locate at point B and be out of the labor force, locate on the segment BC and be a home-based worker, or locate on the segment CD and be an on-site worker. As in the case with Cogan's model, the reservation wage and reservation hours will be lower for home-based work than for on-site work. However, this diagram makes clear the role of fixed costs in the choice between home-based and on-site work: the larger the fixed costs, the further to the left will be the on-site segment of the budget constraint (CD), and the less likely will a person with a given indifference map find it optimal to be on the on-site segment. Similarly, the lower the on-site wage relative to the home-based wage, the less likely is one to choose on-site work over home-based work.

To summarize, the implications of this model are as follows. Fixed costs of working are directly related to a worker's reservation wage and reservation hours. Consequently, a worker's reservation wage and reservation hours for work arrangements that require lower fixed costs, like home-based work, will be lower than for arrangements that require higher fixed costs, like on-site work. Thus, factors that increase a woman's fixed costs of working will be positively related to the likelihood that she will be in the labor force as a home-based worker rather than as an on-site worker. We also expect to observe that for women with a given set of socioeconomic characteristics, her choice of hours as a home-based worker will be lower than as an on-site worker. Further, to the extent that home-based female workers—more than half of whom are self-employed—are less likely than on-site workers to be affected by institutional constraints on work hours or workweeks, we expect them to exhibit greater variability in work hours and workweeks.

The Econometric Model

Our econometric model has four components. The first is a labor force participation equation. The second is a pair of wage equations that predict the "offering wage" a woman can expect for home-based work and for on-site work. The third component is a pair of equations to predict her hours of work, conditional on her choice of labor force state. The last component is a pair of equations predicting weeks worked per year, again conditional on her choice of labor force state. It is assumed that the choice of work site, obtained by maximizing the indirect utility function, is predicated on the woman's having identified the optimal number of work hours associated with each work site.

The empirical model employed here is similar to that used in Hutchens, Jakubson, and Schwartz (1989), Blank (1990), and Hill (1989). The three work states from which women are assumed to choose are

State number   Description

1   Out of the labor force
2   On-site worker
3   Home-based worker

Following Hutchens, Jakubson, and Schwartz, we assume that a woman's utility function can be written as

(1) $U = U(C, L, Z)$,

where C is consumption, L is leisure, and Z is a vector of individual characteristics that affect preferences. The woman will choose the state k which maximizes her utility subject to a budget constraint of the form

(2) $C_k + W_k L_k \leq N + W_k (L^* - L^*_k) - FC_k$, $k = 1,2,3$,

where W_k is the wage rate in work state k, N is nonlabor income, L^* is the total time available to divide between work and leisure, L_k is leisure time in work state k, L^*_k is the reduction in available time associated with work state k (the fixed time costs associated with that work state), and FC_k represents the monetary fixed costs of working in state k. Like Hutchens, Jakubson, and Schwartz (1989), we have normalized the consumption price to 1. As discussed earlier, W_k, L^*_k, and FC_k are assumed to vary with work site.

Let $T_k \equiv (\ln W_k, L^*_k, FC_k)$. The woman's problem is to choose the state k which maximizes her indirect utility function, written as

(3) $V_k = V(T_k|\mathbf{Z})$.

This formulation assumes that an individual's characteristics, $\mathbf{Z}$, are constant across work states (for example, her nonlabor income,[9] presence of preschool children, race, etc). Again following Hutchens, Jakubson, and Schwartz (1989), we assume that the indirect utility function of individual i can be written as the sum of a deterministic part involving T_k, $\mathbf{Z}$, and a stochastic error term and that the deterministic portion of the function is linear

(4) $V_{ik} = \beta_{1k} L_{ik}{}^* + \beta_{2k} FC_{ik} + \beta_{3k} \ln W_{ik} + \mathbf{Z}_i \alpha_k + u_{ik}, \quad k = 1,2,3.$

To estimate Eq. 4 directly, we would need, for each work state, measures of the wage rate and of the monetary and time fixed costs of working. Since estimates of the latter two factors are not available, we substitute for them using the following predicting equations:

(5) $L_{ik}{}^* = U_i \rho_k + e_{1ik}$

(6) $FC_{ik} = U_i \theta_k + e_{2ik},$

where U_i is a vector of predicting variables, some of which may be contained in $\mathbf{Z}_i$. Substituting these into Eq. 4 gives us

(7) $V_{ik} = \beta_{3k} \ln W_{ik} + X_i \gamma_k + v_{ik},$

where X_i is the union of U_i and $\mathbf{Z}_i$; $\gamma_k = \alpha_k + \beta_{1k} \rho_k + \beta_{2k} \theta_k$, α_k is redefined to include zero coefficients for the variables in U_i which are not contained in $\mathbf{Z}_i$, and

(7a) $v_{ik} = \beta_{1k} e_{1ik} + \beta_{2k} e_{2ik} + u_{ik}.$

Further, since we do not have measures of the wage in each labor force state (women are observed in one state only), we predict these wages from estimates of the following equation:

(8) $\ln W_{ik} = Y_i \delta_k + e_{3ik}, \quad k = 2,3,$

where Y_i represents a vector of variables that may overlap X_i. Since Eq. 8 can be estimated only for those women who are actually in the relevant labor force state, the error terms do not satisfy the requirement that their expected value be zero. We adjust for potential selectivity bias by including a selectivity correction factor λ_{ik} as an explanatory variable in Eq. 8.[10] The resulting version of Eq. 8 is estimated with ordinary least sources (OLS), with the standard errors corrected according to the procedure outlined in Lee (1983). Using estimates of Eq. 8, we predict a home-based and on-site wage for each woman in the sample. We then substitute these predicted wages into Eq. 7 to obtain the following "structural" labor force participation equation,

(9) $V_{ik} = \beta_{3k} \ln W_{ik}^* + X_i \gamma_k + v_{ik},$

where $\ln W_{ik}^*$ is the predicted offering wage for woman i in labor force state k.[11]

We estimate the model in Eq. 9, as well as the reduced form version of that equation (used to estimate λ_{ik}), using multinomial logit (see Maddala 1983). Note that instruments for all labor force states are included in the equations for each state. In this way, our econometric model resembles what Hutchens, Jakubson, and Schwartz (1989) refer to as the "universal logit" model. That is, the entire set of variables used to predict the fixed costs and the offering wage for both work states enter the logit function for each work state, and a different set of coefficients is estimated (on the common set of variables) for each work state. The resulting estimates of these coefficients are not affected by the nature of the error structure across labor force states.[12] The fundamental assumption required for this approach is that all of the labor force options are in principle available to all participants.[13]

Finally, we estimate equations to predict hours worked per week and weeks worked per year, conditional on the choice of labor force state. The equation for hours is

(10) $h_{ik} = X_i \eta_k + \zeta_k \ln W_{ik}^* + \xi_k \lambda_{ik} + e_{4ik}, \quad k = 2,3,$

and for weeks,

(11) $w_{ik} = X_i \psi_k + \omega_k \ln W_{ik}^* + \pi_k \lambda_{ik} + e_{5ik}, \quad k = 2,3.$

Eq. 10 is estimated with OLS using the relevant predicted wage and including the relevant selectivity correction factor, and the OLS standard errors are appropriately corrected (Lee 1983).[14] Eq. 11 is estimated using a tobit model because of the clustering of observations at the upper limit of 52 weeks worked per year.[15]

Explanatory Variables

All of the variables described below are listed in Appendix Table 1 with their precise definitions.

Choice of labor force state

Explanatory variables used in the multinomial logit estimates of the choice of labor force state (Eq. 9) are similar to those used in other studies of women's labor supply,[16] but are tailored to fit our focus on work site. They include unearned income, a set of variables to represent home productivity and tastes, a set of variables to proxy the fixed time and money costs of working on site, and the predicted wage in each labor force state.

The variables that represent unearned income and home productivity and tastes are as follows. For unearned income, we use family income less the earnings of the worker (OTHINC). To proxy differences in home productivity and tastes we include the woman's years of schooling (EDUC), her age (AGE), dummy variables that indicate whether she is married with spouse present (MSP), whether she has any children under 6 at home (CU6), whether she has any children between 6 and 17 at home (C617), whether there is someone over 65 in the household (OVER65), whether the woman has a disability that limits the kind or amount of work she can perform (DISAB), whether she is non-Hispanic black (BLACKNH), and whether she is a black or white Hispanic or of another nonwhite race (HISP&OTH) (the excluded class is non-Hispanic white). One additional measure included to represent a woman's home productivity is her husband's wage (S_WAGE) (if she has a spouse present). The higher the husband's wage (which is a measure of his cost of time), the less likely he will contribute to home production and the higher will be the woman's productivity at home.

The proxy measures that index the fixed costs of working on site include some of the home productivity variables described above as well as additional measures. The presence of young children in the household (CU6) is associated with a higher fixed cost of working on site, as is the presence of a disability (DISAB). The presence of older children (C617) or persons over 65 (OVER65) may be associated with either higher or lower fixed costs, depending on whether the older children or older persons in the household require care themselves or are providers of care for young children. Additional fixed cost variables are dummy variables that indicate whether the woman's husband has a mobility or personal care disability (if she has a spouse present) (S_LIM) and whether or not the woman lives in a rural (RURAL) or a rural-farm (FARM) locality. Women living in rural or rural farm areas will experience higher fixed costs of working on site because commuting time to work is likely to be greater in these locales than in urban areas. All of these fixed cost measures are predicted to have a larger deterrent effect on on-site labor force participation than on home-based labor force participation.

Two predicted wage measures are included in the labor force participation equations: the predicted log of the woman's wage in home-based work (LNWPREDH) and her predicted log wage in on-site work (LNWPREDO).[17] We expect LNWPREDH to be positively related to the odds of being a home-based worker and negatively related to the odds of being an on-site worker, and we expect the opposite relationships for LNWPREDO.

In addition to the predicted wage, there is another aspect of compensation that needs to be included in the labor force participation equations: nonwage compensation. An important difference between home-based and on-site work is that home-based workers—who are more likely to be part-time and to be self-employed—are less likely to receive fringe benefits as part of their compensation than are on-site workers.[18] However, the value they will place on any fringe benefits received on their job will depend on whether or not they already receive these benefits through a spouse. To hold constant differences in how women value nonwage compensation we include several proxy variables. MSP will partially capture the likelihood that a woman is receiving fringe benefits through her spouse, as will a dummy variable indicating whether or not the husband received any wage and salary income in the previous year (S_EMP), since a husband with wage and salary income in the previous year is more likely to have received fringe benefits on the job. In addition, the husband's wage (S_WAGE) will be positively correlated with his probability of receipt of fringe benefits.

Finally, we include a dummy variable indicating whether the spouse is a home-based worker (S_HW). This variable may be positively or negatively related to the odds that a woman is a home-based worker. If the couple is engaged jointly in a home-based small business so that there are synergies between the work of the spouses, this variable will be positively related to the odds of being a home-based worker and negatively related to the odds that the woman is an on-site worker. On the other hand, if this variable is a proxy for the husband's (non)receipt of fringe benefits on his job, then it will be negatively related to the odds that the woman is a home-based worker and positively related to her odds of being an on-site worker.

The Conditional Hours and Weeks Equations

The conditional hours worked and weeks worked equations (Eqs. 10 and 11) include most of the same variables discussed above. There are, however, several differences. First, since these equations are conditional on the woman's having chosen the specified work site, we include only the wage specific to that work site. Second, to adjust for the potential selectivity bias we include in each equation the appropriate selectivity adjustment variable (LAMBDAH when the hours or weeks worked of home-based workers are being estimated, and LAMBDAO when the corresponding equations are being estimated for on-site workers), computed from the reduced form logit estimates of the choice of labor force state. Third, three spouse variables that are most relevant for choosing work site rather than hours are excluded from the hours equation: S_LIM, S_EMP, and S_HW. Finally, to allow for the possibility that the wage/hours and wage/weeks relationships can be positive, negative, or can vary in sign over the range of values of the wage, we include in addition to the predicted log wage variable, a squared term of the predicted wage (LNWPREDO2 or LNWPREDH2).

RESULTS

Estimates of the labor force participation equations appear in Table 2, while estimates of the hours worked and weeks worked equations appear in Table 4. (Estimates of the reduced form logits used to obtain the selectivity adjustments are shown in Appendix Table 2.) Because home-based workers are oversampled relative to on-site workers and to those out of the labor force and because the sampling procedure used in the PUMS is not simple random sampling, we use weights in obtaining all of our estimates.[19]

Labor Force Participation Equations

To make the coefficients easier to interpret, rather than presenting logit coefficients in Table 2, we present estimates of the marginal effects of each dependent variable on the probability that an average woman will be in each of the three labor force states (the logit coefficients from which these marginal effects are computed appear in Appendix Table 3). These marginal effects are computed at the overall sample mean values.[20] By construction, the coefficients in the three columns sum to zero (except for rounding error).

In the "On-site employment" column, marginal effects of the independent variables on the probability of on-site labor force participation are very similar to those in other studies of women's labor force participation (in which estimates are dominated by on-site workers, who greatly outweigh home-based workers). Women's on-site labor force participation is positively related to their education and expected wage, and negatively related to their age, their being married with a spouse present, their having children at home, and their having higher unearned income.

Our focus, however, is on showing how women's labor force decisions differ by work site, and the estimates in Table 2 illustrate that these differences are significant in both a statistical and economic sense. First, there is a significant difference in the set of logit coefficients on which the on-site and home-based employment columns are based; that is, the factors that affect the labor force participation decision have significantly different impacts on the two work-site choices. Second, the individual logit coefficients of most of the variables differ

Table 2 Marginal Effects of the Explanatory Variables on the Probability of Being on Each Work State—Structural Model[a]

Variable	Out of the labor force	On-site employment	Home-based employment
Constant[b]	0.148 (11.42)**[c]	−0.069 (−5.30)**	−0.078 (−14.83)**
AGE[b]	0.005 (26.35)**	−0.005 (−26.91)**	−0.0002 (−1.95)
EDUC[b]	−0.011 (−10.09)**	0.012 (10.44)**	−0.001 (−1.76)
MSP[b]	0.127 (23.71)**	−0.130 (−23.84)**	0.003 (0.87)
CU6[b]	0.227 (59.39)**	−0.238 (65.57)**	0.011 (2.12)*
C617[b]	0.039 (14.40)**	−0.042 (−15.45)**	0.003 (3.23)**
BLACKNH [b]	−0.012 (−2.44)*	0.027 (5.38)**	−0.015 (−7.65)**
HISPOTH	0.005 (1.14)	−0.004 (−0.82)	−0.001 (−0.95)
DISAB[b]	0.299 (43.25)**	−0.311 (−48.02)**	0.012 (1.74)
RURAL	−0.013 (−3.85)**	0.011 (3.36)**	0.001 (1.36)
FARM[b]	0.010 (0.92)	−0.020 (−1.70)	0.009 (4.42)**
OVER65	0.016 (2.79)**	−0.017 (−2.94)**	0.001 (0.76)
OTHINC[b]	0.002 (41.74)**	−0.003 (−45.04)**	0.0001 (2.43)*
S_LIM[b]	0.016 (2.00)*	−0.010 (−1.17)	−0.006 (−2.20)*
S_HW[b]	0.058 (5.23)**	−0.094 (−8.33)**	0.036 (19.60)**
S_WAGE	0.000 (2.84)**	−0.0002 (−2.15)*	−0.00004 (−0.53)

(continued)

Table 2 (continued)

Variable	Out of the labor force	On-site employment	Home-based employment
S_EMPL[b]	−0.076 (−16.94)**	0.082 (17.79)**	−0.005 (−2.54)*
LNWPREDO[b]	−0.479 (−23.94)**	0.444 (21.53)**	0.035 (2.75)**
LNWPREDH[b]	0.189 (12.82)**	−0.160 (−10.60)**	−0.029 (−4.59)**
Log likelihood		−79,280.01	

[a] t-statistics are in parentheses and are corrected for the preestimated selectivity correction. Marginal effects are computed at the means of the overall sample from the logit coefficients in Appendix Table 3. Estimates are weighted to adjust for choice-based sampling and the nonrandom nature of the 1990 PUMS.

[b] Variable has significantly different logit coefficients between the two work sites at the 5% level.

[c] * = significant at the 5% level in a two-tailed test.
   ** = significant at the 1% level in a two-tailed test.

significantly between the two work sites (variables with significantly different coefficients are indicated in Table 2 by the subscript letter "b"). Further, as was hypothesized, variables associated with the fixed costs of working on site tend to have significantly greater deterrent effects on on-site labor force participation than on home-based labor-force participation. Being disabled is associated with a 0.31 reduction in the probability of being in the labor force as an on-site worker but does not significantly affect the probability of being a home-based worker. Having a disabled spouse is negatively related to both types of labor force participation, but the negative impact is significantly larger for on-site participation than it is for home-based participation. Having children under 6 is associated with a 0.24 reduction on the probability of being an on-site worker, but with a 0.01 increase in the probability of being a home-based worker. The differential effects of having children aged 6 to 17, while not as great, operate in the same direction, as do the differential effects of having an elderly person living in the household. The location variables, RURAL and FARM, do not provide consistent results. Living in a rural farm area is associated with a reduction in the probability of being in the labor force as an on-site worker as compared to being a home-based worker, but living in a rural nonfarm area yields the opposite result. Overall, however, these results strongly support our hypothesis that factors that are positively associated with the magnitudes of the fixed costs of on-site work will tend to discourage on-site labor force participation in favor of home-based participation.

Although subsidiary to the main focus of this chapter, interesting differences also emerge for the roles of unearned income, marital status, and age. Unearned income is negatively related to the probability of on-site participation but has a slight positive relation to home-based participation. This difference suggests that working at home is preferred to working on-site, and that women use unearned income to "purchase" this preferred work mode. Or, alternatively, working at home might be complementary with time spent in consumption. Put differently, the difference in the marginal effects of unearned income suggests that from a utility point of view, time spent working for pay at home is more similar to leisure than is time spent working outside of the home.[21] A similar implication may be drawn from differences in the marginal effects of marital status and age: the deterrent effects of both marital status and age are also significantly less for home-based work than for on-site work.

We also note differences in the effects of race and educational attainment. Of the two race variables, only BLACKNH has significantly different coefficients for the two work sites. Black non-Hispanic women are significantly more likely than white women to be in the labor force as on-site workers and significantly less likely than white women to be home-based workers.[22] The education effects for the two work sites are also significantly different, with an increase in educational attainment associated with an increase in the probability of on-site employment and a decrease in the probability of home-based employment.[23]

Of the three variables that reflect aspects of the husband's labor force status, two have statistically different coefficients between the two work sites and one does not. Having a husband who is a home-based worker is a significant deterrent to on-site participation but an encouragement to home-based participation. Clearly the issue of fringe benefits is outweighed by the possible synergies when both spouses are home-based workers, possibly because they are joint participants in the same business. As expected, the husband's wage has a negative effect on the odds of working as either an on-site or a home-based worker, versus being out of the labor force. However, the coefficients are not statistically different in the two work sites. The results for the husband's receipt of wage and salary income are the opposite of what we would have expected, but perhaps reflect only the fact that this is an imperfect proxy for receipt of fringe benefits.

Finally, we consider the own wage effects on the choice of labor force participation at each work site. Both predicted wage variables are statistically significant in both labor force sites, but with signs that differ from what we hypothesized: the predicted log of the on-site wage (LNWPREDO) is positively related to the probability of both types of labor force participation, and the predicted log of the home-based wage (LNHPREDH) is negatively related to the probability of both types of labor force participation. The two predicted wage variables are likely to move together (in fact, the correlation between them is 0.93), but this fact does not provide a satisfactory explanation for our results. A more likely explanation is that the predicted wage is an inferior instrument for the actual wage in the case of home-based work than in the case of on-site work. In fact, the adjusted R^2 in the equation predicting the home-based wage is 0.099, as compared to 0.212 for the on-site wage. Further, the wage data used to estimate the earnings function for home-based workers are more likely to be reported with error than in the case of on-site workers.[24] Given these considerations, it is plausible that these unexpected results with regard to predicted wages are a result of relatively greater measurement error in the instrument for the home-based wage.[25]

In order to examine the effects of fixed costs on labor force participation more fully, we compute in Table 3 the effects of changes in these variables on the probabilities of being a home-based or an on-site worker for six prototypical women. The table shows for each prototype the percentage change in the probability of being in the labor force as a home-based or on-site worker associated with a change (from 0 to 1.0) in the value of each of the seven fixed cost proxies. We report the results of these computations for three women with a high school education and varying marital status and age (women 1–3), and for three corresponding women with a college education (women 4–6). Overall,

Table 3 Effect of Fixed-Cost Variables on Predicted Labor Force Participation, by Work Site, for Six Prototypical Women

Variable	Woman 1[a]		Woman 2[b]		Woman 3[c]		Woman 4[d]		Woman 5[e]		Woman 6[f]	
	On-site worker	Home-based worker	On-site worker	Home-based worker	On-site worker	Home-based worker	On-site worker	Home-based worker	On-site worker	Home-based worker	On-site worker	Home-based worker
Base probability	0.922	0.023	0.905	0.028	0.846	0.042	0.938	0.019	0.923	0.023	0.874	0.034
% change in base probability associated with a change in												
CU6	-14	+113	-17	+107	-25	+87	-12	+120	-14	+114	-21	+96
C617	-2	+26	-2	+258	-4	+23	-2	+26	-2	+26	-3	+24
DISAB	-21	+135	-25	+124	-35	+93	-18	+145	-21	+135	-30	+106
RURAL	+0	+6	+0	+6	+0	+6	+0	+6	+0	+6	+0	+6
FARM	-2	+74	-2	+74	-3	+72	-1	+75	-2	+74	-3	+73
OVER65	-1	+9	-1	+9	-1	+9	-1	+9	-1	+9	-1	+9
S_LIM	N/A	N/A	+0	-28	+0	-28	N/A	N/A	+0	-28	+0	-28

[a] Woman 1: Age 25, high school education, not married, or married without a spouse present, white, urban, no children <17, not disabled, no one > 65 in household. Income and predicted wage variables set at means for nonmarried women.
[b] Woman 2: Same as woman 1, except married, spouse present. Wage and predicted income variables set at means for married women.
[c] Woman 3: Same as woman 2, except age 40.
[d] Woman 4: Same as woman 1 except with a college education.
[e] Woman 5: Same as woman 2 except with a college education.
[f] Woman 6: Same as woman 3 except with a college education.

the patterns are quite similar for all six women. In all cases but SP_LIM, proxies associated with higher fixed costs translate into an increase in the probability of being a home-based worker, and in all cases except for RURAL and SP_LIM, into a decrease in the probability of being an on-site worker. Although the basic probability of being home-based is quite low for these prototypical women (between 2 and 4 percent), changes in fixed costs can have a dramatic impact on that probability. For example, for a married 25-year-old woman with a high school education, the presence of children under 6 years old increases the probability of being a home-based worker by 113 percent. For the same prototypical woman, being disabled increases the probability of being in the labor force as a home-based worker by 135 percent. For the comparable woman with a college education, the percentage increases in the probability of home-based labor force participation are also large. Overall, Table 3 supports our contention that the fixed costs of working on-site play a significant role in determining the work site choice of women.

The Conditional Hours Equations

The first and third data columns of Table 4 contain estimates of the conditional hours equations for on-site and home-based workers, respectively. Significant differences in coefficients between work sites in the hours equations are noted with the superscript letters "b" and "e" in the table. Factors that had significantly different coefficients in the labor force participation equations also have, for the most part, significantly different coefficients in the hours and weeks equations, but there is an important difference. Whereas many of the variables that related to family structure had significantly greater deterrent effects for on-site participation than for home-based participation, the sign of the difference between many of these coefficients changes for hours worked. For example, having a child under 6 was a much greater deterrent to labor force participation as an on-site worker than as a home-based worker, but its negative effect on hours worked, conditional on being in the labor force, is larger for home-based work than for on-site work. A similar difference is observed for unearned income and having a disability. In contrast, having an older person in the household, having a ·child between 6 and 17, and living in a rural farm area all act to increase hours of home-based relative to on-site workers. The net effect of all the coefficient differences is that predicted hours for home-based work are lower on average than for on-site work (as is suggested by the theory) and are more variable. What this means is that women are better able to adjust their work hours in home-based work than in on-site work.

This greater flexibility is most easily demonstrated in Figure 2, which illustrates the distribution of predicted weekly hours for home-based workers, predicted alternately from the on-site hours equation and from the home-based hours equation. In generating these predicted distributions of hours worked (and weeks worked, below) in each work state, we include the appropriate LAMBDA among the predictors. In this way, we take each individual's unmeasured characteristics into account. The predicted hours distribution using the home-based hours equation has a wider spread than the distribution computed from the on-site hours equation: a greater proportion of observations are predicted to work fewer than 35 hours per week, or more than 40. For women who actually work at home, the average predicted hours as a home worker are 35.2 with a standard deviation of 4.5, while average predicted hours if the same women were an on-site worker are 36.4 with a standard deviation of 2.7. When we do the same computations for on-site workers or for women out of the labor force, the resulting distributions exhibit the same pattern. (For on-site workers, predicted hours as a home worker would be 36.8 on average, with a standard deviation of 4.2, while predicted hours on-site are 37.9 with a standard deviation of 2.6.) In all cases, the greater spread in the predicted hours distribution for home-based work than for on-site work indicates the greater ability of home-based workers to choose their desired work hours, even if that choice involves a nonstandard workweek.

The Conditional Weeks Equations

Estimates of the two conditional weeks equations appear in the second and fourth data columns of Table 4. The equations are estimated using a tobit specification because of the significant clustering of values at the upper limit of the dependent variable of 52 weeks.[26] Significant differences in the weeks equations are noted with the super-

Table 4 Estimates of Weeks and Hours Supplied, Conditional on Labor Force Participation[a]

Variable	On-site employment		Home-based employment	
	Weekly hours worked	Annual weeks worked	Weekly hours worked	Annual weeks worked
Constant[b,c]	51.615	18.532	76.109	63.623
	(26.86)**[d]	(3.74)**	(47.08)**	(27.26)**
AGE[b,c]	0.050	0.074	−0.107	0.124
	(−8.04)**	(4.71)**	(−8.90)**	(7.38)**
EDUC[b,c]	0.263	−0.663	−0.308	−0.476
	(7.20)**	(−7.07)**	(−6.35)**	(−7.05)**
MSP[b,c]	−0.928	−0.940	−4.583	−2.306
	(−8.67)**	(−3.35)**	(−18.80)**	(−6.80)**
CU6[b,c]	−2.784	−2.512	−5.505	−6.550
	(−14.36)**	(−5.07)**	(−25.60)**	(−22.11)**
C617[b,c]	−1.946	−3.318	−1.284	−1.130
	(−21.52)**	(−14.08)**	(−7.61)**	(−4.83)**
BLACKNH[b]	0.887	−1.446	3.866	1.988
	(6.27)**	(−4.16)**	(8.04)**	(3.15)**
HISPOTH	1.754	−2.149	1.775	−1.111
	(11.88)**	(−5.77)**	(5.62)**	(−2.62)**
DISAB[b,c]	−2.308	−1.129	−3.746	−5.754
	(−5.89)**	(−1.14)	(−9.87)**	(−11.30)**
RURAL[b,c]	−0.066	−0.959	−1.029	0.531
	(−0.63)	(−3.33)**	(−5.38)**	(1.93)*
FARM[b,c]	−0.336	0.587	1.336	5.396
	(−0.92)	(0.57)	(3.34)**	(8.30)**
OVER65[c]	0.207	−1.259	0.770	0.643
	(1.11)	(−2.55)**	(2.10)*	(1.21)
OTHINC[b]	−0.037	−0.018	−0.051	−0.014
	(−16.43)**	(−3.12)**	(−25.10)**	(−4.80)**
S_WAGE	−0.006	−0.0003	−0.008	−0.003
	(−2.55)*	(−0.01)	(−4.72)**	(−0.96)
LNWPREDO[e]	−11.806	48.313	—	—
	(−7.02)**	(11.14)**		
LNWPRDO2[e]	2.798	−10.399	—	—
	(7.77)**	(−11.25)**		

Variable	On-site employment		Home-based employment	
	Weekly hours worked	Annual weeks worked	Weekly hours worked	Annual weeks worked
LNWPREDH[e]	—	—	−15.202	7.748
			(−10.34)**	(3.67)**
LNWPRDH2[e]	—	—	3.840	−1.709
			(8.63)**	(−2.71)**
LAMBDAb[b,c]	−0.863	−8.701	−4.541	−2.188
	(−2.00)*	(−7.84)**	(−15.24)**	(−9.54)**
Adj. R^2/log L	0.05964	−119,438.8	0.06784	−118,937.8

[a] t-statistics in parentheses and are corrected for the preestimated selectivity correction. Hours estimates are weighted to adjust for choice-based sampling and the nonrandom nature of the 1990 PUMS. Weeks equations are estimated using tobit, using the same weighting, but are not selectively corrected.
[b] Denotes significant difference in coefficients between work sites in the hours worked equations at the 5% level.
[c] Denotes significant difference in coefficients between work sites in the weeks worked equations at the 5% level.
[d] * = significant at the 5% level in a two-tailed test.
** = significant at the 1% level in a two-tailed test.
[e] Denotes significant difference in coefficients between work sites of corresponding wage variables in the hours and weeks worked equations at the 5% level.

script letters "c" and "e". The results for weeks are similar to those for hours, although there are fewer variables with coefficients that differ significantly between work sites. As in the case of the hours equations, the net effect of the differences in the coefficients is that the mean of the distribution of predicted annual weeks worked as a home-based worker is lower than the mean of the distribution of predicted weeks worked as an on-site worker. Further, the dispersion of predicted weeks worked is greater for home-based than for on-site work. For example, using the sample of home-based workers, we find that average predicted weeks worked per year are 43.3 with a standard deviation of 2.5 for home-based work, compared to 45.6 with a standard deviation of 2.1 for the same individuals evaluated as on-site workers.

Figure 3 illustrates these differences for home-based workers. As in Figure 2, we show here the distribution of predicted weeks worked

Figure 2 Predicted Hours for Home-Based Workers

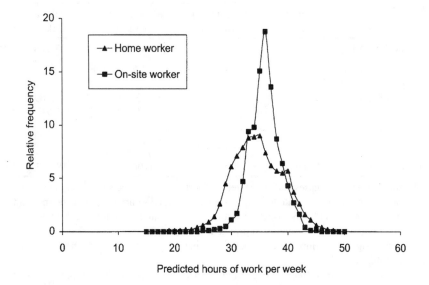

Figure 3 Predicted Weeks for Home-Based Workers

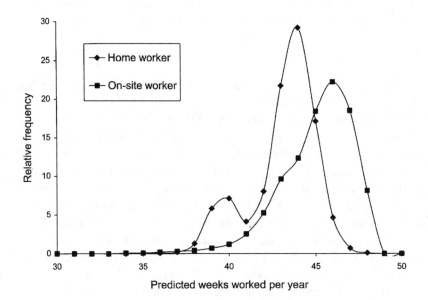

for home-based workers using alternatively the estimates in columns 2 and 4 from Table 4. The figure illustrates the greater spread of the distribution when the equation predicting weeks worked in home-based employment is used. When we do the same calculations for on-site workers or for women out of the labor force, the results are very much the same as in Figure 3. In all three cases, the predicted mean weeks worked is lower for home-based work, and the variability is greater compared to on-site work.

CONCLUSIONS

Home-based work offers women flexibility in work scheduling. The work-at-home option reduces the fixed costs of entering the labor market—the time and money costs of commuting, the costs of work clothing, and the costs of child care while commuting. The lower fixed costs associated with working at home translate into a lower reservation wage for home-based work, so that women who are likely to have large fixed costs associated with working outside of the home—women with young children, women with elderly relatives at home, women who are disabled, or women who live in rural areas that may require substantial commutes to an on-site work location—will be more likely to be in the labor market if they can be home-based workers.

Our estimates are consistent with this hypothesis. When we compute the partial effects of the proxy measures for fixed costs on the probability of being in each labor force state, we find that three of these variables are associated with large and significant increases in the probability of being a home-based worker—having children under 6, being disabled, and living in a rural-farm area. Put differently, the discouraging effect on labor force participation of these fixed costs variables are significantly greater for on-site work than for home-based work. In addition, women with higher levels of unearned income were also more likely to choose home-based versus on-site work, suggesting that this may be a preferred work option for some women.

Another implication of our theoretical discussion is that the lower fixed costs of working at home will result in lower reservation hours and weeks for home-based work. Our estimates provide indirect sup-

278   Edwards and Field-Hendrey

port for this hypothesis: the distributions of predicted weeks and hours for home-based work have lower means and greater dispersions than do the corresponding distributions for on-site work. It appears that home-based workers are better able to adjust their work schedules to accommodate those family circumstances which generate higher fixed costs of working. On average, home-based workers choose to work somewhat less, and they are more likely to choose nonstandard work schedules.

It is interesting to compare our results from the 1990 Census of Population with the views of 24 professional and clerical women in the New York City area who use some type of computer technology in their home-based work (Christensen 1985b). The advantages of home-based work cited by these workers were the flexibility and autonomy in structuring their work and the financial benefits associated with not going to an office. Strikingly, many of the mothers with young children said that they would not be in the labor force at all if they could not work at home.

Home-based work has its detractors. Many still view this as a form of work organization that causes workers to be exploited and mistreated. Even the women surveyed above cite some disadvantages, such as disruption of home and family and an inability to get away from one's work. But it is clear from the findings in this chapter that home-based work has a valuable place in the menu of work options available to women. Women who otherwise would not be able to enter the labor force, either because of home care responsibilities, inconvenient location, or physical disability, choose this option. These women are able to adapt their work schedules to a greater degree than are women working on-site. We believe that women's demand for this work arrangement will continue to grow in the future, especially if the current public concern about the welfare of children and families remains strong.

Notes

Funding for this research was provided by the National Science Foundation, Grant No. SBR-9320820. We thank Andrew Beveridge, Susan Weber, Vadim Shlez, and Deborah

Viola for their assistance in preparing and analyzing the PUMS data, and Julie Hotch-kiss and Cordelia Reimers for helpful discussions.

1. The data for 1960 come from Silver (1989); the data for 1980 come from U.S. Bureau of the Census (1983, Table 122); and the data for 1990 come from U.S. Bureau of the Census (1993, Table 148).

2. One aspect of the choice of home-based work—that it often involves the simulta-neous choice of being self-employed—is not investigated in this chapter, but it is treated explicitly in Edwards and Field-Hendrey (forthcoming).

3. The data and sampling procedure are fully described in U.S. Bureau of the Census (1992).

4. Unemployed women and women with a job but not at work last week are deleted from the sample because there is no way to determine if their desired labor force participation is as a home-based or on-site worker. We also exclude women whose class of worker information is not consistent with their reported earnings—for example, someone who reports herself as self-employed in 1990, yet reports wage and salary income for 1989—and women whose hourly earnings exceed $250.

5. Persons who used more than one mode of transportation were requested to iden-tify the one used for most of the distance.

6. For a more complete discussion of how home-based and on-site workers differ, see Edwards and Field-Hendrey (1996).

7. Child (or other dependent) care costs are not, strictly speaking, a fixed cost of working since they vary with the number of hours worked. The component of these costs attributable to commuting time, however, is a fixed cost.

8. The hourly cost of dependent care may also vary with work site. This possibility could be incorporated into the model by using a "net" wage rate for each work site, net of the hourly cost of dependent care.

9. In this chapter, we treat the labor force decisions and resultant earnings of other family members as exogenous.

10. Our procedure for computing λ_{ik} follows Lee (1983). First we substitute the expression for the wage from Eq. 8 into Eq. 7 to obtain a reduced form multino-mial logit equation predicting labor force status. We obtain the predicted proba-bility of individual i being in labor force state k, P_{ik}, and use it to compute selectivity correction factors for each state, λ_{ik}, by the following procedure:

(A) $H_{ik} = \Phi^{-1}(P_{ik})$

(B) $\lambda_{ik} = \varphi(H_{ik}) / \Phi(H_{ik})$,

where φ and Φ are the PDF and CDF of the standard normal distribution.

11. The procedure described here is similar to Killingsworth (1983, pp. 160–161), but our model has three work states rather than the two considered by Killingsworth.

Note that since the expected value of the offering wage in each work site is being predicted, λ_{ik} is not used as a predictor.

12. We are indebted to George Jakubson for this insight. The issue of correlated errors across labor force states was a concern to us because we have reason to believe that nonzero correlations are likely in our context. For example, Gerson and Kraut (1988), in a personality assessment test given to members of their sample of clerical workers, found that home-based workers had statistically significantly different values concerning gender roles and careers as compared to on-site workers. Views on such issues are just the type of unmeasured factor that create correlations in the errors across labor force states.

13. Hutchens, Jakubson, and Schwartz point out that the major drawback with this model is that it does not meet the condition of allowing one to combine existing estimates with information about a new alternative to make predictions about the probability of choosing that new alternative. This is not a drawback in the context of our problem, since we do not wish to make inferences about work arrangements other than those already discussed in this chapter.

14. We follow this four-step procedure, rather than estimating reduced form equations for the whole system jointly using maximum likelihood as does Blank (1990), in order to obtain explicit estimates of the effect of the on-site and home-based wages on labor force participation, hours, and weeks. This procedure allows us to separate the direct effect on these variables of factors related to fixed costs from the indirect effects that operate through the wage equation.

15. Although λ_{ik} is included as a regressor, so that the coefficient estimates are unbiased, the error variances are not corrected.

16. See, for example, Blank (1988, 1990), Averett and Hotchkiss (1996, 1997), Sorensen (1993), and Zabel (1993).

17. Variables to predict the woman's offering wage in on-site and home-based work are similar to those used by others (see, for example, Blank 1990; Averett and Hotchkiss 1996, 1997; and Neumark and Korenman 1994): age (AGE), age squared (AGE2), education (EDUC), education squared (EDUC2), an age and education interaction term (AGEEDUC), marital status (MSP), number of children (FERT), race (BLACKNH and HISP&OTH), location of residence (RURAL and FARM), whether the woman is disabled (DISAB), variables representing the region of the country (SOUTH, WEST, MW), the manufacturing wage in the state (MFGWAGE), and the unemployment rate in the state (UNEMP). In addition, we include a set of variables to capture the industrial distribution of employment in the state (their definitions are self-evident). One might expect offering wages to be lower in rural areas, at least for on-site work. However, to the extent that one industry that readily lends itself to home-based work, farming, is more prevalent in rural and rural/farm areas, it may be that the offering wage for home-based work will be relatively higher in such areas. Therefore, we include variables representing both residence in a rural area (RURAL) and residence in a rural/farm area (FARM). Precise definitions of all of these variables appear in Appendix Table 1. Also included in each wage predicting equation is the appropriate vari-

able to correct for selectivity bias (LAMBDAH for home-based workers and LAMBDAO for on-site workers), computed from the reduced form logit esti-mates of the choice of labor force state. For estimates and a detailed discussion of these wage equations, see Field-Hendrey and Edwards (2001).

18. Although there is no hard evidence, in the case of home-based employees, it has been suggested that these workers are less likely to have employer-provided fringe benefits (Christensen 1985a). In the case of the self-employed, Devine (1994) documents the much lower proportion of self-employed workers who received health benefits on their jobs, as compared to employees. Blank (1990) documents that part-time workers are much less likely to be included in company pension or health plans.

19. The Census Bureau provides weights to adjust for the nonrandom nature of the PUMS sample. In addition, we weight to take into account our sampling design, which results in home-based workers being 25 times more likely to be in our sam-ple than are on-site workers or women out of the labor force.

20. Marginal effects are computed from the logit coefficients according to the follow-ing formula:

$$\delta_j = \partial P_j / \partial x = P_j \, (\beta_j - \beta),$$

where $\beta = \Sigma P_j \beta_j$.

These marginal effects are actually the derivatives of the probability of being in the specified labor force state with respect to each independent variable. This formula is correct for continuous variables, but not for dummy variables, for which one should compute the effect of a change in the value from 0 to 1.0 by computing the probability of being in the specified labor force state alternatively when the dummy equals 0 and when it equals 1.0, and subtracting the two proba-bilities. Greene (1997, p. 878) shows that the approximation obtained by simply taking derivatives for dichotomous variables, as we do in Table 2, is "often sur-prisingly good." We checked several of our dichotomous variables and found the results to be quite close to the approximation. In Table 3 we use the correct proce-dure for computing the effects of the dummy variables rather than the continuous approximation.

21. Yet another explanation may be that unearned income is an endogenous variable; that is, husbands and wives make labor force choices jointly, and in families in which there is a desire for women to do home-based work, men work longer hours to compensate for their wives' resultant lower earnings.

22. A possible explanation is that many home-based workers are self-employed, and it may be more difficult for black women to obtain the necessary capital.

23. Overall, these results are consistent with findings from the 1980 Census reported by Kraut (1988). He studies only nonfarm white collar employment and estimates a logistic equation to determine which variables were most important in women's choice of home-based work. He finds that the presence of preschool and older

children, especially for married women, and a work-limiting disability were powerful determinants of the odds of a woman's working at home. Age, education, other household income and residence in rural areas were also significant factors. He also finds that, even after holding these factors constant, black women had a lower probability of working at home than did white women.

24. The proportion of observations for which earnings are allocated by the Census Bureau, rather than being reported directly by the woman, is greater for home-based than for on-site workers. Thus, the hourly earnings figure reported in the census will be more subject to error for home-based workers than for on-site workers. This error is compounded by the fact that home-based workers are much more likely than on-site workers to be self-employed, and the earnings of the self-employed are notorious for errors in reporting (Devine 1992).

25. For example, Bound, Jaeger, and Baker (1995) show that if there is a low correlation between an endogenous variable and a potential instrument, even a small correlation between the instrument and the error in the basic equation being estimated can produce a larger inconsistency in the IV estimates than in the OLS estimates.

26. The standard errors in the weeks worked equation estimates are not corrected for the inclusion of the selectivity adjustment variable. In the case of the hours worked equations, we experimented by estimating with and without making the adjustment and found that there was very little difference in result.

References

Averett, Susan L., and Julie Hotchkiss. 1996. "Discrimination in the Payment of Full-Time Wage Premiums." *Industrial and Labor Relations Review* 49: 287–301.

———. 1997. "Female Labor Supply with a Discontinuous, Non-Convex Budget Constraint: Incorporation of a Full-Time/Part-Time Wage Differential." *Review of Economics and Statistics* 79: 461–470.

Blank, Rebecca. 1988. "Simultaneously Modeling the Choice of Weeks and Hours of Work among Female Household Heads." *Journal of Labor Economics* 16: 177–204.

———. 1990. "Are Part-Time Jobs Bad Jobs?" In *A Future of Lousy Jobs? The Changing Structure of U.S. Wages*, Gary Burtless, ed. Washington: The Brookings Institution, pp. 123–164.

Bound, John, David A. Jaeger, and Regina M. Baker. 1995. "Problems with Instrumental Variables Estimation When the Correlation between the Instruments and the Endogenous Explanatory Variable Is Weak." *Journal of the American Statistical Association* 90: 443–450.

Christensen, Kathleen E. 1985a. "Women and Home-Based Work." *Social Policy* 15: 54–57.

_____. 1985b. "Impacts of Computer-Mediated Home-Based Work on Women and Their Families." Unpublished paper, City University of New York Graduate Center.

Cogan, John F. 1981. "Fixed Costs and Labor Supply." *Econometrica* 49: 945–963.

Devine, Theresa J. 1992. "Compensation Composition Constraints and Household Self-Employment Decisions." Unpublished paper, Pennsylvania State University, University Park, Pennsylvania.

_____. 1994. "Characteristics of Self-Employed Women in the United States." *Monthly Labor Review* 117: 20–34.

Edwards, Linda N., and Elizabeth Field-Hendrey. 1996. "What Do We Know about Home-Based Work? Data from the 1990 Census of Population." *Monthly Labor Review* 119: 26–34.

_____. Forthcoming. "Home-Based Work and Women's Labor Force Decisions." *Journal of Labor Economics*.

Field-Hendrey, Elizabeth and Linda N. Edwards. 2001. "Why Do Home-Based Workers Earn Less? An Analysis of Earnings of Home-Based and On-Site Women Workers." Unpublished paper, City University of New York.

Gerson, Judith, and Robert E. Kraut. 1988. "Clerical Work at Home or in the Office: The Difference It Makes." In *The New Era of Home-Based Work*, Kathleen Christensen, ed. Boulder, Colorado: Westview Press, pp. 49–64.

Greene, William H. 1997. *Econometric Analysis*. 3rd. ed. New York: Macmillan.

Hersch, Joni, and Leslie S. Stratton. 1994. "Wages and the Division of Housework Time for Employed Spouses." American Economic Association, *Papers and Proceedings* 84: 118–125.

Hill, M. Anne. 1989. "Female Labor Supply in Japan: Implications of the Informal Sector for Labor Force Participation and Hours of Work." *Journal of Human Resources* 24: 143–161.

Hutchens, Robert, George Jakubson, and Saul Schwartz. 1989. "AFDC and the Formation of Subfamilies." *Journal of Human Resources* 24: 597–628.

Killingsworth, Mark R. 1983. *Labor Supply*. New York: Cambridge University Press.

Kraut, Robert. 1988. "Homework: What Is It and Who Does It?" In *The New Era of Home-Based Work*, Kathleen Christensen, ed. Boulder, Colorado: Westview Press, pp. 30–48.

Lee, L. 1983. "Generalized Econometric Models with Selectivity." *Econometrica* 51: 507–512.

Maddala, G.S. 1983. *Limited Dependent and Qualitative Variables in Econometrics*. Cambridge: Cambridge University Press.

Neal, Margaret B., Nancy J. Chapman, Berit Ingersoll-Dayton, and Arthur C. Emlen. 1993. *Balancing Work and Caregiving for Children, Adults, and Elders*. New York: Sage Publications.

Neumark, David, and Sanders Korenman. 1994. "Sources of Bias in Women's Wage Equations." *Journal of Human Resources* 29: 379–405.

Silver, Hillary. 1989. "The Demand for Homework: Evidence from the U.S. Census." In *Homework: Historical and Contemporary Perspectives on Paid Labor at Home*, Eileen Boris and Cynthia R. Daniels, eds. Urbana, Illinois: University of Illinois Press.

Sorensen, Elaine. 1993. "Continuous Female Workers: How Different are They from Other Women?" *Eastern Economic Journal* 19: 15–32.

Sundt, Leslie A. 1989. "Involuntary Employment and Labor Market Constraints upon Women." Unpublished paper, University of Arizona.

U.S. Bureau of the Census. 1983. *1980 Census of Population: General Social and Economic Characteristics, Part I, United States Summary*. Washington, D.C.: U.S. GPO.

_____. 1992. *1990 Census of Population and Housing: Public Use Microdata Samples, U.S. Technical Documentation*. Washington, D.C.: Bureau of the Census.

_____. 1993. *1990 Census of Population: Social and Economic Characteristics: United States (1990 CP-2-1)*. Washington, D.C.: U.S. GPO.

U.S. Department of Labor. 1991. *Employment and Earnings*. Washington, D.C.: Bureau of Labor Statistics.

U.S. President. 1996. *Economic Report of the President, 1996*. Washington, D.C.: U.S. GPO.

Zabel, Jeffrey. 1993. "The Relationship between Hours of Work and Labor Force Participation in Four Models of Labor Supply Behavior." *Journal of Labor Economics* 11: 387–416.

Table A1   Variable Definitions[a]

Variable	Definition
AGE	Age
AGE2	Age squared
EDUC	Years of schooling[b]
EDUC2	Years of schooling squared
AGEEDUC	Age times years of schooling
OTHINC	Total family income − earned income of individual
MSP	Dummy variable which equals 1 if woman is married with spouse present
FERT	Number of children
CU6	Dummy variable which equals 1 if one or more children under 6 years old is present in the household
C617	Dummy variable which equals 1 if one or more children between 6 and 17 years is present in the household
BLACKNH	Dummy variable which equals 1 if woman is black, non-Hispanic
HISP&OTH	Dummy variable which equals 1 if woman is Hispanic, Asian, or other non-white race
DISAB	Dummy variable which equals 1 if woman has a disability which restricts the kind or amount of work she can do
RURAL	Dummy variable which equals 1 if woman lives in a rural area
FARM	Dummy variable which equals 1 if woman lives in a rural farm area
OVER65	Dummy variable which equals 1 if there are person(s) over 65 years old in the household
S_HW	Dummy variable which equals 1 if the woman's spouse is a home-based worker
S_LIM	Dummy variable which equals 1 if the woman's spouse has a mobility or personal care limitation
S_WAGE	Spouse's average hourly earnings computed from 1989 annual earnings, weeks worked in 1989, and hours worked in the census week
S_EMPL	Dummy variable which equals 1 if the woman's spouse reported wage and salary income in 1989

(continued)

Table A1 (continued)

Variable	Definition
LNWPREDO	Log of predicted hourly earnings in on-site work
LNWPRDO2	Square of LNWPREDO
LNWPREDH	Log of predicted hourly earnings in home-based work
LNWPRDH2	Square of LNWPREDH
MW	Dummy variable which equals 1 if the woman lives in the Midwest
SOUTH	Dummy variable which equals 1 if the woman lives in the South
WEST	Dummy variable which equals 1 if the woman lives in the West
MFGWAGE[c]	Average hourly earnings in 1989 of production workers in manufacturing in the state
UNEMP[d]	Unemployment rate in the state in 1990

Industrial distribution of employment in 1990 by state
(agriculture is excluded industry)[d]

FORESTRY	Percentage of employment in forestry and fisheries
MINING	Percentage of employment in mining
CONSTRUC	Percentage of employment in construction
MFG	Percentage of employment in manufacturing
TRANS	Percentage of employment in transportation, communications and other public utilities
WHLESALE	Percentage of employment in wholesale trade
RETAIL	Percentage of employment in retail trade
FINANCE	Percentage of employment in finance, insurance, and real estate
SERVICES	Percentage of employment in services
PUBADMIN	Percentage of employment in public administration

[a] All variables taken from the 1990 PUMS unless otherwise indicated.
[b] This variable was coded as a continuous variable from the classes provided in the census.
[c] U.S. Department of Labor (1991, Table C-8).
[d] U.S. Bureau of the Census (1993, Tables 149 and 151).

Table A2 Reduced Form Logit Coefficients for Labor Force Choice[a,b]

Variable	On-site workers	Home-based workers
Constant	0.004	−5.046
	(0.01)	(−3.11)**
AGE	0.136	0.195
	(14.33)**	(6.60)**
AGE2	−0.002	−0.002
	(−15.40)**	(−6.82)**
EDUC	0.027	0.021
	(1.56)	(0.36)
EDUC2	0.009	0.008
	(19.35)**	(5.54)**
AGEEDUC	−0.001	−0.001
	(−3.31)**	(−1.06)
MSP	−0.628	−0.163
	(−23.26)**	(−1.97)*
CU6	−1.157	−0.334
	(−61.86)**	(−6.27)**
C617	−0.176	−0.036
	(−10.66)**	(−0.74)
FERT	−0.143	−0.037
	(−26.03)**	(−2.22)*
BLACKNH	−0.034	−1.024
	(−1.48)	(−9.32)**
HISP&OTH	−0.159	−0.475
	(−6.67)**	(−6.18)**
DISAB	−2.200	−1.253
	(−78.93)**	(−13.60)**
RURAL	−0.098	0.069
	(−5.76)**	(1.39)
FARM	−0.153	0.501
	(−2.58)*	(4.44)**
OVER65	−0.117	0.024
	(−3.81)**	(0.25)
OTHINC	−0.012	−0.002
	(−43.94)**	(−1.24)

(continued)

Table A2 (continued)

Variable	On-site workers	Home-based workers
S_LIM	−0.066	−0.384
	(−1.51)	(−2.42)*
S_HW	−0.362	1.696
	(−6.00)**	(19.58)**
S_WAGE	−0.001	−0.003
	(−3.34)**	(−0.75)
S_EMPL	0.412	0.039
	(17.13)**	(0.60)
MW	0.142	0.308
	(4.55)**	(3.48)**
SOUTH	0.087	0.119
	(2.24)*	(0.10)
WEST	−0.076	0.273
	(−2.35)*	(2.94)**
MFGWAGE	−0.016	−0.032
	(−1.51)	(−1.09)
UNEMP	−0.129	−0.173
	(−12.72)**	(−6.05)**
FORESTRY	0.207	0.294
	(4.99)**	(2.64)**
MINING	−0.005	0.047
	(−0.34)	(1.02)
CONSTRUC	0.004	−0.050
	(0.27)	(−1.24)
MFG	−0.008	−0.178
	(−1.41)	(−1.20)
TRANS	0.079	−0.180
	(−6.07)**	(−4.90)**
WHLESALE	0.034	0.151
	(1.42)	(2.17)*
RETAIL	−0.032	−0.027
	(−3.13)**	(−0.96)
FINANCE	−0.007	−0.001
	(−0.60)	(−0.04)

SERVICES	0.014	0.019
	(1.71)	(0.93)
PUBADMIN	–0.018	0.033
	(–1.78)	(1.25)

[a] t-Statistics are in parentheses. All logit coefficients refer to the odds of being in the specified labor force category versus being out of the labor force. Estimates are weighted to adjust for choice-based sampling and the nonrandom nature of the 1990 PUMS.

[b] * = Significant at the 5% level in a two-tailed test.

** = Significant at the 1% level in a two-tailed test.

Table A3 Structural Logit Coefficients for Labor Force Choice[a,b]

Variable	On-site work	Home-based work
Constant[c]	−0.684	−4.825
	(−9.98)**	(−24.43)**
AGE[c]	−0.026	−0.007
	(−27.00)**	(−2.25)*
EDUC[c]	0.059	0.002
	(10.35)**	(0.10)
MSP[c]	−0.684	−0.358
	(−24.30)**	(−4.20)**
CU6[c]	−1.234	−0.320
	(−68.63)**	(−6.23)**
C617[c]	−0.212	0.035
	(−14.88)**	(0.86)
BLACKNH[c]	0.082	−0.771
	(3.27)**	(−6.83)**
HISPOTH	−0.026	−0.093
	(−1.06)	(−1.18)
DISAB[c]	−1.621	−0.533
	(−49.39)**	(−4.98)**
RURAL	0.065	0.121
	(3.75)**	(2.33)*
FARM[c]	−0.068	0.451
	(−1.13)	(3.83)**
OVER65	−0.088	0.008
	(−2.85)**	(0.08)
OTHINC[c]	−0.013	−0.002
	(−46.28)**	(−1.40)
S_LIM[c]	−0.078	−0.408
	(−1.80)	(−2.57)*
S_HW[c]	−0.360	1.704
	(−6.05)**	(19.82)**
S_WAGE	−0.001	−0.003
	(−2.97)**	(−0.71)
S_EMPL[c]	0.417	0.019
	(17.45)**	(0.30)

Variable	On-site work	Home-based work
LNWPREDO[c]	2.524 (23.75)**	3.829 (11.58)**
LNWPREDH[c]	−0.974 (−12.39)**	−2.322 (−9.93)**
Log likelihood	−79,280.01	

[a] t-Statistics are in parentheses and are corrected for the preestimated selectivity correction. Estimates are weighted to adjust for choice-based sampling and the nonrandom nature of the 1990 PUMS. All logit coefficients refer to the odds of being in the specified labor force category versus being out of the labor force.

[b] * = Significant at the 5% level in a two-tailed test.

** = Significant at the 1% level in a two-tailed test.

[c] Denotes significant difference in coefficients between work sites at the 5% level.

10
A Comparative Analysis
of Moonlighting in Canada
and the United States

Jean Kimmel
W.E. Upjohn Institute for Employment Research

Lisa M. Powell
Queen's University

Moonlighting is a small but significant aspect of labor market activity of North America. Moonlighting, or multiple job-holding, is defined by a worker who holds more than one job. The worker may be job-packaging; that is, adding a part-time job to a full-time job, or the total hours of work on all jobs may still be less than what would usually be considered to be full-time hours. The incidence of moonlighting and the characteristics of moonlighters have been examined periodically by researchers in both Canada (Webber 1989; Cohen 1994; Krahn 1995; Pold 1995) and the United States (Sekscenski 1980; Stinson 1986, 1990; Levenson 1995). Researchers have also sought to examine the determinants of moonlighting, using econometrics to examine hypotheses such as primary job hours constraints, liquidity constraints, and job heterogeneity (Shishko and Rostker 1976; Krishnan 1990; Lilja 1991; Abdukadir 1992; Paxson and Sicherman 1996; Powell and Boucher 2001; Conway and Kimmel 1998; Kimmel and Conway 2001;).

This chapter will analyze moonlighting in a comparative context in Canada and the United States. Because the United States and Canada have interdependent economies with such broad similarities, the two countries serve as a useful basis for comparison. According to Card and Freeman (1993, p. 191), ". . . few countries offer a more natural pairing of policies and institutions or for uncovering the reasons for differences in outcomes than the United States and Canada."

The chapter begins by providing detailed descriptive evidence concerning various aspects of moonlighting behavior in both countries. These descriptive analyses include an examination of differences across sex, age, education, marital status, occupation, industry, etc. Within this static comparison we are able to discuss reasons for moonlighting based on information reported by individual workers. We then seek further information regarding the determinants of moonlighting and the structure of primary job (PJ) and secondary job (SJ) wages by using regression analyses. We estimate separate PJ and SJ wage equations for each country and use them to construct predicted wages for use in a probit model for moonlighting.

The following section of this chapter provides a static cross-country comparison of moonlighting with respect to a variety of characteristics. The next section provides an econometric analysis of the determinants of moonlighting, and the last section concludes the chapter.

COMPARISON OF MOONLIGHTING BEHAVIOR BETWEEN CANADA AND THE UNITED STATES

Here we examine the incidence and distribution of moonlighting across country and sex in 1991. We consider various demographic characteristics, including age, education, marital status, and the presence of children in the household, and we use a sample of nonmoonlighters as a basis for comparison. Next, we describe the extent to which moonlighters are self-employed or hold temporary or union jobs, as well as the incidence and distribution of moonlighting for occupations and industries. Also analyzed in this section are wages on both jobs and total hours worked. Then we relate two basic motivations for moonlighting—primary job constraints and heterogeneous jobs—to reported reasons for taking a second job. Finally, we present multivariate analyses to explain the structure of primary and secondary job wages as well as the probability of moonlighting.[1]

The United States data are drawn from the May Current Population Survey (CPS), which contains a special supplement with information on multiple jobs. The CPS is a randomly drawn U.S. sample of households. Only those rotation groups eligible for the supplement are included in these analyses. And, only individuals between the ages of 17–64 are included in our subsample. In the 1991 data, the full sample is comprised of 14,727 workers, 941 of whom moonlight. Broken down by sex, the full sample includes 7,896 male workers and 6,831 female workers.

The Canadian data used in this section are drawn from the Survey of Work Arrangements (SWA) which is a supplement to the November 1991 Labour Force Survey (LFS). While the LFS does flag multiple job-holders, the SWA provides additional information on work patterns, primary job union membership, occupational and industrial distributions of secondary jobs, secondary job wages, and the reason for moonlighting. Certain data in the SWA are available only for paid employees, and these cases are noted in our tables. Our subsample includes those individuals aged 17–64 and omits unpaid family workers. Thus, our Canadian sample contains 29,875 workers, 13,500 of whom are female and 16,375 are male. Among all workers, 1,606 individuals are multiple job-holders.

While both survey designs aim for the resulting samples to be purely random representations of the two countries' populations, both samples suffer from some systematic nonresponse and over/underrepresentation of particular segments of the population. Therefore, all of the summary statistics presented in this chapter are weighted.[2]

Who Moonlights?

The discussion in this section will relate to data given in Tables 1, 2, and 3. Table 1 shows moonlighting rates; that is, the percentage of different groups of workers who moonlight. The numbers in Table 2 are distributions, showing the percentage of all moonlighters who fall in the given subcategory, defined by a characteristic such as educational level or marital status. For example, Table 2 shows that 65.9 percent of all Canadian moonlighters are married. Table 3 is interpreted just like Table 2, except Table 3 focuses on employed nonmoonlighters.

The incidence of moonlighting in Canada and the United States by different individual characteristics are given in Table 1. Overall, U.S. workers are more likely to moonlight than Canadian workers, at 6.01 percent in the United States and 5.04 percent in Canada.[3] While female

Table 1 Incidence of Moonlighting in Canada and the United States, by Characteristics and Sex (%)

Characteristics	Canada			United States		
	Both sexes	Males	Females	Both sexes	Males	Females
All individuals	5.04	4.82	5.31	6.01	6.56	5.34
Age						
17–24	5.42	4.34	6.58	5.43	6.06	4.74
25–44	5.15	5.07	5.24	6.57	7.10	5.91
45–64	4.61	4.56	4.67	5.14	5.67	4.48
Education						
None or elementary	3.37	3.50	3.18	3.10	3.13	3.06
High school	4.29	4.02	4.56	5.03	5.41	4.60
Some post-secondary/diploma	6.07	5.75	6.43	7.22	8.32	6.08
University degree	6.21	5.90	6.63	8.04	8.86	6.93
Marital status						
Married	5.02	5.05	4.97	5.96	7.06	4.43
Never married	5.11	4.34	6.09	5.83	5.75	5.94
Other	5.06	4.31	5.59	6.58	5.38	7.44
Children aged 0–5	5.07	5.06	5.10	6.26	7.89	3.90
Self-empl. PJ[a] (unincorporated + incorporated)	6.60	5.99	8.03	4.89	5.17	4.17
Self-empl. PJ (unincorporated)	7.32	6.84	8.22	3.71	4.01	3.04
Self-empl. PJ (unincorporated, no help)	7.16	5.74	9.36	N/A[c]	N/A	N/A
Temporary job PJ[b]	7.12	5.54	8.90	N/A	N/A	N/A
Union member PJ[b]	4.52	4.89	4.03	6.99	7.47	6.26
Occupation PJ						
Managerial	5.39	5.62	5.16	6.54	7.56	5.36
Clerical	5.54	5.64	5.51	6.15	6.70	6.02

Characteristics	Canada			United States		
	Both sexes	Males	Females	Both sexes	Males	Females
Sales	4.91	4.74	5.11	5.28	6.81	3.92
Service	5.33	5.32	5.33	7.35	9.84	5.45
Primary	8.69	7.86	12.32	6.30	5.97	8.45
Processing	4.03	4.18	3.39	4.98	5.10	4.65
Construction, transportation and material handling	3.16	2.94	5.49	4.44	4.49	3.97
Industry PJ						
Agriculture	8.96	9.13	8.53	7.40	7.34	7.66
Other primary	4.33	4.42	3.77	3.58	4.40	0.00
Manufacturing, nondurable	3.98	3.82	4.26	4.94	4.78	5.20
Manufacturing, durable	2.33	2.16	3.01	5.32	5.90	3.63
Construction	3.64	2.95	9.59	3.74	3.70	4.30
Transportation	3.89	3.44	5.16	6.32	6.62	5.60
Wholesale trade	4.30	4.47	3.93	7.14	7.25	6.87
Retail trade	5.39	6.04	4.76	4.52	5.28	3.78
Finance	5.26	3.56	6.33	4.82	5.58	4.20
Community services	6.97	8.64	6.20	7.59	9.91	6.55
Personal services	4.50	2.64	5.45	5.00	4.72	5.12
Business services	5.26	5.82	4.52	6.00	6.52	5.06
Public administration	4.83	5.96	3.40	10.00	12.81	5.95
Number of moonlighters	1,606	877	729	941	536	405
Full sample	29,875	16,375	13,500	14,727	7,896	6,831

[a] PJ = primary job.
[b] Available for Canada only for employees on PJ.
[c] N/A = data not available.

**Table 2 Characteristics of Moonlighters in Canada and the United
States, by Characteristics and Sex**

Characteristics	Canada[a]			United States		
	Both sexes	Males	Females	Both sexes	Males	Females
Age (%)						
17–24	16.6	13.2	20.3	13.1	12.8	13.7
25–44	58.7	60.0	57.3	63.3	63.1	63.7
45–64	24.7	26.8	22.4	23.5	24.1	22.6
Education (%)						
None or elementary	15.4	18.3	12.1	6.8	7.2	6.1
High school	20.4	18.7	22.3	33.2	31.6	35.7
Some postsecondary/ diploma	44.5	42.5	46.8	26.3	25.8	27.2
University degree	19.7	20.6	18.7	33.7	35.4	31.0
Marital Status (%)						
Married	65.9	70.8	60.7	60.9	69.0	47.6
Never married	26.5	24.1	29.1	23.7	21.5	27.1
Other	7.5	5.1	10.2	15.4	8.8	25.3
Children aged 0–5 (%)	17.9	20.2	15.3	20.0	24.8	12.8
Family income ($)	N/A[b]	N/A	N/A	43,925	46,665	39,834
Self-empl. PJ (unincorporated+ incorporated) (%)	18.4	22.3	14.1	9.1	11.5	5.5
Self-empl. PJ (unincorporated) (%)	13.2	15.3	10.9	5.2	6.5	3.3
Self-empl. PJ (unincorporated, no help) (%)	9.2	8.5	9.9	N/A	N/A	N/A
Temporary job PJ[c] (%)	7.2	6.1	8.3	N/A	N/A	N/A

Characteristics	Canada[a]			United States		
	Both sexes	Males	Females	Both sexes	Males	Females
Union member PJ[c] (%)	33.3	40.7	26.0	20.4	21.6	18.5
Total weekly hours	43.3	48.2	37.9	51.9	56.6	44.8
Distribution of total hours (%)						
0–29	15.3	9.3	22.0	7.6	3.8	13.3
30–39	22.6	14.6	31.4	7.6	3.7	13.6
40–49	25.1	25.1	25.2	30.1	24.4	38.6
50+	36.9	51.1	21.5	54.7	68.1	34.5
Mean hourly wage PJ[b] (C$)	13.7	15.9	11.8	13.41	14.61	11.71
Hourly wage SJ[d] (C$)						
Under 5.00	3.1	2.4	3.6	15.7	14.8	17.0
5.00–6.99	25.5	21.3	28.4	20.9	14.2	29.9
7.00–9.99	21.4	27.0	17.6	17.9	20.4	14.5
10.00–13.99	22.7	22.3	23.0	14.4	17.9	9.9
14.00–19.99	10.5	12.0	9.5	13.8	12.5	15.6
20.00 +	16.8	15.1	17.9	17.2	20.2	13.2
Mean hourly wage SJ[c] (C$)	12.1	12.1	12.1	14.66	16.97	11.58

[a] Canadian information available only for moonlighters who are employees on secondary job (SJ).

[b] N/A = data not available.

[c] Available information only for paid employees on primary job (PJ).

[d] Available information only for paid employees on SJ.

Table 3 Summary Statistics for Nonmoonlighting Workers in Canada and the United States, by Characteristics and Sex

Characteristics	Canada			United States		
	Both sexes	Males	Females	Both sexes	Males	Females
Age (%)						
17–24	15.4	14.7	16.2	14.6	13.9	15.5
25–44	57.5	56.9	58.2	57.6	57.9	57.2
45–64	27.2	28.4	25.7	27.7	28.2	27.2
Education (%)						
None or elementary	23.4	25.6	20.7	13.6	15.7	11.0
High school	24.2	22.6	26.2	40.1	38.7	41.8
Some postsecondary/ diploma	36.6	35.2	38.3	21.6	20.0	23.7
University degree	15.8	16.6	14.8	24.6	25.6	23.5
Marital status (%)						
Married	66.4	67.4	65.1	61.5	64.5	58.0
Never-married	26.1	26.9	25.2	24.5	24.7	24.2
Other	7.5	5.8	9.7	14.0	10.8	17.8
Children aged 0–5 (%)	17.8	19.25	16.0	19.2	20.4	17.8
Family income ($)	N/A[a]	N/A	N/A	44,248	44,94	43,405
Self-empl. PJ (unincorporated+ incorporated) (%)	13.8	17.7	9.1	11.3	14.8	7.1
Self-empl. PJ (unincorpated) (%)	8.8	10.5	6.8	8.6	10.8	5.9
Self-empl. PJ (unincorporated, no help) (%)	6.3	7.1	5.4	N/A	N/A	N/A
Temporary job PJ (%)	4.7	5.0	4.5	N/A	N/A	N/A

Characteristics	Canada			United States		
	Both sexes	Males	Females	Both sexes	Males	Females
Union member PJ (%)	35.4	37.8	32.8	16.7	18.3	14.7
Mean total weekly hours	35.45	38.65	31.6	39.3	42.2	35.9
Distribution of hours (%)						
0–29	22.3	13.4	32.9	12.8	7.0	19.8
30–39	32.7	28.7	37.5	10.8	6.2	16.4
40–49	32.7	40.3	23.6	61.5	65.3	57.0
50+	12.4	17.6	6.0	14.9	21.5	6.8
Mean hourly wage PJ (C$)	14.53	15.92	13.13	12.89	14.53	11.07

a N/A = data not available.

workers in Canada have higher moonlighting rates than their male counterparts (5.31 percent versus 4.82 percent), the opposite is true in the United States (5.34 percent versus 6.56 percent). Note, however, that females in Canada and the United States moonlight at approximately the same rate. The U.S. male moonlighting rate is 1.74 percentage points higher than the Canadian male rate, a 36 percent difference.

The moonlighting age profile also is different across the two countries. For male and female workers combined, Canadian moonlighting rates peak for the youngest workers, while U.S. moonlighting rates peak for the middle-age workers (ages 25–44). The moonlighting rates for young workers (ages 17–24) are essentially identical across the two countries, at 5.4 percent. This pattern is altered when the sample is broken down by sex. Canadian male moonlighters are like their U.S. male counterparts, moonlighting at the highest rates during the middle ages. It is the Canadian female moonlighters driving their aggregate age profile: they are most likely to moonlight while they are young. Female moonlighters in the United States follow the same age/moonlighting profile as their male counterparts, moonlighting at the highest rates during the middle ages.

Further information regarding moonlighting patterns over the life cycle can be discerned from Table 2.[4]   Over half of all moonlighters are prime-age workers, and in the United States this figure approaches two-thirds. The life-cycle distribution of moonlighting across sex is quite similar for both countries. As shown in Table 3, compared with nonmoonlighters, U.S. moonlighters are somewhat more likely to be between the ages of 25 and 44.

As seen in Table 1, for Canadian and U.S. workers, male and female, the incidence of moonlighting rises with higher levels of education. For those with a university degree (16 or more years of education for U.S. workers), 6.21 percent of Canadians and 8.04 percent of U.S. workers moonlight. For lesser-educated workers, moonlighting rates are below 4 percent in both countries. Comparing Tables 2 and 3, nonmoonlighters are considerably more likely to have low levels of education compared to moonlighters. This implies that moonlighting is not mostly comprised of the most disadvantaged workers, contrary to what is often implied by the popular media. On the contrary, because of the rising marginal valuation of each additional foregone hour of leisure, if the substitution effect dominates, then those who are most likely to moonlight, *ceteris paribus*, would be those with the relatively greatest wage opportunities on the second job. Additionally, higher-educated workers are more likely to be salaried on their primary jobs rather than hourly paid, so extra hours worked on the primary job will not increase earnings. Overall, moonlighting is undertaken by relatively higher-educated workers. This finding is consistent with Levenson (1995).

One of the characteristics with the most significant differences in the incidence of moonlighting by sex is marital status. In particular, U.S. females who are divorced, separated, or widowed (the "Other" marital status category) moonlight at a rate of 7.44 percent, higher than the 5.38 percent rate for like U.S. male workers. No single marital status category for males has a moonlighting rate as high as for the "Other" females. In Canada, two marital status categories for females exhibit higher moonlighting rates than for any of the three marital status groups for the Canadian males. Females who have never married have a 6.09 percent incidence of moonlighting, while 5.59 percent of females who are divorced, separated, or widowed moonlight.

Table 2 shows that about two-thirds of moonlighters are married, reflecting the relatively high percentage of married workers in the general working population. In both Canada and the United States, male moonlighters are more likely to be married, at 66 percent for Canadians and 61 percent for the United States. However, the gender differences are striking for the United States, where 69 percent of male moonlighters are married but only 48 percent of female moonlighters are married. The extent to which these numbers are driven by overall labor market statistics can be seen in Table 3, where the distribution across marital status is quite similar to that found for the nonmoonlighters. The only substantive difference is for females, where the marriage rate for employed nonmoonlighters is 10 percent higher than the rate for moonlighters.

As is typical in most standard labor supply issues, the presence of young children (aged 0–5 years) is associated with less moonlighting for females but more moonlighting for males. That is, male workers with young children are more likely to moonlight than male workers in general, and the opposite is true for females. This pattern holds for both Canada and the United States, although the sex pattern is stronger in the United States. For men, the income effect of children is stronger, but for females the substitution effect is stronger, implying that the relative valuation of work and leisure causes women to work less when they have young children. Therefore, women with young children are less likely to moonlight as well. As seen in Table 2, Canadian male moonlighters are about 20 percent less likely to have young children than U.S. male moonlighters, while Canadian female moonlighters are more likely to have young children than their U.S. counterparts. Nonmoonlighters (Table 3) are about equally as likely to have young children overall in the two countries, but there is more of a sex difference in the United States, where female nonmoonlighters are nearly 50 percent more likely to have young children than female moonlighters. The distribution of moonlighting across characteristics broken down by marital status and gender is given in Table 4.

Looking at marital status and the presence of young children combined (U.S. numbers, not shown in the tables), reveals that the bulk of the higher moonlighting rates for male workers with young children is associated with the higher moonlighting rates for married or once-married males. In fact, divorced fathers of young children moonlight at

Table 4 Characteristics of Moonlighters, by Marital Status and Sex

Characteristics	Canada			United States			
	Married	Never married	Other	Married	Never married	Divorced	Other
Females							
Age (%)							
17–24	9.9	48.7	0.9	4.0	42.9	1.0	0.7
25–44	64.9	39.2	63.9	75.9	51.8	54.4	53.4
45–64	25.2	12.1	35.3	20.1	5.3	44.6	45.9
Education (%)							
None or elementary	12.2	12.8	9.8	7.8	3.7	4.1	5.6
High school	25.1	15.3	25.8	33.0	27.0	51.2	50.0
Some postsecondary/ diploma	46.0	45.6	55.6	28.3	33.1	14.4	18.7
University degree	16.7	26.3	8.8	30.9	36.2	30.4	25.7
Children aged 0–5 (%)	23.6	0.8	7.6	20.3	4.9	7.2	7.0
Family income ($)	N/A[a]	N/A	N/A	45,973	37,253	31,932	30,427
Self-empl. PJ (unincorporated + corporated) (%)	18.7	9.9	8.7	9.0	1.7	1.7	2.9
Self-empl. PJ (unincorporated) (%)	13.5	6.4	7.9	5.5	0.6	0.3	2.0
Self-empl. PJ (unincorporated, no help) (%)	12.0	6.4	7.6	N/A	N/A	N/A	N/A
Temporary job PJ (%)	5.0	14.4	8.2	N/A	N/A	N/A	N/A
Union member PJ (%)	30.4	16.4	30.6	19.1	10.0	27.7	26.4
Mean total weekly hours	37.24	38.62	39.45	41.6	46.4	50.3	49.4

	Canada			United States			
Characteristics	Married	Never married	Other	Married	Never married	Divorced	Other
Distribution of total hours (%)							
0–29	25.0	18.0	14.9	19.4	11.7	5.0	3.6
30–39	29.4	38.8	22.7	16.3	12.6	5.6	9.3
40–49	26.2	19.7	34.7	38.2	34.4	44.0	43.9
50+	19.4	23.6	27.7	26.1	41.2	45.5	43.2
Mean hourly wage, PJ ($)	12.88	9.84	11.61	11.17	11.84	13.04	12.52
Hourly wage,[b] SJ (%)							
Under 5.00	2.8	4.2	5.8	13.7	25.6	12.3	12.8
5.00–6.99	19.2	40.3	34.4	31.7	31.2	27.3	25.5
7.00–9.99	16.1	16.5	27.6	16.8	16.2	6.2	8.6
10.00–13.99	25.8	21.6	14.8	6.4	9.0	14.0	16.8
14.00–19.99	15.6	1.4	5.9	17.5	7.0	24.6	21.9
20.00+	20.5	16.1	11.4	14.0	10.9	15.7	14.5
Mean hourly wage, SJ ($)	13.51	10.77	10.12	11.79	10.14	13.42	12.83
Number of observations	499	159	71	196	113	62	96
Males							
Age (%)							
17–24	4.2	42.3	0.0	5.9	40.5	0	0
25–44	62.9	51.2	61.4	64.9	55.9	63.3	66.8
45–64	32.9	6.5	38.6	29.3	3.6	36.7	33.2
Education (%)							
None or elementary	20.4	13.1	14.8	6.4	9.7	7.6	8.1
High school	18.7	19.9	13.8	32.1	31.6	28.1	27.6
Some post-secondary/ diploma	40.5	46.8	48.4	26.1	21.5	36.8	33.4

(continued)

Table 4 (continued)

	Canada			United States			
Characteristics	Married	Never married	Other	Married	Never married	Divorced	Other
University degree	20.5	20.2	23.0	35.5	37.2	27.5	30.9
Children aged 0–5 (%)	28.1	1.2	1.3	34.6	0.3	8.1	6.8
Family income ($)	N/A	N/A	N/A	51,196	35.444	37,979	36,813
Self-empl. PJ (unincorporated + incorporated) (%)	26.5	9.9	21.7	11.5	12.5	1.4	9.0
Self-empl. PJ (unincorporated) (%)	17.3	9.6	13.1	5.5	9.8	0	5.5
Self-empl. PJ (unincorporated, no help) (%)	8.9	7.8	7.0	N/A	N/A	N/A	N/A
Temporary job PJ (%)	3.4	10.8	16.2	N/A	N/A	N/A	N/A
Union member PJ (%)	42.8	33.1	54.6	25.1	14.7	12.7	10.4
Total weekly hours	50.27	42.19	47.09	58.4	51.4	54.4	54.4
Distribution of total hours (%)							
0–29	5.4	21.3	7.4	7.4	9.4	1.3	6.1
30–39	13.7	15.2	24.1	24.1	9.5	3.6	2.8
40–49	23.4	29.4	28.8	28.8	29.0	21.2	23.8
50+	57.6	34.2	39.8	39.8	52.1	74.0	67.3
Hourly wage, PJ (C$)	17.59	10.74	23.22	15.72	11.22	14.92	14.13
Hourly wage, SJ (C$)							
Under 5.00	4.1	0	0	15.0	17.3	4.9	7.8
5.00–6.99	10.1	41.8	8.3	10.9	18.4	16.8	25.3
7.00–9.99	26.1	29.8	19.1	20.7	24.3	12.3	9.1

	Canada			United States			
Characteristics	Married	Never married	Other	Married	Never married	Divorced	Other
10.00–13.99	26.6	15.9	18.4	18.3	16.7	14.8	17.7
14.00–19.99	14.4	9.3	3.5	14.2	9.1	14.0	10.3
20.00+	18.7	3.1	50.8	21.0	14.2	37.2	29.9
Hourly wage SJ (C$)	13.3	9.04	17.54	17.95	13.32	19.58	22.67
Number of observations	691	153	33	365	121	38	50

[a] N/A = data not available.
[b] In Canadian dollars.

more than twice the rate of all workers, 12.88 percent. Presumably the financial pressures of alimony or single-parenting play an important role here. Relating marital status and the presence of young children for females in the United States, married women with young children have the lowest moonlighting rate (3.72 percent), while unmarried women without young children moonlight at the highest rate, nearly 8 percent.

Canadians who are self-employed are much more likely to moonlight than the typical Canadian worker. However, in the United States, workers who are self-employed in their primary jobs are less likely to moonlight. The corresponding rates of moonlighting for those self-employed in their primary jobs are 6.6 percent for Canadian workers and 4.9 percent for U.S. workers. Comparing moonlighters to non-moonlighters (Table 3), the difference across the two countries is striking. While U.S. moonlighters are less likely to be self-employed than nonmoonlighters, Canadian moonlighters are much more likely to be self-employed.

Workers in Canada who hold temporary primary jobs moonlight at a rate greater than the overall moonlighting rate, 7.12 percent versus 5.04 percent. And female temporary workers are 50 percent more likely to moonlight than the typical female worker. Comparing moonlighters to nonmoonlighters, moonlighters are considerably more likely to hold temporary primary jobs.

The patterns of moonlighting for those workers unionized on their primary jobs differs between Canada and the United States. Unionized male workers are more likely to moonlight than all male workers, but this increased moonlighting incidence is only 0.07 percentage points for male workers in Canada, but equals a 0.91 point difference for U.S. male workers. Canadian females who are unionized on their primary jobs have significantly lower moonlighting rates than the overall female rate, but the opposite is true for U.S. females. This might reflect the differences in unionization rates and the types of workers unionized between Canada and the United States. In our 1991 data, Canadian males and females were unionized at rates of 39.7 percent and 34.1 percent, respectively. However, in the United States, males and females were unionized at much lower rates, 18.5 percent and 14.9 percent, respectively.

From Table 2, 33.3 percent of Canadian moonlighters and 20.4 percent of U.S. moonlighters are unionized on their primary jobs; that is, Canadian moonlighters are more than 50 percent more likely than their U.S. counterparts to be unionized. In Canada, male moonlighters are considerably more likely to be unionized than females, but the rates across sex in the United States are fairly similar. Compared to non-moonlighters (as seen in Table 3), the differences across sex for Canada persist. Canadian male workers who moonlight are more likely to be unionized than their nonmoonlighting counterparts, but the opposite is true for females. The result for males is somewhat counterintuitive, given the greater than 20 percent boost to wages associated with holding a union job (Riddell 1993). However, union workers are more likely to work full time, and female moonlighters are less likely than males to combine a full-time with a second part-time job. For the United States, unionization rates for moonlighters and nonmoonlighters are fairly close, but like the Canadian males, moonlighters are more likely to be unionized.

As one might expect, moonlighting rates vary across occupations and industries.[5] In Canada, by far the highest moonlighting rate for both men and women is the Primary occupation (7.86 percent and 12.32 percent), which includes farming, forestry, fishing, and mining. Of course, relatively few workers overall are employed in this occupation. The managerial and professional technical occupation (referred to as Managerial in the tables) is the most common occupation for

workers of both sexes in both countries. Male workers in this occupation are a bit more likely to moonlight than workers overall. However,
Canadian female workers in the Managerial occupation are less likely
to moonlight, while the rate for this occupation for U.S. females is
nearly identical to their overall moonlighting rate.

One of the occupations most frequently talked about in discussions
of moonlighting is sales; however, only U.S. males in sales moonlight
at relatively high rates. Sales become more important as the occupation choice for the second job. Approximately 40 percent of female
moonlighters in both countries hold second jobs in sales. For males, 37
percent and 25 percent of moonlighters in Canada and the U.S., respectively, moonlight in sales. A second occupation prevalent in moonlighting jobs is the Professional/Skilled occupation; one-third of U.S.
male moonlighters hold second jobs in Semiskilled/Unskilled jobs.

Turning to PJ industries, relatively high moonlighting rates are seen
in Agriculture and Community Services in all four samples. In fact, 45
percent of U.S. females are employed in primary jobs in Community
Services, which is a broadly defined industry category that includes
professional services and entertainment. And U.S. males employed in
the industry of Public Administration also moonlight at a high rate. For
the second job, by far the most common industry is Services.

The final section in Table 2 shows the percentage of moonlighters
whose second job occupation or industry are the same. Occupation-
switching between the PJ and SJ (seen as a relatively low percentage in
the table) occurs with different occupations for men than women. For
men employed in a clerical occupation in their second job, only about
one-fourth were employed in the same PJ occupation. For women,
only about one-fourth of those employed in a Semiskilled/Unskilled
occupation were employed in the same occupation in the primary job.
For U.S. females, about three-fourths of those employed in Sales and
Service second jobs are occupation-switchers. Industry-switching is
most prevalent for those employed in Retail Trade for the second job.

Information concerning wages on both jobs and total weekly hours
is given in Table 2. On average, U.S. male and female moonlighters
work more total hours per week (at 57 and 45 total hours, respectively)
than their Canadian counterparts (at 48 and 38 hours, respectively).
These averages are nearly 10 hours per week higher than the average
hours worked per week for nonmoonlighters. Additionally, moonlight-

ers have a much greater percentage working more than 50 hours per week than nonmoonlighters. Approximately 50 percent of Canadian male moonlighters and two-thirds of U.S. male moonlighters work more than 50 hours per week. Relatively few nonmoonlighters work this many hours. These numbers suggest that many moonlighters face significant time pressures.

Male moonlighters earn on average $15.90 per hour on the PJ in Canada and $14.60 per hour on the PJ in the U.S.[6] Hourly wages for female moonlighters are nearly equal on average in Canada and the U.S., with Canadian moonlighters earning $11.80 per hour on average and U.S. moonlighters earning $11.71. Compared to nonmoonlighters, moonlighters in three of the four samples earn more per hour on average. Only U.S. female moonlighters earn less per hour on their PJ than do nonmoonlighters.

Secondary job wages are much higher on average for U.S. males ($16.97 per hour) than Canadian males ($12.10), but the opposite is true for females. This might explain in part the higher moonlighting rate for males in the United States. Canadian females earn $12.10 per hour on their SJ while U.S. females earn $11.58 per hour. Surprisingly, Canadian males and females earn identical SJ hourly wages on average. However, as is seen from the SJ wage distribution, 32 percent of Canadian females are low wage (defined as a SJ wage less than $7.00 per hour) while only 24 percent of Canadian males are low wage. In the U.S., 29 percent of male moonlighters are low wage workers, as opposed to 47 percent of U.S. females. With respect to earnings capacity on both jobs, U.S. females seem to be at the greatest disadvantage.

Why Moonlighters Take Second Jobs

Why do workers in the United States and Canada moonlight? The evidence cited so far shows that there are many reasons, reflecting many factors, including age, education, marital status, and household composition. As explained by Conway and Kimmel (1998), the reasons for multiple-job holding can be summarized as constraints on the primary job (insufficient hours or earnings) or heterogeneous jobs (different jobs provide different nonpecuniary benefits to the worker.) These sorts of reasons for moonlighting can be identified in both the Canadian and U.S. data sources because individual workers report specific reasons in the survey for taking a second job. These findings are given in Table 5 and include the following responses: to meet regular household expenses, pay off debts, buy something special, save for the future, gain experience or build up a business, or enjoys the work of the second job.

While there are some similarities between the two countries, some differences can be seen, particularly in how the aggregate figures break down into their sex components. Combining the first and second categories gives the percentage of moonlighting attributable to financial hardship. Approximately 45 percent of Canadian moonlighters and 42 percent of U.S. moonlighters report moonlighting due to financial hardship. And Canadian male moonlighters are somewhat more likely than U.S. male moonlighters to take a second job due to financial hardship—45.6 percent versus 39.2 percent. The rates for females are similar for the two countries, and U.S. women are more likely to moonlight due to financial hardship than U.S. men. Combining the first four categories provides a more comprehensive picture of the percentage of moonlighters who are choosing to take a second job for financial reasons, or for PJ constraints, as alluded to earlier. Canadian

Table 5   Main Reasons for Undertaking Moonlighting in Canada and the United States (%)

	Canada			United States		
	Both sexes	Males	Females	Both sexes	Males	Females
Meet regular household expenses	33.7	33.4	33.9	31.2	28.0	36.0
Pay off debts	11.3	12.2	10.5	11.0	11.2	10.7
Buy something special	4.6	4.5	4.7	7.2	6.7	7.9
Save for the future	12.4	12.8	12.1	10.7	11.1	10.1
Gain experience/build business	10.8	9.7	11.5	7.8	7.1	8.7
Enjoys the work of SJ	15.0	14.6	15.3	13.9	15.2	11.9
Other	12.3	12.7	12.0	18.4	20.8	14.7

NOTE: Canadian information in this table pertains only to moonlighters who were "employees" in their second job.

males are more likely than U.S. males to moonlight for financial reasons (62.9 percent versus 57 percent), but the opposite is true for women (61.2 percent versus 64.7 percent). However, both rates are fairly close.

The last two specific categories identify those moonlighters who have taken a second job because there is some characteristic of that second job that does not exist on the PJ.[7] From the two general moonlighting motivations listed earlier, this is the heterogeneous jobs motive. Canadian and U.S. workers moonlight for this reason at fairly substantial rates—25.8 percent for Canadians, and 21.7 percent for U.S. moonlighters. Breaking this down by sex reveals a more substantial discrepancy between female moonlighters—27.3 percent for Canadians and 20.6 percent for U.S. moonlighters. Overall, while financial motivations are most important in moonlighting, the heterogeneous jobs motive is important for a substantial percentage of individuals.

In summary, there are several findings of note in this section. Moonlighting is most prevalent among relatively higher educated workers, and unmarried females are most likely to moonlight. Also, the bulk of moonlighting is undertaken for financial reasons. There are two major differences between moonlighting in Canada and the United States. First, U.S. workers overall are about 20 percent more likely to moonlight than Canadian workers, while females in the two countries moonlight at comparable rates. Second, U.S. moonlighters work on average more total hours per week than Canadian workers, but moonlighters in all cases work considerably more hours per week than non-moonlighters.

ECONOMETRIC ANALYSES

In addition to the descriptive analyses using the summary statistics, we seek further information regarding moonlighting patterns and the structure of PJ and SJ wages using regression analyses. Previous econometric studies of moonlighting behavior include Shishko and Rostker (1976), Krishnan (1990), Lilja (1991), Abdukadir (1992), Paxson and Sicherman (1996), Conway and Kimmel (1998), Kimmel and Conway (2001), and Powell and Boucher (2001). First, to determine what factors are important in determining the level of wages in each of the two jobs, we estimate ordinary least squares (OLS) wage equations for both the PJ and SJ wages. Because SJ wages are observed only for those holding a secondary job, we include an econometric sample selection term to account for this selection on positive SJ wages in this equation. We refer to this term as Lambda, and it is the standard Heckman (1979) sample selection correction term.[8]   The two wage equations are written out in summary form below.

PJ wage = dummy variables for age categories; dummy variables for education categories; dummy variable for young children;[9] regional dummies; industry dummy variables.

SJ wage = dummy variables for age categories; dummy variables for education categories; dummy variable for presence of young children;[10]   regional dummies; lambda.

These specifications reflect a standard human capital model of wages in which the level of education and years of experience (proxied by age in our data) are expected to contribute positively to wages. Additionally, in the regressions for females, an additional dummy variable for the presence of young children in the family is included as a proxy for intermittent work history (Blau and Beller 1988). And, the regional dummies are included to control the effect of regional differences in labor market demand conditions. Industry dummy variables are included in the PJ wage equation but not the secondary wage equation because the industry of the SJ is not available for all workers, so the results could not be used to predict the SJ wage for nonmoonlighters.

PJ and SJ wage equations are estimated separately by country and sex. Results from these regressions are given in Tables 6 and 7. Because the equations are estimated with the natural logarithm of the wage as the dependent variable, coefficient values reflect percentage returns to the different characteristics.[11]   Additionally, for each categorical dummy variable, the coefficient is interpreted in comparison to the excluded category. Only coefficients with statistical significance of 10 percent or greater are discussed in text.

Table 6 OLS Log PJ Wage Equations in Canada and the United States[a,b]

Variables	Males		Females	
	Canada	United States	Canada	United States
Intercept	2.1808***	1.7012***	2.2388***	1.7278***
	(113.256)	(68.907)	(128.569)	(75.602)
Age 25–34	0.2967***	0.2732***	0.1929***	0.2450***
	(22.986)	(15.603)	(15.935)	(14.068)
Age 35–44	0.4496***	0.4521***	0.2795***	0.3172***
	(33.302)	(25.015)	(22.264)	(17.737)
Age 45+	0.4585***	0.5103***	0.2611***	0.2980***
	(32.585)	(28.325)	(19.528)	(17.625)
High school	0.1172***	0.2138***	0.1394***	0.2040***
	(9.867)	(13.047)	(11.453)	(11.201)
Some postsecondary	0.2063***	0.3520***	0.2177***	0.3378***
	(19.345)	(19.023)	(19.075)	(17.047)
University degree	0.4382***	0.6215***	0.4950***	0.5772***
	(29.444)	(33.000)	(32.077)	(28.110)
Number of children	—	—	−0.0162***	−0.0287***
			(−4.389)	(−4.986)
Region 1[c]	−0.2427***	0.1248***	−0.2136***	0.1179***
	(−19.632)	(8.363)	(−18.076)	(8.274)
Region 2	−0.0557***	0.0261*	−0.0333***	0.0051
	(−4.692)	(1.755)	(−2.799)	(0.353)
Region 3	−0.1417***	0.0982***	−0.1179***	0.1148***
	(−10.200)	(6.485)	(−9.094)	(7.749)
Region 4	−0.3537***	—	−0.0489***	—
	(−2.271)		(−3.306)	
Region 5	0.2196	—	−0.0353**	—
	(1.391)		(−2.246)	
Agriculture	−0.2943***	−0.3375***	−0.3699***	−0.1641***
	(−8.736)	(−7.951)	(−9.460)	(−2.404)
Other primary	0.2576***	0.2738***	0.0142	0.1043
	(11.816)	(5.547)	(0.298)	(1.235)
Manufacturing, nondurable	0.0711***	0.1724***	−0.1733***	−0.0203
	(4.018)	(7.348)	(−9.621)	(−0.911)
Manufacturing, durable	0.0888***	0.2351***	−0.0988***	0.0927***
	(5.091)	(11.449)	(−3.801)	(4.027)

Variables	Males		Females	
	Canada	United States	Canada	United States
Construction	0.1072***	0.2234***	–0.1696***	0.0471
	(5.664)	(9.769)	(–4.490)	(0.902)
Transportation	0.0928***	0.2501***	0.0607***	0.1840***
	(5.206)	(11.047)	(2.927)	(7.226)
Wholesale trade	–0.0539***	0.1052***	–0.2530***	0.0022
	(–2.533)	(3.740)	(–9.314)	(0.063)
Retail trade	–0.1888***	–0.0988***	–0.3979***	–0.2327***
	(–10.481)	(–4.651)	(–30.579)	(–14.796)
Finance	0.0848***	0.2162***	–0.0771***	0.0705***
	(3.074)	(7.681)	(–4.540)	(3.498)
Personal services	–0.3748***	–0.1158***	–0.5313***	–0.3456***
	(–15.913)	(–2.721)	(–36.377)	(–13.048)
Business services	–0.0566***	0.0526**	–0.1695***	–0.0191
	(–2.622)	(1.983)	(–9.163)	(–0.696)
Public administration	0.1581***	0.1856***	0.0637***	0.1675***
	(8.673)	(7.164)	(3.999)	(6.604)
R^2	0.4026	0.3961	0.4375	0.3425
Number of observations	8,643	6,477	8,846	6,210

[a] * = 10% statistical significance.
  ** = 5% statistical significance.
  *** = 1% statistical significance.
[b] t-Statistics are in parentheses.
[c] In Canda, the regions are 1) Atlantic, 2) Quebec, 3) Manitoba and Saskatchewan, 4) Alberta, 5) British Columbia. In the United States, the regions are 1) Northeast, 2) Midwest, 3) West.

Table 7 OLS Log SJ Wage Equations in Canada and the United States[a,b]

	Males		Females	
Variables	Canada	United States	Canada	United States
Intercept	1.9828***	2.2316***	1.4408***	2.0342***
	(4.939)	(2.906)	(5.998)	(3.467)
Age 25–34	0.1619*	0.1481	0.2741***	0.2042*
	(1.694)	(1.128)	(3.733)	(1.886)
Age 35–44	0.4153***	0.3407**	0.3090***	0.2379**
	(3.740)	(2.241)	(4.061)	(2.071)
Age 45+	0.2518*	0.5074***	0.1924**	0.1721
	(1.853)	(3.308)	(2.131)	(1.333)
High school	0.1535	0.0836	0.1410	0.0556
	(1.419)	(0.467)	(1.587)	(0.310)
Some	0.2696***	0.2134	0.3553***	0.2017
postsecondary	(2.668)	(1.029)	(4.302)	(1.039)
University degree	0.4828***	0.3305	0.5535***	0.4641***
	(3.880)	(1.536)	(5.350)	(2.399)
Number of children	—	—	0.0139	0.0450
			(0.679)	(1.157)
Region 1[c]	–0.1889	–0.333	–0.2143***	–0.1140
	(–1.620)	(–0.245)	(–2.374)	(–1.087)
Region 2	–0.0107	–0.0593	–0.0952	–0.1505
	(–0.094)	(–0.481)	(–0.811)	(–1.344)
Region 3	–0.2241*	0.1868	–0.0792	0.0731
	(–1.905)	(1.532)	(–1.095)	(0.665)
Region 4	–0.0239	—	–0.2470***	—
	(–0.186)		(–2.837)	
Region 5	–0.1507	—	–0.0625	—
	(–1.120)		(–0.636)	
Lambda	–0.0209	–0.1708	1.2921*	–0.1120
	(–0.131)	(–0.532)	(1.839)	(–0.486)
R^2	0.2807	0.1420	0.2503	0.1720
Number of observations	161	223	280	248

---

[a]   * = 10% statistical significance.
   ** = 5% statistical significance.
   *** = 1% statistical significance.
[b] t-Statistics are in parentheses.
[c] In Canada, the regions are 1) Atlantic, 2) Quebec, 3) Manitoba and Saskatchewan,
   4) Alberta, 5) British Columbia. In the United States, the regions are 1) Northeast,
   2), Midwest, 3) West.

Starting with the PJ wage equation, as expected, age is positively associated with wages across the board, with older workers receiving increasingly larger wage boosts. The one exception to this rule is U.S. females, where the middle age category receives the highest wage boost. This could be due to the fact that entry level wages for female workers have been relatively higher in the past 20 years or so (thereby shifting up the entire wage profile for these workers), a wage increase not enjoyed by the older U.S. female workers.

The wage returns to education rise with higher education levels, as predicted by human capital theory. For men, Canadian and U.S. workers receive 12 percent and 24 percent wage boosts, respectively, for having finished high school. This is a wage premium relative to workers who have failed to complete high school. See that the returns to finishing high school for U.S. males is twice as high as that for Canadian males. This reflects a fact of the U.S. labor market that has contributed to growing wage inequality in the United States. For female workers, the returns to completing a high school education for Canada and the United States are 14 percent and 20 percent, respectively. In all cases, the wage return rises with the higher education levels. So, for males, having completed some postsecondary education is associated with a 21 percent and 35 percent return for Canadian and U.S. workers, respectively. Those two returns are 22 percent and 34 percent for females. Finally, having finished a university degree (or 16 or more total years of education in the United States) is associated with 44 percent and 62 percent returns for Canadian and U.S. men, respectively, and 50 percent and 58 percent returns for women. In each case, the returns to the different level of education is higher in the United States. The returns across sex are quite close, with the most noticeable being the returns to men and women in the United States for having completed college. Here, men receive a 4 percent larger return than the women workers.

As predicted by theory, having young children (associated with a greater disrupted work history) has a negative impact on wages for both Canadian and U.S. female workers. The negative impact is almost double for the U.S. females, but the absolute magnitude in both cases is quite small. And, as expected, region of residence is important. Canadian workers living in Ontario receive the highest wage return, as do workers living in the Northeast and the West in the United States.

The overall explanatory power of the PJ wage equations is quite high in all four cases, with R^2 ranging in value from 0.34 up to 0.44. The explanatory power of the SJ wage equations is much weaker, with R^2 ranging in value from 0.14 to 0.28. And fewer of the *a priori* hypotheses for the specific variables hold in this equation. There is a fairly strong return to age (the proxy for experience), but the additional proxy for experience for females (the dummy variable for the presence of young children) is not significant in either case. Education is not strongly related to wages for any of the four samples. For Canadians (both males and females), there is a significant return for having some postsecondary education as well as a college degree, with the females receiving the higher returns. For the United States, the only case of a significant education coefficient is for females with a university degree. Here, the return is 46 percent, but it is not as large as it is for Canadian female moonlighters. While no U.S. regions are significant, for Canadian males, living in Manitoba or Saskatchewan is associated with lower wages (relative to Ontario), as is living in the Atlantic Provinces or Alberta for females. The only sample for whom sample selection is significant is Canadian females. That is, for this group, the probability of moonlighting is significantly positively correlated with higher SJ wages.

Results from these two wage equations are used to construct predicted wages for use in a probit model for moonlighting. The probit equation is written out in summary form below.

Probability of moonlighting = (PJ wage; SJ wage; dummy variables for age categories; dummy variables for education categories; dummy variable for young children; total number of children; dummy variables for marital status).

The probit model transforms a discretely measured dependent variable (here, a 0–1 dummy variable equaling one for moonlighters) into a continuous probability.

The results for the probit model of moonlighting are given in Table 8. Probit coefficients are given, then probit derivatives. For the two wage measures, elasticities are also given.[12] *Ceteris paribus*, one would expect that higher primary job wages would be associated with a lower probability of moonlighting. Indeed, in each of the two cases in which the PJ wage is significant, it is significantly negative. For males in the United States and Canada, those with higher primary job wages are less likely to moonlight. The PJ wage elasticity is fairly large in both cases: –0.81 for males in Canada and –1.18 for males in the United States. For females, both PJ wage coefficients are positive with very large standard errors.

As a standard wage employment effect, we would expect that the coefficient on the SJ wage would be positive; that is, we would expect those individuals with a higher predicted secondary job wage to be more likely to take a second job. This coefficient is negative and insignificant in three of four cases, but in the one case where it is significant, for females in Canada, the coefficient is positive. The corresponding SJ wage elasticity is 1.26.

For Canadian males, age is not significantly related to the probability of moonlighting. But for Canadian females, older workers are increasingly less likely to moonlight. (Recall that the coefficient is interpreted in relation to the excluded category, which is the youngest age group.) For workers in the United States, the only significant relationship between age and the probability of moonlighting is found with females, who are less likely to moonlight if they are older than 45 years of age.

The coefficients for the education variables are interpreted relative to the excluded category of the lowest education level, fewer than 12 years of education. Having more education increases the probability of moonlighting for Canadian males and U.S. males and females. Interestingly, having more education is not significantly related to increased moonlighting probabilities for Canadian females.

Having young children can be expected to have different effects on men than women, due to traditional family roles. We would expect fathers to be more likely to moonlight due to an income effect; that is,

Table 8 Moonlighting Probit Regressions[a,b,c]

Regressors	Canada		United States	
	Males	Females	Males	Females
Intercept	−0.3144	−2.9380***	−0.6243	1.2681*
	(−0.464)	(−6.575)	(−0.777)	(−1.671)
	−0.0129	−0.1952	−0.0447	−0.0994
PJ wage	−0.3692*	0.1296	−0.5683***	0.1102
	(−1.809)	(0.927)	(−2.846)	(0.518)
	−0.0151	0.0086	−0.0407	0.0086
	[−0.8110]	[0.2749]	[−1.1810]	[0.2163]
SJ wage	−0.4555	0.6028*	−0.0998	−0.5245
	(−1.213)	(1.887)	(−0.304)	(−1.530)
	−0.0186	0.0400	−0.0071	−0.0411
	[−1.0005]	[1.2606]	[−0.2075]	[−1.0291]
Age 25–34	−0.1188	−0.3646***	0.0423	0.0194
	(−0.928)	(−3.117)	(−0.342)	(0.144)
	−0.0049	−0.0242	−0.0030	0.0015
Age 35–44	0.0032	−0.4661***	−0.0387	−0.0283
	(0.017)	(−3.559)	(−0.209)	(−0.180)
	0.0001	−0.0310	−0.0028	−0.0022
Age ≥ 45	−0.2114	−0.4991***	0.0221	−0.2805*
	(−1.203)	(−4.078)	(0.096)	(−1.867)
	−0.0086	−0.0332	0.0016	−0.0220
Education = 12	0.3178***	0.0227	0.3704***	0.2858**
	(2.904)	(0.237)	(3.094)	(2.092)
	0.0130	0.0015	0.0265	0.0224
Education 13–15	0.3801***	−0.0830	0.6518***	0.4909***
	(2.910)	(−0.624)	(4.335)	(2.957)
	0.0156	−0.0055	0.0466	0.0385
Education ≥ 16	0.6915***	−0.2493	0.8501***	0.6142***
	(3.406)	(−1.235)	(4.309)	(2.537)
	0.0283	−0.0166	0.0608	0.0481
Preschool children	−0.0041	−0.0354	0.0038	−0.2679***
	(−0.041)	(−0.422)	(0.039)	(−2.652)
	−0.0002	−0.0023	0.0003	−0.0210
Number of children	−0.0159	−0.0034	0.0258	0.1013***
	(−0.504)	(−0.129)	(0.698)	(2.457)
	−0.0006	−0.0003	0.0018	0.0079

Regressors	Canada		United States	
	Males	Females	Males	Females
Single	−0.0045	0.1420*	−0.0679	0.2272***
	(−0.046)	(1.946)	(−0.693)	(2.527)
	−0.0002	0.0094	−0.0049	0.0178
Not married/Other	0.1154	0.3203***	−0.0063	0.3723***
	(0.746)	(3.759)	(−0.055)	(4.773)
	0.0047	0.0213	−0.0004	0.0292
Log–likelihood	−776.271	−1,208.044	−949.876	−1,008.746

[a] These regressions exclude those self-employed on their PJ or SJ. Uses log wages from log wage equations.

[b] Presents coefficients first, then t-statistics in parentheses, then derivatives. For the two wages, elasticities are given in brackets.

[c] * = 10% statistical significance.

   ** = 5% statistical significance.

   *** = 1% statistical significance.

having young children would be expected to increase the stresses on the family budget. For women, we would expect that having young children would raise the opportunity cost of working, implying a substitution effect, therefore reducing the probability of moonlighting. The only case in which this expectation is upheld is for females in the United States, where having young children significantly decreases the probability of holding a second job. But these expectations are not contradicted in any of the other cases, because the coefficients are not statistically significant. The number of children would be expected to have somewhat the same role in the moonlighting choice, with a less strong negative impact on females. The results show that having more children actually increases the probability of moonlighting for females in the United States. This implies that for these women, while the substitution effect dominates in the case of young children, the income effect dominates for total children.

We already saw in the previous descriptive analyses that marital status is strongly linked to moonlighting behavior. But in a regression framework we are able to determine the importance of marital status after controlling for the effect of other factors. Controlling these effects, the role that marital status plays in the moonlighting choices of women is still evident. For both Canadian and U.S. females, being never-married or once-married both are significantly positively related to the probability of moonlighting. It is likely that some of this effect would have been reduced had income been included as a variable, but still the importance of marital status is clear. Thus, within our multivariate analyses, the wage regressions reveal that the structure of SJ wages is more ambiguous than PJ wages, because while the expected wage return to experience is found, no consistent SJ wage return to education can be seen. And, the moonlighting probit equation shows the importance of PJ wages in the moonlighting choice, with those males having higher PJ wages being less likely to moonlight. And, *ceteris paribus*, those with higher education levels are more likely to moonlight. Finally, unmarried females are more likely to moonlight as well.

CONCLUSIONS

In this chapter, we have described and compared moonlighting behavior in Canada and the United States. What are the major findings? First, education plays a major role in moonlighting, with higher educated workers more likely to moonlight. Second, about two-thirds of moonlighters take a second job for financial reasons. Third, total hours worked per week are much higher for moonlighters than non-moonlighters, and hourly wages on the primary job are higher for all moonlighters except U.S. females. Fourth, unmarried females and married males are most likely to moonlight. Finally, there is evidence that workers moonlight due to both primary job constraints and job heterogeneity.

Now, how does moonlighting behavior differ between Canada and the United States? First, overall moonlighting rates are higher in the United States than in Canada, although females in both countries moonlight at approximately the same rate. Second, U.S. moonlighters tend to be older on average than Canadian moonlighters, while Canadian moonlighters tend to be somewhat more educated. Third, total hours worked are considerably higher in the United States than in Canada. So what are the reasons for the differences between Canada and the United States? One factor contributing to the higher moonlighting rate in the

United States is higher U.S. divorce rates. Males in the United States are more likely to be unmarried fathers (custodial or not), and these fathers moonlight at very high rates. Canadians might moonlight less overall in part due to the higher unemployment rates in Canada. With such an excess supply of labor, both primary and secondary jobs are hard to find.

Finally, what are the implications of all these numbers? Why do we care about moonlighting? To put it succinctly, moonlighting itself is not so much a problem as it is a symptom of a broader labor market problem. Two issues are of most importance here: time pressures faced by moonlighters and their families, and the degree to which moonlighting reflects perceived financial hardship. First, because total hours worked for moonlighting are considerably higher than for nonmoonlighters, rising moonlighting rates imply increased time pressures faced by individuals and families. For children, this implies increases in nonparental child care. Second, moonlighters clearly face financial pressures. They do not tend to be lower-income workers, so their financial concerns extend beyond the basics of minimal shelter and food to more middle class concerns such as home ownership and saving for retirement and their children's college educations. While these pressures are not as desperate as those faced by low-income workers, they probably reflect for many moonlighters the desire to achieve the standard of living they enjoyed during their upbringing. For divorced mothers, they reflect a desire to maintain the lifestyle experienced during the previous marriage. And the plight of moonlighters reflects the growing frustrations of today's workers who feel they are working more for less.

Notes

The authors would like to thank Rebecca Jacobs for superb research assistance and Claire Black for secretarial support. Also, we are grateful to the Household Surveys Division at Statistics Canada for kindly providing us with Labour Force Survey data.

1. The primary job is the job with the higher weekly hours. Hereafter we use PJ and SJ to denote the primary and secondary jobs.
2. The U.S. CPS weight used is the multiple job-holder (supplement) weight. This weight corrects for nonresponse in general, as well as nonresponse that varies systematically by class of worker.

3. These rates differ from the rates implied by the raw data, but again, this is due to the weighting necessary to assure that the summary statistics reflect the populations in the two countries.

4. For example, in Canada, 16.6 percent of all moonlighters are between the ages of 17 and 24 years.

5. U.S. three-digit industry and occupation SIC codes were matched to the broader categories reported in the Canadian data.

6. Wages are measured in Canadian dollars.

7. This discussion ignores the final category of Other. It is not possible to assign these individuals to either of the two general categories with any certainty. In fact, a small percentage of these moonlighters are not truly holding a second job because they are changing jobs and so probably only hold two jobs during a short overlapping time period.

8. Lambda is constructed from the results of a reduced form probit in which the dependent variable takes on the value of 1.0 if the individual moonlights, and takes the value of 0 otherwise. Any worker self-employed on the primary or secondary job is excluded from all these regression analyses.

9. This variable is included just in the regressions for females.

10. See previous note.

11. Also, recall that the wages are measured in Canadian dollars, using the 1991 exchange rate. According to Card and Freeman (1993), using purchasing-power parity figures would yield similar results.

12. Note that income is excluded because it is unavailable in the Canadian data.

References

Abdukadir, Gulnaz. 1992. "Liquidity Constraints as a Cause of Moonlighting." *Applied Economics* 24: 1307–1310.

Blau, Francine D., and Andrea H. Beller. 1988. "Trends in Earnings Differentials by Gender, 1971–1981." *Industrial and Labor Relations Review* 41(4): 513–529.

Card, David, and Richard B. Freeman. 1993. "Small Differences That Matter: Canada vs. the United States." In *Working under Different Rules*, Richard B. Freeman ed. Chicago: The University of Chicago Press, pp. 189–222.

Cohen, Gary L. 1994. "Ever More Moonlighters." *Perspectives on Labour and Income* (Autumn): 31–38.

Conway, Karen Smith, and Jean Kimmel. 1998. "Male Labor Supply Estimates and the Decision to Moonlight." *Labour Economics* 5(2): 135–166.

Heckman, James. 1979. "Sample Selection Bias as a Specification Error." *Econometrica* 47: 153–162.

Kimmel, Jean, and Karen Smith Conway. 2001. "Who Moonlights and Why? Evidence from the SIPP." *Industrial Relations* 40(1): 89–121.

Krahn, Harvey. 1995. "Non-standard Work on the Rise." *Perspectives on Labour and Income* (Winter): 35–42.

Krishnan, Pramila. 1990. "The Economics of Moonlighting: A Double Self-Selection Model." *Review of Economics and Statistics* 72(2): 361–367.

Levenson, Alec. 1995. "Where Have All the Part-Timers Gone? Recent Trends and New Evidence on Moonlighting." Working paper 951, Milken Institute for Job and Capital Foundation, Santa Monica, California.

Lilja, Reija. 1991. *The Problematic and Unproblematic Second Job.* Discussion paper No. 107, Labor Institute for Economic Research, Helsinki.

Paxson, Christina H., and Nachum Sicherman. 1996. "The Dynamics of Dual Job Holding and Job Mobility." *Journal of Labor Economics* 14(3): 357–393.

Pold, Henry. 1995. "Families and Moonlighting." *Perspectives on Labour and Income* (Summer): 7–8.

Powell, Lisa M., and Nathalie Boucher. 2001. "Duration Analysis of Multiple Job-Holders." Unpublished paper.

Riddell, Craig W. 1993. "Unionization in Canada and the United States: A Tale of Two Countries." In *Small Differences that Matter: Labor Markets and Income Maintenance in Canada and the United States*, David Card and Richard B. Freeman, eds. Chicago: The University of Chicago Press, pp. 109–148.

Sekscenski, Edward S. 1980. "Women's Share of Moonlighting Nearly Doubles during 1969–79." *Monthly Labor Review* 103(5): 36–39.

Shishko, Robert, and Bernard Rostker. 1976. "The Economics of Multiple Job Holding." *American Economic Review* 66(3): 298–308.

Stinson, John F., Jr. 1986. "Moonlighting by Women Jumped to Record Highs." *Monthly Labor Review* 109(11): 22–25.

_____. 1990. "Multiple Job-Holding Up Sharply in the 1980s." *Monthly Labor Review* 113(7): 3–10.

Webber, Maryanne. 1989. "Moonlighters." *Perspectives on Labour and Income* (Winter): 21–30.

11
Large Companies and the Changing Use of Temporary Workers
Trends and Impacts on
Financial Measures of Performance

Shulamit Kahn, Fred Foulkes, and Jeffrey Heisler
Boston University

Over the past decade, there has been a large increase in the number of people employed in temporary work. For instance, in July of 1996, the number of employees in the Standard Industrial Classification code for "help supply services" (7,363) was estimated in the U.S. Bureau of Labor Statistics (BLS) Establishment Survey as 2.38 million people (U.S. BLS 1996)—an increase from 0.6 percent of the labor force in 1985 to 2.0 percent in mid 1996.[1] In the early 1990s, many analysts believed that this was a phenomenon born of the last recession that would reverse itself in the subsequent expansion. Instead, this trend has continued at varying pace throughout the decade. BLS projects that the somewhat larger category of "personnel supply" will be the seventh-fastest growing industry between 1994 and 2005, with growth projected at 58 percent (Staffing Industry Analysts 1996).

This chapter uses the results from a random survey of human resource executives from large companies around the country to consider why companies are changing their uses of temporary workers. The chapter then correlates the intensity of temporary use with financial measures of profitability. The sample is quite small, so it is more suggestive than definitive. Remarkably, some statistically significant correlations do arise even within this small sample. Although it is impossible to deduce causality from correlation, the results somewhat suggest that strategic uses of temporaries may increase operating margins and company value.

The study also considers a case study of two firms in a narrowly defined manufacturing industry. These firms radically increased their

use of temporaries, hiring all entry-level production workers as temporaries who then—if successful—transition into permanent employment
after three months. Financial measures of performance after the policy
change indicate that the companies either did equally well or worse
than the previous period, suggesting that this use of temporaries was
either neutral or harmful to the companies' bottom lines.

DESCRIPTION OF SURVEY

The focus of this section is large companies' usage of temporary
employees. In the first phase of our research, we conducted in-depth,
open-ended interviews with human resource executives from several
large companies to get a sense of the role of temporary staff within
their organizations. We also spoke to a large number of executives
from within the staffing industry to get their perspectives and insights
into industry trends. We defined temporary workers as those paid by a
temporary agency or temporaries directly hired by their company. We
specifically asked them to exclude all others, including contract workers.[2]

Although chosen primarily for their accessibility rather than for
aspects of their temporary usage, these preliminary interviews were not
in any way a representative, random sample. To obtain a representative
sample of large companies, we chose companies randomly from the
Fortune 500 Industrials and other *Fortune* lists (banking, savings,
financial, retail, service, transportation, and utilities) and identified a
senior human resource executive in that company, generally the human
resource vice president.

Through a letter, we solicited these companies' participation in an
extended telephone interview and asked for a contact within the company most familiar with the company's use of temporaries. We followed up with telephone calls in June 1995, conducting 35 30-minute
interviews from this sample. This represents a response rate of 22 percent. Of the nonrespondents, 29 refused in writing or over the phone to
participate in the research, generally because of time constraints or
company policy not to participate in surveys.[3] In the other cases, we
failed to reach the appropriate person after several phone calls.

Given the high level of the executives whom we were contacting, a low response rate is expected. A crucial question is whether there is any nonresponse bias in the responses. The most likely bias would be that companies with innovative temporary policies are more likely to respond. While this is a possibility, the factors arguing against this bias are the nature of the reasons given for nonresponse and the fact that the most common case of nonresponse was simply failure to make any contact with the relevant person.

The actual respondent from each company was a person familiar with the company's use of temporaries. When the company's use of temporaries was decentralized, we were generally put in contact with someone who was familiar with only a portion of the company's temporaries, typically those used at corporate headquarters. Respondents ranged from senior vice presidents to employment specialists. In the completed telephone interviews, we followed a seven-page script/questionnaire that included both open-ended and forced-choice questions.[4] The small size of this sample means that any hypothesis test is likely to be rejected unless differences are quite large.

One of the companies surveyed was a southern U.S. fibers/textiles firm. We discovered that this company had made a sudden shift toward the exclusive use of temporaries for all entry-level production jobs. In order to conduct a time-series event study of this firm, we conducted a telephone survey of seven other comparable firms, i.e., nonunionized, southern, publicly traded companies in the fiber/textiles industry. This additional sample was taken from the Compustat listing of companies in three similar four-digit industry codes. We identified 12 companies (other than our original one) that had headquarters in southern states. Of these, we were able to interview seven.

RESULTS: CHANGES IN THE ROLE OF TEMPORARIES

Labor force surveys indicate an increase in the number of temporary workers in the United States. This increase is evident in our sample of large firms as well. Along with the changing numbers of temps, there were also changes in other aspects of temp usage. As the first row of Table 1 indicates, the increased usage of temporaries was by no

Table 1 Percentage of Sample Who Changed Use of Temporaries

	Increased >100%	Increased somewhat (10%–100%)	Small or no change (<10% change)	Decreased a lot (>10%)
[Over the past 3 to 5 years, have you increased or decreased the number of temporaries that you hire?] Does this represent a change in the percent of total employment?	8.6	28.6	37.1	25.7
Has the length of stay of temps changed over the past 3 to 5 years?	0.0	38.2	52.9	8.8
In the past 3 to 5 years, have there been changes in the percent of (full-time regular) hires who began working at your company as a temp?[a]	9.4	18.8	71.9	0.0

	% changed
[In what kinds of situations does your company use temps?] Has this changed over the past 3 to 5 years?	44.1
[What kinds of jobs do you use temporaries for?] Has this changed over the past 3 to 5 years?	46.8
Have you used this same source of temps over the past 3 to 5 years, or does this represent a change?[b]	50.0

NOTE: Wording in brackets varies from the actual questions used in the survey.

[a] Wording different from actual question, which culminated a series of questions about the number of temps hired permanently and the number of total employees hired into comparable jobs.

[b] This number excluded changes in vendors' identities that weren't accompanied by other changes in the source, such as a change in the number of agencies used.

means universal. The proportion of firms that substantially increased their use of temps (37 percent) is just equal to the proportion with a small or no change. While each of these categories is larger than the proportion that decreased their use of temps, fully one-quarter of the firms in the sample did substantially decrease their use of temps.

At the extreme, some companies have moved to hiring only, or primarily, temporaries for large numbers of jobs within their companies. We observed two variants of this policy. In one, temporary workers may stay only a limited length of time, which in some companies is as long as two years. In the second variant, temporaries who perform well transfer over to regular jobs after some period, often specified up front. Reading the business press and talking to human resource (HR) executives, we identified quite a few companies that are hiring only temporaries for large classes of jobs. These include Dell Computer, Hewlett-Packard, DEC, and Microsoft. At Dell, approximately 3,000 of the company's 10,000 employees are temporary. At Hewlett-Packard and DEC, 30–35 percent of their manufacturing jobs are being done by temporary employees. Many of these publicized examples are at newer, rapidly growing, and changing organizations. What is particularly surprising, however, is that even in a sample of 35 randomly chosen companies, we found two companies that are hiring only temporaries into a large class of entry-level jobs.

The changing role of temps is evidenced not only in their numbers, but also in their roles. Other surveys have documented shifts in the occupational distribution of temporaries. The typical image of a temporary as a "Kelly Girl," a female secretary, characterized a majority of temporaries 20 years ago but no longer does. By 1994, only 40 percent of the payroll for temporary help services went to office/clerical occupations (Steinberg 1994). In our sample, we found that while almost all companies used temps for secretarial/clerical positions, 80 percent also used temporaries for other kinds of jobs. One source of growth highlighted in surveys such as the National Association of Temporary Service's (NATS) is in the "light industrial" category, including production work and unskilled manual labor. Forty percent of the companies in our survey use temps for these occupations. In fact, Blank (1998) found that the temporary help industry has approximately the same proportion of people in blue-collar occupations as does the general labor force. Given the fact that blue-collar temporaries tend to be unskilled, we can infer that a much higher proportion of temps are in unskilled blue-collar jobs than in the general labor force.

Table 1 also shows the number of companies that changed their use of temps in other ways. Ninety-four percent of our sample changed their use of temporaries in one of the ways listed in the six rows of

Table 1. Forty percent changed more than three of these six aspects of temporary use.

Forty-four percent of the companies indicated that they are using temporaries in different kinds of situations than they had previously. Table 2 lists the kinds of situations in which these companies report using temporaries. The situation that best fits the traditional view of a temporary is someone hired as a replacement for a temporary absence. Most companies continue to use temps for this purpose. Several employers reported expansion of this need due to changing medical and family leave policies.

The business press has adjured companies to use temps as part of a "strategic staffing" plan (e.g., Denka 1994). In essence, a strategic staffing plan is one where employment policies are seen as a part of a company's strategic plan and where alternatives to full-time regular staffing are actively considered at a general level rather than as ad hoc or reactive decisions. The list of situations in our sample in which large companies use temporaries suggests that companies are in fact using "strategic staffing," or at least claiming to. Practically all (91 percent) use temporaries not just for temporary replacement of absences but also as a deliberately chosen alternative to permanent employment designed to further the firm's profitability. Other than absence replacement, the other reasons listed in Table 2 suggest that companies see temporary labor as a solution to two kinds of variance in labor demand: foreseen variance and unforeseen and uncertain variance.

Table 2 Situations in Which Large Companies Use Temporaries

Reasons for hiring temporaries	% of companies
Replacement or temporary absences, medical leave	88.6
Temporary projects	88.2
To bypass head-count restrictions	51.4
Seasonal fluctuations	50.0
New projects	48.6
To screen for permanent jobs	31.4
Downsizing, termination	25.7
Buffer against layoffs	22.9

One major source of foreseen variance is temporary or special projects. The largest use of temporaries reported in the survey is to staff temporary projects, where "temporary" projects can last as long as two years or more. Temporary projects include start-ups, e.g., for new stores or new computer systems. Rather than hiring a regular employee and, upon completion of the project, either finding them alternative positions or paying them a severance package, companies are turning to temporary employees who do not impose the same future responsibilities.

Many companies with labor demands that fluctuate considerably over the year are decreasing labor costs by using temporaries seasonally. For instance, temporaries are being used to harvest fruit in Florida and to process the February rush of annual proxy statements for a large investment bank. One HR manager explained, "We don't staff for peaks any longer." Half of the sample use temporaries for seasonal fluctuations. Both the seasonal needs and temporary projects introduce fully anticipated variance into labor demand. Temps are a logical solution.

When companies face uncertainties about future employment needs, they also sometimes use temporaries to address these uncertainties. Twenty percent of our sample use temporaries when they are uncertain whether new products will take off or what their need will be for a new endeavor. For 23 percent of the companies, temps are being used to provide a buffer to protect the jobs of core, regular employees in the event of unforeseen shifts in product demand.

To an economist, these uses of temporaries do not seem surprising. In fact, it seems more surprising that temporaries were not always used to solve problems of variance and uncertainty.

Temporary Assignments as a Recruiting and Hiring Mechanism

A final major motivation for the use of temps is the avoidance of many of the costs of poor job matches. In all jobs, both the employer and the new employee take time to learn about whether this job is a good match. Unsuccessful matches tend to be terminated by one party or the other. There are many costs of mismatches that fall on the employer, the employee, and society. Some of these costs can be avoided by having new entrants begin in the company as an employee of a temporary agency. First, risk to the employee is lower. If this job does not work out, the employee is given another placement by the temporary agency.[5] For the employer, severance pay, long dismissal procedures, and increased unemployment compensation premia are avoided. Moreover, managers don't have to be put in the difficult emotional position of firing someone, or of being responsible for someone's loss of livelihood. Recruiting costs, such as attracting candidates or conducting drug and criminal screens, are not lost when a particular match does not work out. Societally, unemployment compensation is not incurred when the temporary is reassigned. Finally, in some of the companies we interviewed, it was clear that temporary agencies often had "economies of scale" in recruiting and could simply attract and process candidates more efficiently than some companies. On the other hand, the use of temporaries as a hiring mechanism may be a way for companies to change the implicit or explicit employment contracts with potential employees or to evade government policies.[6]

In our sample, 94 percent of companies responded that they have permanently hired people who began as temporaries. The survey also provides some evidence of increasing use of temps as a hiring mechanism. Thirty-one percent of companies reported that their permanent hiring of temporaries has increased over the past five years. Not a single company responded that their permanent hiring of temporaries has decreased.

This increased hiring is also being documented by temporary agencies. Manpower reports that in 1993, they themselves transitioned 150,000 temps into regular jobs. One mid-sized temporary agency with whom we talked has done an informal poll and found that between 30 and 35 percent of their assignments could change to permanent. In a 1994 National Association of Temporary Staffing (NATS) survey, more than one-third of temporary employees reported being offered a regular job by a firm for which they had an assignment (NATS 1994). In a more recent NATSS survey of former temporaries, 21 percent had found permanent jobs as a result of their temporary position.[7]

Permanent hiring of temporaries occurs in two conceptually different ways—temp-to-hire and temp-to-perm. In the former, the hiring is an unforeseen and unplanned consequence: supervisors are impressed by a temp, or temps get inside tracks to a job listed within the company.

This hiring of temporary employees generally tends to be a small but not inconsequential part of a company's total hiring. Of companies that did not do temp-to-perm, on average only 24 percent of new employees in the jobs comparable to those staffed by temps began as temps.

In temp-to-perm, companies hire temporaries with the intention of transitioning them into regular employment if the match is successful. Thirty-one percent of companies responded that one reason they hire temps is to screen for permanent employees (Table 2). In these companies, on average more than half of people hired into these specific job categories began as temps. As one sample respondent put it, "Now, even low-level supervisors know this is another way to recruit, one of their bag of tricks. In the past, it was not a concept they knew of or thought of."

Temp-to-perm will be a profit-maximizing strategy when temporary agencies are able to attract an ample supply of qualified candidates, and when an extended trial period is a particularly helpful way to screen candidates. Not surprisingly, then, in our interviews with companies, we saw temp-to-perm most commonly used for "light industrial," i.e., relatively unskilled blue-collar jobs—where work habits tend to be of prime importance in determining the success of an employee—and in white-collar jobs that are based on speed and accuracy, such as billing and telephone operators. For one company, the supply of light-industrial employees available through temporary companies was greater than the company itself could otherwise recruit.[8]

The screening aspect of this process is quite clear from the interviews. Only workers who "work out" become regular employees. If temporaries can provide a way of screening employees that incurs less mobility costs, it seems clearly Pareto superior. Once again, economists are more challenged to explain why these methods were not used previously, rather than to explain why they are being used now. The answer is not to be found in labor market tightness. The unemployment rate at the time was 5.5 percent, neither particularly high nor particularly low.

Temporaries and Downsizing

The survey provides some evidence that decreased firm demand for labor, due either to slow sales or to cost-cutting in the face of increased competition, is correlated with an increased use of temporaries. A test of the correlation between downsizing and changes in their proportional use of temps is significant at the 20 percent level. Of the 53 percent of companies in our sample that reported some downsizing in the past five years, fully 78 percent changed their proportional use of temporaries, while only 50 percent of companies that did not downsize changed their usage. A recent survey by Olsten cited in *Business Wire* (1996) found that slightly more than half of firms that report downsizing say that they use temps to address staffing issues.

However, different companies make very different kinds of decisions about temporaries while downsizing. Downsizing companies are more likely to both increase and decrease their use of temporaries than companies who did not downsize. Of downsizing firms, 50 percent increased their use of temps while 28 percent decreased them; among the other companies, 31 percent increased their use of temps while 19 percent decreased them.[9]

The small sample that report downsizing does not lend itself to statistical analysis. If we consider these 16 companies as case studies, we come up with suggestions of the kinds of factors that have led at least some companies to modify their temporary usage during periods of contraction. If temps are used to protect full-time employees from layoffs, we would expect the number of temps to fall drastically during downsizing. While this occurred in some companies, in our small sample the numbers indicate that decreased use of temps was less common than increased use.

One factor that was repeatedly mentioned for increased use of temps was the presence of head-count restrictions—limits imposed on line managers on the number of people allowed on payroll (Table 2). Head-count restrictions are a common mechanism used by central management to control costs incurred by line managers. A head count has the advantage of being an easily measurable cost item that is not affected by conditions outside the line manager's control, such as fluctuating market wage rates or materials prices. However, as companies move to greater usage of temporaries and part-time workers, head-count restrictions should adjust to reflect these new institutions. While it may be profit-maximizing for companies to impose head-count restrictions on permanent employees to limit their permanent employment, head-count restrictions should not create managerial incentives to hire temporaries into jobs that are most profitably staffed by permanent employees.

In some companies we interviewed, head-count restrictions included temps; in others, the restrictions applied only to permanent employees, and consequently managers used temps to evade these restrictions. In fact, 53 percent of our sample said that avoiding head-count restrictions (presumably of permanent employees) *was* a factor in its use of temps. Of the nine companies that chose to increase their (proportional) usage of temporaries during a contraction of employment, six attributed the growth in their use of temporaries at least partially to head-count restrictions. An HR manager in one company, for instance, reported that a hiring freeze has led line managers to hire a temp when an extra person was needed. In another company, the interviewed HR executive told how line managers had to "play games with head count when, head-count considerations aside, regular hiring would have made much more sense." These examples suggest that head-count restrictions introduced inefficiencies. However, head-count restrictions on permanent employees may be optimal for the company that wanted "to keep their future long-run commitment to new employees low."

Hourly Labor Costs and the Increasing Use of Temps

The previous sections suggest that temporary workers are increasingly being used to promote efficiency in a variety of ways and thus raise profitability. An additional way that temporaries might impact profitability is through their direct costs. Temporaries receive lower benefits than their "permanent" counterparts. In our sample, all but two companies say that benefit levels for temps are lower than for regular employees, with the vast majority placing them much lower or nonexistent.[10] Other authors have also documented the low benefit coverage for temporary workers, including BLS (1995) and Axel (1995).

The hourly rates reviewed by the temporaries are sometimes lower than the regular employees they replace but sometimes higher, both in our survey and in comprehensive labor force surveys, such as the CPS data analyzed in Segal and Sullivan (1995). However, companies pay a large margin to cover temporary agencies' costs. Totaling the savings in benefits, different hourly rates, and agencies' margins, do companies save on hourly compensation costs when they use temporaries? Sixty-three percent of companies believe that they do, with half of the others believing that either there is no saving or that temps cost more than regular employees.

Yet, even for many of the companies that save on compensation costs, respondents volunteer the information that costs do not enter into their decisions to use temporaries. One executive seemed quizzical when I asked him about direct cost savings and said, "We don't look at it that way."

Does Productivity and Product Quality Suffer?

Hour for hour, ignoring slack periods when permanent workers may be underutilized, do temporaries work as efficiently as permanent workers and produce similar quality products? Only extensive case studies can really answer this question. Companies differed on their perceptions of the overall productivity of temporaries. Seventeen percent of the companies listed the temporary's lack of commitment among the three biggest problems with temporary employees. One respondent noted a perception among his supervisors that temporary employees were not as qualified, but wondered whether this was due to the fact that the supervisor did not feel "ownership" of these employees.

Yet many employers mentioned the increasing skill and quality levels of temporaries. In fact, several employers believe that temporaries often worked harder than regular employees because they hoped thereby to obtain a permanent placement. Both our survey and a recent *Conference Board* survey (Axel 1995) found that the most frequently mentioned difficulty with temporary workers was that they lacked the skills and training to do the job. In our survey, 23 percent of employers mentioned this.

These mixed perceptions suggest a high variation among temporaries, with average quality varying from company to company as well as from market to market, depending on supply/demand conditions in the specific occupational labor market, as well as on the skill of the temporary agency in screening applicants.

Have Things Really Changed?

It is instructive to compare our survey with the survey of HR executives conducted in 1986 by Katharine Abraham and the Bureau of National Affairs (Abraham 1988). That survey included a somewhat different universe, including some smaller companies along with the large sample of large firms. In addition, that survey explicitly included on-call workers. Nevertheless, there are many similar results in the two surveys. Executives in 1986 also used temporaries for special projects, seasonal needs, and to provide a buffer for regular staff against downturns in demand, long before HR executives were using the term "strategic staffing" for policies regarding temporaries. The proportion using temporaries for at least one of those purposes was lower in that earlier survey, although only marginally so.

Twenty-three percent of the companies in the 1986 survey said that one reason they use temps was to "identify good candidates for regular jobs," similar to the proportion in our 1995 sample that use temp-to-perm, or the proportion in the recent *Conference Board* survey (Axel 1995) that respond that they use temps to screen candidates for future employment.

Since the universes are different, trends can only be suggestive. Yet it is striking that in these aspects, the two surveys point to little change between 1986 and 1995, despite claims of the survey's HR executives to the contrary. However, there are some significant differences between the surveys that may suggest real differences in temporary usage. Thus, there is a difference between surveys in temporaries as a proportion of the companies' total employment. The mean of this proportion in the 1986 sample was 1.5 percent, while the mean in the present sample is 2.3 percent. A much larger difference is evident at the extreme: 2 percent of the companies in the 1986 survey reported using 10 percent temps or more, while in our sample, 9 percent of companies used 10 percent or more.

The second major difference seen is the length of stay of temporaries. In the 1986 survey, only 7 percent of the companies reported that the mean duration of the typical assignment was three months or greater. In our survey, 40 percent reported typical lengths in this range, while a recent NATS survey found that 55 percent of temporary assignments last 11 weeks or more (NATS 1994). Thus, the two surveys are suggestive of a recent shift toward usage of more temporaries and of temporaries for longer periods, although research on directly comparable samples is necessary to confirm this result.

Finally, we note that although the same number of companies report that they use temps to identify good candidates for regular jobs or for purposes like special projects or seasonal fluctuations, it does not preclude the possibility of major changes in the ways companies conceive and decide both the temp-to-perm and "strategic staffing" uses of temps. Moreover, the increase in the number and use-intensity of temps suggest that although the number of companies using temps for these purposes may not have changed, the extent that they use temps in these ways undoubtedly has.

RESULTS: THE USE OF TEMPORARIES AND FINANCIAL MEASURES OF PERFORMANCE

If temporaries improve a firm's performance, we should see this reflected in the company's profits or other financial measures. This impact could, at least hypothetically, be measured by a cross-sectional comparison of the performance of companies that differ in their use of temporaries. Alternatively, it could be measured by comparing the financial performance for companies (or industries) before and after a change in their use of temporaries. In this section, we pursue both methods.

The cross-sectional analysis will be plagued by two different kinds of conceptual problems, causality and heterogeneity issues. A positive correlation between the use of temporaries and financial success might indicate that the use of temporaries increases a company's profitability. However, it could instead indicate that companies that are likely to be profitable (e.g., dynamic, growing companies) choose or need to turn to temporaries for some of their staffing needs.

The great degree of heterogeneity of companies on a wide variety of other dimensions is likely to make this exercise akin to searching for a needle in a haystack. Research has shown that it is extremely difficult to detect financial impacts of changes in human resource practices.[11] Additionally, temporaries are used in many different ways and situations, and they are not likely to have similar impacts in all contexts.

A time-series analysis of companies can avoid some aspects of these problems. First, by comparing periods before and after a change in policy, we can mitigate the causality issue. Second, by looking at individual companies (relative to industry trends) we can remove some of the heterogeneity. Pursuing the analogy, the time-series analysis is akin to finding a button in a haystack: there are still many confounding issues, but we have slightly increased the likelihood of finding some impact.

We have chosen to look at three measures of financial performance. Market price per share (P) summarizes all publicly available information and expectations for the company. However, the share price will reflect all of the activities of the firm, such as acquisitions, making it an extremely noisy series for measuring the impact of temporary policy. We also examine variables that attempt to measure the ongoing profitability of the enterprise: earnings and operating margin (OPM). Earnings are measured as primary earnings per share (EPS) before extraordinary items, i.e., one-time events such as acquisitions and divestitures. OPM is the ratio between operating income and sales. This ratio measures the impact of cost of goods sold (COGS) and sales, general, and administrative expenses (SGA), which include labor costs, on the company's profitability. Although neither of these measures are affected by events like acquisitions, they are affected by changes in accounting practices.

Cross-Sectional Analysis

For the 35 different companies in our sample, we correlated a variety of aspects of temporary usage with the financial variables, the latter considered both in 1994 levels and in five-year (1989–1994) changes.[12] The results can be summarized succinctly.

1) A seven-value index of changing usage of temps, from large cuts in the use of temps to large increases, is generally unrelated to all financial variables with the following exception: companies that had high earnings per share[13] at the beginning of the five-year period were significantly more likely to increase their temporary usage ($P = 0.02$). A two-value index of whether or not a company substantially increased its use of temps was also correlated with increasing share prices ($P = 0.10$).

2) The correlation between temps as a proportion of total employment and the change in share price over the five-year period was positive and highly significant ($P = 0.01$); the proportion of temps was also positively related to the change in EPS over the period at a lower significance level ($P = 0.17$). However, it was not correlated with levels of either EPS or OPM, nor with the change in OPM.

3) We constructed an index for increased use of temporaries as a strategic staffing plan by counting the number of "strategic" changes the company made, including increasing use of temporaries, changing sources of temporaries, changing situations in which use temporaries, increasing the length of temporaries' stays, increasing hiring of temporaries as permanent employees, and changing the occupations in which temporaries are hired. This "strategic temp changes" variable was positively correlated with various measures of firms' profitability in 1994, although only at marginal significance levels (with OPM $P = 0.10$; with EPS $P = 0.07$). However, it was not correlated with the *change* in share price, OPM, or EPS.

4) Many specific increases in strategic temp usage may have been positively correlated with the level of OPM in 1994, although the significance levels were marginal: changing occupations ($P = 0.11$); changing situations where use temps ($P = 0.22$); increasing permanent hiring through temps ($P = 0.28$).

Overall these findings suggest that the use of temporaries, particularly in "strategic" ways, is correlated with positive financial outcomes. Certain "strategic" changes in policies regarding temps may have led to high OPMs. High and/or increasing use of temps may have led to increasing share prices during the early 1990s. Alternatively, the causality may have run in the opposite direction. For instance, companies with high operating margins may have been more likely to make "strategic" changes in their use of temps.

The latter direction of causality is suggested by the fact that companies with high EPS at the beginning of the period later increased their temp usage. On the other hand, changes in temp usage is not correlated with other beginning financial values, such as OPM.

Time-Series Case Studies

In our random survey, we identified one company in the South's fibers/textiles industry that made a sudden shift towards the exclusive use of temporaries for all entry level production jobs. These temporaries are moved into permanent jobs after three months if they "work out." We then surveyed seven other comparable firms, i.e., nonunionized, southern publicly-owned companies in the fiber/textiles industry. Of these seven, one company had suddenly increased its usage of temporaries for entry-level jobs.

All of these eight companies faced tight labor markets. In the face of this tight supply, they were forced to hire poorer quality employees than they usually did. The temp-to-perm option allowed them to screen workers in a situation where screening was particularly important. The two companies that chose this option believed that the temporary agencies could do a better job of attracting workers in a tight labor market than could the company itself. The companies that had not chosen to use temp-to-perm tended to cite company-culture kinds of reasons, such as "It builds good will," and "We have pride in our people and value long-term relationships."

We calculated financial measures for these two companies, denoted A and B, using the other six companies as controls. By studying these companies with radical changes in their use of temporaries, we increased the likelihood of the policy having an impact. By narrowly defining both industry and region, we eliminated some of the variation across firms, increasing the likelihood of detecting any effect. For each company, we estimated time series regressions on quarterly data for the change in the log of share price and the change in earnings per share (EPS):

(1) $\ln(P_t / P_{t-1}) = \beta_0 + \beta_1 D_t + \beta_2 \ln(P_{c,t} / P_{c,t-1}) + \Sigma \beta_I Q_i + e$

(2) $\Delta EPS_t / S_t = \beta_0 + \beta_1 D_t + \beta_2 \Delta EPS_{c,t} / S_{c,t-1} + \Sigma \beta_I Q_i + e$

where S_t is a scaling factor to account for differences in share price,[14] $P_{c,t}$ is the average share price at time t for the six control companies, $EPS_{c,t}$ is the average EPS at time t for the six control companies, D_t is a dummy variable that takes the value 1 for all quarters after the change in policy, and Q_i are seasonal dummy variables.[15] The sample period was from March 1984 through March 1996. However, when the earlier period fit particularly poorly, estimations are reported for the period of March 1988 through March 1996. The results are presented in Tables 3 and 4.

Company A's large change in temporary usage occurred in the beginning of 1995. The results indicate that this point did not mark a watershed in either share price or EPS. Thus, the post-change dummy variable is not distinguishable from 0 in any of the four equations (with t-statistic always considerably less than 1.0). An F-test of the hypothesis that the pre-change years accurately fits the post-change quarters could not be rejected ($F = 0.39$, P-value $= 0.85$ for the share price model; $F = 0.19$, P-value $= 0.96$ for the EPS model).[16]

Graphs corroborate that the 1995–1996 quarters look remarkably similar to previous periods. A model based only on trends in comparable companies and quarterly dummies fits the timing of both share price and EPS swings.[17] The graph of the EPS indicates a slight change in the seasonality of the series in the mid 1990s: the change in earnings is somewhat less variable than it had been previously and the peak has moved from the third to the first quarter. However, the change seems to have occurred in 1994, prior to the specific introduction of temporaries, and can be traced to a major change in product mix discussed in the company's annual report.

Company B changed its temping policies in the fall of 1994. During 1995, this company did worse than would be predicted based on

Table 3 Case Study: Impact of Large Increase in Temporary Usage in a Large Fiber/Fabric Manufacturing Company's Production Workers—Company A[a]

Dependent variable	$\ln(P_t / P_{t-1})$		$\Delta EPS/P_{t-1}$	
Time period	1984:2–1996:1	1988:1–1996:1	1984:2–1996:1	1984:2–1996:1
No. of observations	48	33	48	48
Dummy for temp change	0.014	0.039	0.003	0.002
	(0.069)	(0.065)	(0.011)	(0.009)
Average for 6 control companies	0.377	0.607	0.020	–0.010
	(0.222)	(0.236)	(0.072)	(0.055)
Constant	–0.030	–0.041	–0.017	–0.018
	(0.042)	(0.047)	(0.007)	(0.005)
Q1	0.046	0.035	0.007	0.009
	(0.061)	(0.065)	(0.010)	(0.008)
Q2	0.110	0.120	0.031	0.034
	(0.059)	(0.066)	(0.010)	(0.007)
Q3	–0.029	–0.053	0.030	0.031
	(0.058)	(0.065)	(0.009)	(0.007)
R^2 adj.	0.19	0.21	0.21	0.53
Durbin-Watson statistics	1.86	2.05	2.69	1.82
MA[b] terms?	No	Yes	No	Yes

[a] Standard errors in parentheses.
[b] Three-quarter moving average.

Table 4 Case Study: Impact of Large Increase in Temporary Usage in a Large Fiber/Fabric Manufacturing Company's Production Workers—Company B[a]

Dependent variable	$\ln(P_t / P_{t-1})$		Δ EPS/P_{t-1}	
Time period	1984:3–1996:1	1988:1–1996:1	1984:3–1996:1	1988:1–1996:1
No. of observations	47	33	47	33
Dummy for temp change	–0.135 (0.111)	–0.133 (0.074)	–0.007 (0.013)	–0.006 (0.003)
Average for 6 control companies	0.817 (0.388)	0.224 (0.292)	0.075 (0.095)	–0.004 (0.020)
Constant	0.073 (0.075)	0.100 (0.060)	0.009 (0.009)	0.003 (0.075)
Q1	–0.016 (0.106)	–0.041 (0.071)	–0.027 (0.013)	–0.016 (0.106)
Q2	–0.004 (0.105)	–0.086 (0.082)	–0.013 (0.013)	–0.004 (0.105)
Q3	–0.050 (0.103)	–0.140 (0.082)	0.018 (0.012)	–0.050 (0.103)
R^2 adj.	0.05	0.20	0.16	0.59
Durbin-Watson statistics	2.05	1.93	1.32	2.01
MA[b] terms?	Yes	Yes	No	No

[a] Standard errors in parentheses.
[b] Three-quarter moving average.

seasonality and the six control companies. Thus, in the best of the two-share price equations reported in Table 4, the t-statistic of the postchange dummy variable is –1.79 (significant at the 10 percent level). The F-test of whether the latter period fits the earlier model is $F = 1.59$, which has a P-value of 0.20. Similarly, the actual EPS/P_{t-1} is lower than what would be predicted based on industry trends and seasonality (t-statistic = –2.17). The F-test for the similarity of the postchange period is 6.94 ($P = 0.0003$). Annual reports suggest that the company was being affected by a wide variety of other factors in

1995, including several major acquisitions and major capital outlays for modernized production facilities.

Thus, in these two companies, the period of intensive use of temporaries as a hiring device was accompanied by very different profitability. In one, the radical HR change could not be detected in share price or earnings, except that perhaps we saw a slightly dampened variability in earnings. In Company B, the radical HR change accompanied other aggressive changes in the company's assets and direction. Thus while Company B fared far worse during the period of increased use of temporaries, it is difficult to attribute this to the HR policy change.

CONCLUSIONS AND FUTURE DIRECTIONS

This chapter finds that many large companies surveyed are using temporaries in different ways than they had previously. Many are hiring more temporaries and are hiring them to serve different purposes than previously. Temps are being hired not just to replace temporary absences, but also as a strategic solution to both foreseen and unforeseen variability in labor demand. As a result, temps are being hired to a wider variety of jobs, and are staying at assignments for longer periods of time. Moreover, temporary help is being increasingly used as a recruiting and screening mechanism to find permanent employees. Additional research is warranted to document these changes among a larger sample of companies of varying sizes.

Both individual companies and labor market researchers find it difficult to find a measurable impact of HR policies on profitability or costs. The cross-sectional results here suggest that there may be some correlation between strategic use of temporaries and positive financial outcomes. While this is in no way indicative of causality, they provide a beginning shred of evidence that "strategic staffing" may increase operating margins and company value.

On the other hand, the time-series case study suggests either no impact or a negative impact for manufacturing companies choosing to hire all entry-level production workers as temps. The somewhat contradictory conclusions from the cross-sectional and time-series estimates are in no way mutually exclusive: a selective use of temporaries might be profitable while a more blanket approach might be counter-productive. However, the time-series results for two companies primarily corroborate the general fact that the financial impact of even major changes in HR policies tends to be eclipsed by other changes occurring within companies.

Nevertheless, executives at large companies who have increased their usage of temporaries are convinced that it has increased their profitability, particularly by giving them additional flexibility. The overall rising usage of temporaries in a wider variety of jobs and situations is a testament to their conviction in the financial benefits of temps.

It seems clear that, absent government intervention, this growth of temporaries in the workforce will continue. Many factors, from global competition to the need for flexibility and the quick availability of qualified personnel, drive this change. In light of these changes, both companies and government should reexamine whether policies written for more static and permanent labor markets make sense in the light of these changes. Researchers should assist this process of reexamination by studying the impact of these changes on companies, on individuals, and on labor market outcomes.

Notes

1. Alternatively, a February 1995 supplement to the Current Population Survey estimated that 1.0 percent of employed workers were paid by temporary help agencies, while an additional 1.7 percent of the employed were on-call workers and day laborers, for a total of 2.7 percent of the workforce in temporary work. This measure, however, excludes direct-hire temporaries but may include some non-temporaries who work for temporary agencies. The Bureau of Labor Statistics also estimated various definitions of contingent workers. The broadest definition encompassing all workers who don't expect their jobs to last, including contract workers and self-employed, comprised 4.9 percent of total employed.
2. We did not explicitly mention on-call workers, although we did ask respondents to include people hired for temporary work from in-house listings of available temporary workers.
3. One executive was able to schedule an appointment six months hence but no sooner.
4. Because of confidentiality agreements, we are not using company names in this chapter. When company names appear, the information is not from our sample itself but from public sources.

5. Owners of temporary agencies have told us that while they do not ignore the employee's unsuccessful experience, neither does a single unsuccessful match lead an agency to drop an employee from its roster.

6. Thus, rather than using temporaries to avoid severance pay or to avoid paying benefits, companies could change their own policies for the probationary period. Seen this way, the movement toward using temps as probationary workers may simply be an expedient way for companies to, in effect, renegotiate the contracts of new employees. Moreover, the use of temporaries in this way may allow companies to avoid government policies such as unemployment compensation experience-rating or the threat of suit for discriminatory practices if dismissed during the probationary period. The case law regarding coemployment of temporary workers is still evolving.

7. Reported in *Staffing Industry Report*, January 1996. Note that NATSS changed its name between these two surveys to National Association of Temporary and Staffing Services.

8. This occurred in the textile/fiber company that is the focus of our case study later in this chapter (Company A).

9. A χ^2 test of downsizing versus increasing, decreasing, or keeping temps steady is significant at the 24 percent level.

10. One of these two companies has a pool of in-house temps that tend, de facto, to be continually employed.

11. When HR policies have been shown to have impacts, it is usually when many aspects of management change simultaneously. Similarly, we would be most likely to find an impact when the firm is simultaneously adopting an entire "strategic staffing" approach.

12. The surveys in the cross-section were all carried out in 1995, and asked about changes in the previous three to five years.

13. All earnings-per-share numbers are standardized by the share price.

14. Two scaling factors were considered: the share price (P_{t-1}) and the average share price of the company over the sample period (P_{avg}). While reported results use the former, all results are similar for both measures. Another way to think of these earnings measures is as a return on equity, where the return is based on actual share price rather than "book value." OPM was not available for quarterly data.

15. Quarterly dummies are included in the share price as well as in EPS equations to capture the January effect. Note also that when Durbin-Watson statistics indicated serial correlation, we included three-quarter moving average terms, which fit better than autoregressive terms.

16. Results using the alternative EPS measure are similar to those reported here both in the case of Company A and Company B.

17. Company A's share price variability is greater than for the six firms' average share price, as would be expected, because a portfolio with offsetting idiosyncratic risks will exhibit lower return variability than a single investment.

References

Abraham, Katharine. 1988. "Flexible Staffing Arrangements and Employers' Short-term Adjustment Strategies." In *Employment, Unemployment and Labor Utilization*, Robert Hart, ed. Boston: Unwin Hyman, pp. 288–311.

Axel, Helen. 1995. "Contingent Employment." *The Conference Board HR Executive Review* 3(2): 1–3.

Blank, Rebecca. 1998. "Contingent Work in a Changing Labor Market." In *Generating Jobs: How to Increase Demand for Less-Skilled Workers*, Richard B. Freeman and Peter Gottschalk, eds. New York: Russell Sage Foundation, pp. 258–294.

Business Wire. 1996. "Record Number of North American Businesses are Understaffed," http://www.businesswire.com. January 31.

Denka, Andrew. 1994. "Achieve Better Management through Strategic Staffing." *Managing Office Technology* 39(3): 10.

National Association of Temporary Services. 1994. *1994 Profile of the Temporary Workforce*. Alexandria, Virginia: National Association of Temporary Services.

Segal, Lewis, and Daniel Sullivan. 1995. "The Temporary Labor Force." Federal Reserve Bank of Chicago *Economic Perspective* 19(2): 2–19.

Staffing Industry Analysts, 1996. *Staffing Industry Report* 7(1): 10.

Steinberg, Bruce. 1994. *The Temporary Help Industry: Annual Update*. Alexandria, Virginia: National Association of Temporary Services.

U.S. Bureau of Labor Statistics. 1995. "Contingent and Alternative Employment Arrangements." *Bureau of Labor Statistics News* (August): 2.

_____. 1996. "Current Labor Statistics: Employment of Workers on Nonfarm Payrolls by Industry." *Monthly Labor Review* 119(9): 67.

Cited Author Index

The italic letters *f*, *n*, or *t* following a page number indicate that the cited name is within a figure, note, or table, respectively, on that page.

Abdukadir, Gulnaz, 293, 312, 324
Abraham, Katharine, 339, 350
Alsalam, Nabeel, 97
Altonji, Joseph G., 36n1, 38, 76, 96,
    218, 248
Anderson, K., 161, 169, 173, 177
Aronson, Robert L., 247n1, 248
Averett, Susan L., 251, 280n16, 280n17,
    282
Axel, Helen, 337, 338, 339, 350

Baker, Michael, 183, 190, 212, 212n1-4,
    213
Baker, Regina M., 282, 282n25
Batt, Rosemary, 95n2, 97
Beck, S., 159, 160, 172, 177
Becker, Gary S., 16, 37n11, 39, 134,
    138, 154
Bélanger, 44, 46t, 63
Beller, Andrea H., 313, 324
Benimadhu, Prem, 37n5, 38
Benjamin, Dwayne, 183, 190, 212n1,
    212n2, 212n4, 213
Berger, Mark C., 76, 96
Betcherman, G., 160, 161, 174, 177
Blank, Rebecca, 251, 260, 280n16,
    280n17, 281n18, 282, 331, 350
Blank, Rebecca M., 218, 232, 248
Blau, Francine D., 313, 324
Boaz, R., 160, 177
Boskin, M., 158, 177
Boskin, Michael, 191, 213
Boucher, Nathalie, 293, 312, 325
Bound, John, 282, 282n25
Breslau, Naomi, 137, 154
Breslaw, J., 161, 169, 173, 177
Bronstein, A., 160, 174, 178
Browning, M., 37n2, 38
Bulow, Jeremy I., 125n1, 126

Burbidge, John, 212n2, 213
Burbridge, J.B., 36n1, 40
Burkhauser, R., 161, 169, 173, 177
Burr, J., 159, 179
Burtless, G., 163, 172, 178
Burton, Lawrence, 83, 94, 95n6, 96

Card, David, 293, 324, 324n11
Caron, C., 177
Celebuski, Carin A., 83, 94, 95n6, 96
Chapman, Nancy J., 284
Christensen, Kathleen E., 278, 281n18,
    283
Cogan, John F., 257, 283
Cohen, Gary L., 293, 324
Conaty, Joseph C., 97
Conway, Karen Smith, 293, 310, 312,
    324, 325
Cordova, E., 160, 174, 178
Corman, Hope, 75, 81, 96

Dale, A., 159, 180
Deaton, A., 37n2, 38
Denka, Andrew, 332, 350
Denton, Frank T., 37n5, 39, 44, 63
Devine, Theresa J., 218, 247n1, 247n2,
    247n7, 247n9, 248, 249, 281n18,
    282n24, 283
Doeringer, P., 157, 159, 161, 169, 176,
    178

Edwards, Linda N., 279n2, 279n6,
    281n17, 283
Eide, Eric, 76, 96
Emlen, Arthur C., 284
Even, William, 101, 112, 127
Field-Hendrey, Elizabeth, 279n2, 279n6,
    281n17, 283

Subject Index

The italic letters *f, n,* or *t* following a page number indicate that the subject information is in a figure, note, or a table, respectively, on that page.

About the Institute

The W.E. Upjohn Institute for Employment Research is a nonprofit research organization devoted to finding and promoting solutions to employment-related problems at the national, state, and local levels. It is an activity of the W.E. Upjohn Unemployment Trustee Corporation, which was established in 1932 to administer a fund set aside by the late Dr. W.E. Upjohn, founder of The Upjohn Company, to seek ways to counteract the loss of employment income during economic downturns.

The Institute is funded largely by income from the W.E. Upjohn Unemployment Trust, supplemented by outside grants, contracts, and sales of publications. Activities of the Institute comprise the following elements: 1) a research program conducted by a resident staff of professional social scientists; 2) a competitive grant program, which expands and complements the internal research program by providing financial support to researchers outside the Institute; 3) a publications program, which provides the major vehicle for disseminating the research of staff and grantees, as well as other selected works in the field; and 4) an Employment Management Services division, which manages most of the publicly funded employment and training programs in the local area.

The broad objectives of the Institute's research, grant, and publication programs are to 1) promote scholarship and experimentation on issues of public and private employment and unemployment policy, and 2) make knowledge and scholarship relevant and useful to policymakers in their pursuit of solutions to employment and unemployment problems.

Current areas of concentration for these programs include causes, consequences, and measures to alleviate unemployment; social insurance and income maintenance programs; compensation; workforce quality; work arrangements; family labor issues; labor-management relations; and regional economic development and local labor markets.